새 교과서 반영
중등 내신
완벽 대비서

GRAMMAR

Level **3**

Grammar 공감 Level 3

지은이 넥서스영어교육연구소
펴낸이 임상진
펴낸곳 (주)넥서스

출판신고 1992년 4월 3일 제311-2002-2호 ®
10880 경기도 파주시 지목로 5
Tel (02)330-5500 Fax (02)330-5555

ISBN 978-89-6790-846-1 54740
      978-89-6790-843-0 (SET)

가격은 뒤표지에 있습니다.
잘못 만들어진 책은 구입처에서 바꾸어 드립니다.

www.nexusEDU.kr
NEXUS Edu는 넥서스의 초·중·고 학습물 전문 브랜드입니다.

※집필에 도움을 주신 분
  :김현진 선생님, 정혜영 선생님, 임현주 선생님, 임재원 선생님, 오선행 선생님

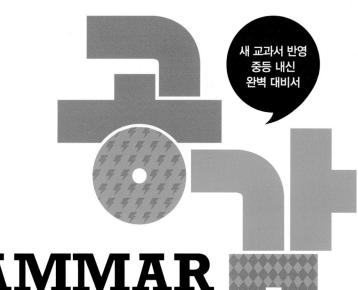

새 교과서 반영
중등 내신
완벽 대비서

GRAMMAR

넥서스영어교육연구소 지음

Level 3

NEXUS Edu

Grammar Gong Gam helps you...

Get high scores
2,500여 개의 전국 중학교 기출 문제를 분석하여 반영한 review test를 제공함으로써 내신 성적을 향상시켜 줍니다.

Obtain a wide vocabulary
풍부한 어휘 리스트를 제공, 기본적인 어휘 실력을 향상시켜 줍니다.

Nurture your English skills
최신 개정 교과서를 분석 반영한 문법 설명을 수록, 2,500여 개에 달하는 전국 중학교 최신 기출 문제를 분석하여 반영한 문제를 수록, 중등 과정에서 알아야 하는 풍부한 어휘를 제공함으로써 종합적인 영어 실력을 향상시켜 줍니다.

Get writing skills
서술형 평가 코너를 따로 수록해 새로운 교수 평가 방법에 대비할 수 있게 해 줍니다.

Get speaking skills
영어 회화로도 활용 가능한 예문을 제공하여 영어 말하기 능력을 향상시켜 줍니다.

Acquire good English sense
2,000여 개의 충분한 연습 문제를 풀어보게 해줌으로써 문법 감각을 습득시켜 줍니다.

Master the essentials of grammar
최신 교과서를 분석하여 반영한 문법 설명으로, 내신에 필수 불가결한 문법을 학습하게 해 줍니다.

Features

내신에 꼭 필요한 핵심 문법 사항들을 알기 쉽게 단계별로 설명하였습니다. 실용적인 예문과 간결하고 정확한 문법 설명을 제시하여 대표 예문만 봐도 문법의 개념을 이해할 수 있습니다. 시험에 꼭 나오는 문법 내용이 자연스럽게 반복되어 충분한 학습 효과를 볼 수 있습니다.

Plus α & Tips
핵심 문법 사항 이외에 추가로 심화 문법 사항과 학생들이 특히 주의해야 할 사항을 정리하였습니다.

Check-up
학습한 핵심 문법을 올바로 이해하였는지 바로 확인할 수 있는 문제로, 핵심 문법 사항만 숙지하였다면 누구나 쉽고 재미있게 풀 수 있는 기본 문제들로 구성하였습니다.

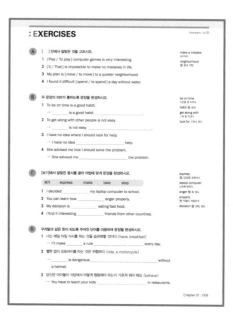

Exercises
해당 Unit에서 학습한 문법 사항을 다양한 유형의 주관식 문제를 통해 완벽하게 정리할 수 있도록 하였습니다. 단순 암기한 내용을 가지고 푸는 것이 아니라 직접 응용해서 써 보고 생각해 볼 수 있도록 구성하였습니다.

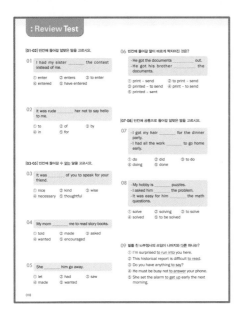

Review Test

해당 Chapter에서 학습한 내용을 통합형 문제 유형을 통해서 다시 한 번 정리할 수 있도록 하였습니다. 실제 학교 시험과 동일한 유형의 문제들로 구성하여 내신을 완벽하게 대비할 수 있습니다. 스스로 자신의 취약한 부분을 점검하며 문법에 대한 자신감을 기를 수 있습니다.

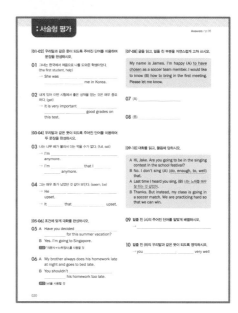

서술형 평가

최신 교수 평가 방법에 대비할 수 있도록 서술형 평가 코너를 따로 마련하였습니다. 학교 내신 시험에 자주 나오는 유형의 서술형 문제를 통해서 어떤 문제가 나와도 대비할 수 있도록 하였으며 학생들의 사고력과 창의력도 길러줍니다.

Workbook (서술형 대비)

본책에서 학습한 내용을 다양한 서술형 문제를 통해서 핵심 문법 사항을 충분히 연습할 수 있도록 하였습니다. 숙제나 자습을 통해 문법 사항을 최종 정리하며 복습할 수 있는 좋은 기회가 될 수 있습니다.

정답 및 해설

기존의 어렵고 복잡한 설명에서 벗어나 간결하고 정확한 설명을 통해서 해설집만 보고도 핵심 문법 정리를 한눈에 할 수 있도록 하였습니다.

Contents

Chapter 1

부정사

명사적 쓰임

1. 명사적 쓰임: to부정사는 문장에서 주어, 목적어, 보어로 쓰인다.

To see is to believe. [주어] 보는 것이 믿는 것이다. (백문이 불여일견)

I like **to watch** sci-fi movies. [목적어] 나는 공상 과학 영화 보는 것을 좋아한다.

My wish is **to help** the people in need. [보어] 나의 소망은 어려운 사람들을 돕는 것이다.

2. 가주어, 가목적어 it: 주어나 목적어로 쓰인 to부정사가 긴 경우, 주어나 목적어 자리에 it을 쓰고 to부정사를 문장의 뒤로 보낸다.

It is important **to have** healthy eating habits. 건강한 식습관을 가지는 것은 중요하다.
가주어   진주어

I found **it** difficult **to exercise** regularly. 나는 규칙적으로 운동하는 것이 어렵다는 것을 알았다.
       가목적어   진목적어

3. 「의문사+to부정사」: 문장에서 명사구 역할을 하며, 「의문사+주어+should+동사」와 바꿔 쓸 수 있다.

Now, tell me **what to do**. 이제 제가 무엇을 해야 할지 말해 주세요.
= what I should do

Let me know **when to start**. 언제 시작해야 할지 알려 주세요.
= when I should start

Can you show me **where to find** a pet shop?
= where I should find
애완동물 용품점을 어디서 찾을 수 있는지 알려 주실 수 있어요?

He taught me **how to drive**. 그는 나에게 운전하는 법을 가르쳐 주었다.
= how I should drive

I don't know **who(m) to ask**. 누구에게 물어야 할지 모르겠다.
= who(m) I should ask

It is hard to decide **which to buy**. 어떤 것을 살지 결정하는 것은 어렵다.
= which I should buy

> **Tips**
> 구어체에서는 whom 대신 who를 주로 사용한다.

Check-up   ☐ 안에서 알맞은 말을 고르시오.

---

1 It is hard | see / to see | stars in Seoul.

2 You should decide where | going / to go | right now.

3 My goal is | improve / to improve | my English skills.

: EXERCISES

A [   ] 안에서 알맞은 것을 고르시오.

1 [Play / To play] computer games is very interesting.

2 [It / That] is impossible to make no mistakes in life.

3 My plan is [move / to move] to a quieter neighborhood.

4 I found it difficult [spend / to spend] a day without water.

make a mistake
실수하다

neighborhood
(명) 동네, 지방

B 두 문장의 의미가 통하도록 문장을 완성하시오.

1 To be on time is a good habit.

→ _____ is a good habit _____.

2 To get along with other people is not easy.

→ _____ is not easy _____.

3 I have no idea where I should look for help.

→ I have no idea _____ help.

4 She advised me how I should solve the problem.

→ She advised me _____ the problem.

be on time
시간을 잘 지키다

habit (명) 습관

get along with
~와 잘 지내다

look for 구하다, 찾다

C [보기]에서 알맞은 동사를 골라 어법에 맞게 바꿔 문장을 완성하시오.

보기	express	make	take	stop

1 I decided _____ my laptop computer to school.

2 You can learn how _____ anger properly.

3 My decision is _____ eating fast food.

4 I find it interesting _____ friends from other countries.

express
(동) (감정을) 표현하다

laptop computer
노트북 컴퓨터

anger (명) 화, 분노

properly
(부) 적절히, 적절하게

decision (명) 결정, 결심

D 우리말과 같은 뜻이 되도록 주어진 단어를 이용하여 문장을 완성하시오.

1 나는 매일 아침 식사를 하는 것을 습관화할 것이다. (have, breakfast)

→ I'll make _____ a rule _____ _____ _____ every day.

2 헬멧 없이 오토바이를 타는 것은 위험하다. (ride, a motorcycle)

→ _____ is dangerous _____ _____ _____ _____ without
   a helmet.

3 당신은 아이들이 식당에서 어떻게 행동해야 하는지 가르쳐 줘야 해요. (behave)

→ You have to teach your kids _____ _____ _____ in restaurants.

UNIT 02 형용사적, 부사적 쓰임

1. 형용사적 쓰임

(1) 명사 수식: to부정사는 명사의 뒤에서 명사를 꾸며 주는 형용사 역할을 한다.

This is a good place **to start** your trip. 이곳은 너의 여행을 시작하기에 좋은 장소이다.

We all need someone **to talk to**. 우리 모두 대화를 나눌 누군가가 필요하다.

(2) 「be+to부정사」: '가능, 예정, 의무, 의도, 운명'의 의미로 쓰이고, be to용법이라고도 부른다.

Love **is** not **to be bought** with money. [가능] 사랑은 돈으로 살 수 없다.

The class meeting **is to take** place tomorrow. [예정] 학급 회의가 내일 열릴 예정이다.

You **are to complete** the work by next month. [의무] 너는 다음 달까지 그 일을 끝내야 한다.

If you **are to succeed**, be diligent. [의도] 만약 네가 성공하고자 한다면 부지런하라.

He **was** never **to return** to his country again.

[운명] 그는 다시는 조국으로 돌아오지 못할 운명이었다.

2. 부사적 쓰임: to부정사는 동사나 형용사를 수식하며, '목적, 결과, 감정의 원인, 판단의 근거' 등의 의미로 쓰인다.

She goes jogging every day **to stay** healthy. [목적] 그녀는 건강을 유지하기 위해 매일 달리기를 한다.

He grew up **to be** a famous violinist. [결과] 그는 자라서 유명한 바이올리니스트가 되었다.

I am pleased **to meet** you in person. [감정의 원인] 직접 만나 뵙게 되어 영광입니다.

The man is foolish **to do** such a thing. [판단의 근거] 그런 짓을 하다니 그 남자는 어리석구나.

My father is hard **to please**. [형용사 수식] 나의 아버지는 기쁘게 해 드리기가 어렵다.

Plus α

목적을 의미하는 to부정사는 in order to나 so as to로 바꿔 쓸 수 있다.

I deleted the data **to protect** my personal information. 내 개인 정보를 보호하기 위해 그 자료를 삭제했다.

= in order to protect

= so as to protect

Tips

to부정사 뒤에 전치사를 필요로 하는지 아닌지는 to부정사 뒤에 목적어를 놓아 보면 알 수 있다.

talk to someone (O)

~~talk someone~~ (X)

write with a pen (O)

~~write a pen~~ (X)

Check-up   안에서 알맞은 말을 고르시오.

1 I'm cold. I need something warm wear / to wear .

2 A new leader is be / to be elected soon.

3 I am sorry keep / to keep you waiting.

: **EXERCISES**

A [ ] 안에서 알맞은 것을 고르시오.

1 Sally was surprised [receive / to receive] a letter from her cousin.

2 This is the list of things [shopping / to shop] for today.

3 He studied hard [achieve / to achieve] his goal.

4 I have a better way [hand / to handle] this problem.

shop for ~을 사러 가다
achieve
(동) 달성하다, 성취하다
handle (동) 다루다

B 두 문장의 의미가 통하도록 문장을 완성하시오.

1 If you intend to wake up early, you should go to bed early.

→ If you are _____ _____ _____ early, you should go to bed early.

2 There was going to be a war soon.

→ There was _____ _____ a war soon.

3 She was destined not to come home again.

→ She was never _____ _____ home again.

4 You should finish the project by 6 o'clock.

→ You are _____ _____ the project by 6 o'clock.

intend to
~하려고 생각하다
be destined
~로 운명 지어지다

C 밑줄 친 부분에 유의하여 해석을 완성하시오.

1 I'm happy to work with her.

→ 나는 그녀와 함께 _____ 기쁘다.

2 Andy went to the airport to see his cousin off.

→ Andy는 그의 사촌을 _____ 공항에 갔다.

3 I'm glad to meet you here today.

→ 오늘 여기서 당신을 _____ 기쁩니다.

4 She woke up to find herself famous.

→ 그녀는 일어나 보니 자신이 유명해진 것을 _____.

D 우리말과 같은 뜻이 되도록 주어진 단어를 이용하여 문장을 완성하시오.

1 그 문제들 중 몇 개는 풀기 어려웠다. (solve, difficult)

→ Some of the questions were _____ _____ _____.

2 나는 같이 놀 친구들이 필요하다. (play)

→ I need some friends _____ _____ _____.

3 Washington으로 가는 기차는 3시 45분에 도착할 것이다. (arrive)

→ The train to Washington is _____ _____ at 3:45.

UNIT 03 to부정사의 시제, 태, 의미상 주어

1. to부정사의 시제

(1) 「**to+동사원형**」: 주절의 동사와 to부정사의 시제가 같을 때 사용하며 '단순부정사'라고 부른다.

He **seems to be** sick. 그는 아픈 것 같다.
➡ It **seems** that he **is** sick.

He **seemed to be** sick. 그는 아픈 것 같았다.
➡ It **seemed** that he **was** sick.

(2) 「**to+have p.p.**」: 주절의 동사보다 to부정사의 시제가 앞설 때 사용하며 '완료부정사'라고 부른다.

He **seems to have been** sick. 그는 아팠던 것 같다.
➡ It **seems** that he **was[has been]** sick.

He **seemed to have been** sick. 그는 아팠던 것 같았다.
➡ It **seemed** that he **had been** sick.

2. to부정사의 수동태: 「to+be p.p.」 「to+have been p.p.」

She has homework **to be done** by Friday. 그녀는 금요일까지 마쳐야 하는 숙제가 있다.
I am pleased **to have been chosen** as a dean. 학장으로 선택되어 기쁩니다.

3. 의미상의 주어: to부정사를 행하는 주체를 나타낼 때 쓴다.

(1) 「**for+목적격**」: 일반적인 형용사 뒤에 쓴다.
It is <u>difficult</u> **for me** <u>to learn</u> snowboarding. 나에게 있어 스노보드를 배우는 것은 어려운 일이다.

(2) 「**of+목적격**」: 사람의 성질이나 태도를 칭찬하거나 비평하는 의미의 형용사 뒤에 쓴다.
☆ kind, wise, nice, polite, rude, foolish, brave, thoughtful 등
It is so <u>kind</u> **of you** <u>to send</u> me a thank-you card.
나에게 감사 카드를 보내다니 너는 정말 친절하구나.

(3) **의미상 주어의 생략**: 행위자가 일반적인 사람인 경우 주로 생략한다.
It is dangerous <u>to swim</u> in the river. 강에서 수영하는 것은 위험하다.

> **Plus α**
>
> to부정사의 부정형:
> 「not/never+to+동사원형」
>
> He told me **not to mention** anything about it.
> 그는 나에게 그것에 대해서 아무 것도 언급하지 말라고 말했다.

Check-up ☐ 안에서 알맞은 말을 고르시오.

1 It seems that she likes her job so much.
　→ She seems ☐ to like / to have liked ☐ her job so much.

2 It was very brave ☐ for / of ☐ you to do that.

3 I expect him ☐ not to / to not ☐ do anything.

: EXERCISES

A   [   ] 안에서 알맞은 것을 고르시오.

1   It is so sweet [for / of] you to help me carry my baggage.

2   It was necessary [for / of] me to follow her words.

3   She seems [to live / to have lived] in the city as a child.

4   I was upset [to punish / to be punished] by the teacher.

baggage 몡 짐, 수하물
follow
통 (충고, 지시 등을) 따르다
punish 통 벌주다

B   두 문장의 의미가 통하도록 문장을 완성하시오.

1   It seems that she was surprised to see me.

→ She seems ＿＿＿＿＿＿＿＿＿＿ surprised to see me.

2   It seems that he is occupied with his work.

→ He seems ＿＿＿＿＿＿＿＿＿ occupied with his work.

3   It seemed that he had lived a hard life.

→ He seemed ＿＿＿＿＿＿＿＿＿ a hard life.

4   It seemed that she was tired of doing the same thing.

→ She seemed ＿＿＿＿＿＿＿＿＿ tired of doing the same thing.

be occupied with
～으로 바쁘다
be tired of
～에 싫증이 나다

C   주어진 단어를 어법에 맞게 바꿔 문장을 완성하시오.

1   It will be easy ＿＿＿＿＿＿＿ to solve the puzzle by yourself. (you)

2   It is nice ＿＿＿＿＿＿＿ to lend me her new suitcase. (she)

3   My mom wants my room ＿＿＿＿＿＿＿ before I go to bed. (clean)

4   I expect this work ＿＿＿＿＿＿＿ as soon as possible. (finish)

by oneself 혼자서
suitcase 몡 여행 가방
as soon as possible
가능한 한 빨리

D   우리말과 같은 뜻이 되도록 주어진 단어를 이용하여 문장을 완성하시오.

1   그는 그녀를 잘 아는 것처럼 보인다. (seem)

→ He ＿＿＿＿＿ ＿＿＿＿＿ ＿＿＿＿ her very well.

2   그가 중국어로 의사소통하는 것은 불가능하다. (communicate)

→ It is impossible ＿＿＿＿ ＿＿＿＿ ＿＿＿＿ ＿＿＿＿ in Chinese.

3   이 상을 받게 되어서 매우 영광입니다. (award)

→ I'm so honored ＿＿＿＿ ＿＿＿＿ ＿＿＿＿ this prize.

목적격보어로 쓰이는 부정사

1. 「동사+목적어+to부정사」

☆ want, allow, tell, ask, order, expect, advise, enable, force, encourage 등

He never **allows** kids **to touch** the machine.
그는 절대 아이들이 그 기계를 만지는 것을 허락하지 않는다.

The teacher **advised** us **to check** the answers again.
선생님께서 우리에게 답을 다시 확인하라고 조언하셨다.

2. 「지각동사+목적어+동사원형」

☆ 지각동사: feel 느끼다   see 보다   listen to 듣다   hear 듣다
　　　　　 watch 보다   look at 보다   smell ~하는 냄새가 나다   notice 알아차리다

I **felt** someone **stare** at my back. 나는 누군가가 내 등을 응시하는 것을 느꼈다.

She **listened to** the orchestra **play** *Moonlight Sonata*.
그녀는 오케스트라가 '달빛 소나타'를 연주하는 것을 들었다.

3. 「사역동사+목적어+동사원형」

☆ 사역동사: let, make, have ~에게 …하도록 하다[시키다]

Please **have** someone **bring** me a glass of water. 누가 나에게 물 한 잔만 가져다주게 해 주세요.

They didn't **let** me **go**; they **made** me **stay** there. 그들은 나를 못 가게 하고 그곳에 머물게 했다.

Plus α

1 「have/get+목적어+p.p.」: 목적어와 목적격보어의 관계가 수동일 때 사용한다.
　 Make sure to **get** it **done** by tomorrow. 내일까지 그 일이 완료되도록 하세요.
　 Don't forget to **have** my shirt **ironed**. 내 셔츠를 다리는 것을 잊지 마세요.

2 「get+목적어+to부정사」: get은 '~에게 …하게 하다'라는 사역의 의미를 갖지만 목적격보어 자리에 to부정사를
　 쓴다. 또한 to부정사 자리에 '-ing'가 올 수도 있다.
　 It **got** me **to think**. 그것이 나로 하여금 생각하게 만들었다.
　 → It **got** me **thinking**.

3 「help+목적어(+to)+동사원형」: help의 목적격보어 자리에는 to부정사와 동사원형 둘 다 올 수 있다.
　 He **helped** me **(to) move** to a new house. 그는 내가 새집으로 이사하는 것을 도왔다.

Tips

「지각동사+목적어+-ing」:
진행의 의미를 강조
I felt <u>someone</u> **staring** at
my back.
누군가가 내 등을 응시하고 있
는 것을 느꼈다.

「지각동사+목적어+p.p.」:
목적어와 목적격보어의 관계
가 수동일 때 사용
I saw <u>his car</u> **parked** in
front of his house.
나는 그의 집 앞에 그의 차가
주차되어 있는 것을 보았다.

Check-up　　☐ 안에서 알맞은 말을 고르시오.

1 I expect the world ☐ be / to be ☐ a better place to live in.

2 Don't make me ☐ get / to get ☐ disappointed in you.

3 Don't you smell something ☐ burning / to burn ☐?

: EXERCISES

A [   ] 안에서 알맞은 것을 고르시오.

1 The trainer made me [do / to do] 10 push-ups.

2 I heard my dog [bark / to bark] loudly in the back yard.

3 Do you want the door [to paint / to be painted] green?

4 Language enabled humans [be / to be] a better species.

push-up 명 팔 굽혀 펴기
bark 동 (개가) 짖다
enable
동 ~을 할 수 있게 하다
species 명 종(種)

B 주어진 단어를 어법에 맞게 바꿔 문장을 완성하시오.

1 I felt something _____ on my leg. (crawl)

2 Mom told Dad _____ smoking. (quit)

3 They never expected the war _____. (come)

4 The accident made me _____ how careless I was. (realize)

crawl 동 기다, 기어가다
come
동 일어나다, 발생하다, 오다
accident 명 사고
careless 형 부주의한
realize 동 깨닫다

C 두 문장의 의미가 통하도록 문장을 완성하시오.

1 Don't stop her telling the truth.

→ Let her _____ the truth.

2 I saw Charlie when he was talking to Grace.

→ I saw Charlie _____ to Grace.

3 My mom said I could use her cell phone.

→ My mom allowed me _____ her cell phone.

talk to ~에게 이야기하다
allow 동 허락하다

D 우리말과 같은 뜻이 되도록 주어진 단어를 이용하여 문장을 완성하시오.

1 그 학생들로 하여금 줄을 서도록 해 주세요. (have, stand in line)

→ _____ _____ _____ _____ _____ _____ , please.

2 누나가 나에게 방 청소를 하라고 말했다. (tell, clean)

→ My sister _____ _____ _____ _____ the room.

3 나는 누군가가 어둠 속에서 걸어 나오는 것을 보았다. (see, someone, walk)

→ I _____ _____ _____ out of the dark.

UNIT 05 too ~ to, enough to, 기타 표현

1. 「too+형용사[부사]+to부정사」: 너무 ~해서 …할 수 없다

「so+형용사[부사]+주어+can't[couldn't]」

She is **too** <u>shy</u> **to** <u>act</u> on the stage. 그녀는 너무 수줍어해서 무대에서 연기할 수 없다.

➡ She is **so** <u>shy</u> **that she can't** <u>act</u> on the stage.

He walked **too** <u>slow</u> **to** <u>arrive</u> there on time. 그는 너무 천천히 걸어서 제시간에 그곳에 도착할 수 없었다.

➡ He walked **so** <u>slow</u> **that he couldn't** <u>arrive</u> there on time.

2. 「형용사[부사]+enough+to부정사」: ~할 만큼 충분히 ~하다

「so+형용사[부사]+주어+can[could]」

He is <u>strong</u> **enough to** <u>lift</u> the big rock. 그는 그 큰 바위를 들어 올릴 만큼 힘이 세다.

➡ He is **so** <u>strong</u> **that he can** <u>lift</u> the big rock.

She ran <u>fast</u> **enough to** <u>be</u> a world champion. 그녀는 세계 챔피언이 될 만큼 빨리 뛰었다.

➡ She ran **so** <u>fast</u> **that she could** <u>be</u> a world champion.

3. 독립부정사: 주로 문장 앞에 와서 문장 전체를 수식하는 to부정사

to tell the truth 사실을 말하자면	to begin with 우선
to make matters worse 설상가상으로	needless to say 말할 필요도 없이
so to speak 말하자면	strange to say 이상하게 들리겠지만
to be frank with you 솔직히 말하자면	to be brief 간단히 말하면
to make a long story short 요약해서 말하면	to be sure 확실히

To tell the truth, I have no idea about the issue.
사실을 말하자면, 나는 그 문제에 대해 아는 바가 없다.

To make matters worse, it started to rain.
설상가상으로, 비가 오기 시작했다.

Needless to say, parents should protect their children.
말할 필요도 없이, 부모는 자식을 보호해야 한다.

Vogue is, **so to speak**, a bible in the fashion industry.
말하자면 Vogue는 패션 업계의 필독서이다.

Plus α

1 「enough+명사」 충분한 vs. 「형용사+enough」 충분히

Do we have **enough** <u>water</u> for three days? 우리에게 3일 동안 마실 충분한 물이 있나요?

I'm <u>old</u> **enough** to drink beer. 난 맥주를 마실 만큼 충분히 나이가 들었다.

2 「so that+주어+동사」 ~할 수 있도록 vs. 「so+형용사[부사]+that +주어+can[could]」 매우 ~해서 ~할 수 있다

Raise your hands **so that** I can see you. [목적] 내가 너를 볼 수 있도록 손을 들어라.

He prepared for the test **so** perfectly **that** he could pass it. [결과] 그는 시험에 매우 완벽하게 준비해서 시험에 합격할 수 있었다.

Check-up ☐ 안에서 알맞은 말을 고르시오.

1 He woke up | late too / **too late** | to catch the flight.

2 Her grades are | enough good / **good enough** | to receive a scholarship.

3 | Begin with / **To begin with** |, I have no time to do it.

: EXERCISES

A 주어진 단어를 알맞게 배열하여 문장을 완성하시오.

1 This tea is _____. (too, to, hot, drink)

2 I was _____ to your message. (too, to, busy, reply)

3 The girl is _____ safe in the pool. (enough, to, stay, careful)

4 This candle is _____ a day. (enough, to, long, last)

reply
(동) 응답하다, 대답하다
careful (형) 주의 깊은
last (동) 지속되다

B 두 문장의 의미가 통하도록 문장을 완성하시오.

1 He is so bored that he can't do the same job every day.

→ He is _____ the same job every day.

2 They were so angry that they couldn't calm down.

→ They were _____.

3 She is so confident that she can be a good leader.

→ She is _____ a good leader.

4 She danced so well that she could be a professional dancer.

→ She danced _____ a professional dancer.

bored (형) 지루해 하는
calm down 진정하다
confident
(형) 자신에 찬, 자신감 있는
professional
(형) 전문가의

C 밑줄 친 부분에 유의하여 해석을 완성하시오.

1 <u>To make matters worse</u>, he left his wallet at home.

→ _____, 그는 집에 지갑을 두고 왔다.

2 <u>To tell the truth</u>, he is not an honest man.

→ _____, 그는 정직한 사람이 아니다.

3 <u>Needless to say</u>, we should respect the elderly.

→ _____, 우리는 노인을 공경해야 한다.

D 우리말과 같은 뜻이 되도록 주어진 단어를 이용하여 문장을 완성하시오.

1 그는 운전을 할 수 있을 만큼 충분히 나이가 들었다. (old, drive)

→ He is _____ _____ _____ _____ a car.

2 나는 너무 졸려서 눈을 뜰 수가 없었다. (sleepy, open)

→ I was _____ _____ _____ _____ my eyes.

3 솔직히 말하자면 나는 여행을 갈 충분한 돈이 없다. (frank)

→ _____ _____ _____ _____ _____,

I don't have enough money for the trip.

[01-02] 빈칸에 들어갈 알맞은 말을 고르시오.

01
> I had my sister _____ the contest instead of me.

① enter　　② enters　　③ to enter
④ entered　　⑤ have entered

02
> It was rude _____ her not to say hello to me.

① to　　② of　　③ by
④ in　　⑤ for

[03-05] 빈칸에 들어갈 수 <u>없는</u> 말을 고르시오.

03
> It was _____ of you to speak for your friend.

① nice　　② kind　　③ wise
④ necessary　　⑤ thoughtful

04
> My mom _____ me to read story books.

① told　　② made　　③ asked
④ wanted　　⑤ encouraged

05
> She _____ him go away.

① let　　② had　　③ saw
④ made　　⑤ wanted

06 빈칸에 들어갈 말이 바르게 짝지어진 것은?

> · He got the documents _____ out.
> · He got his brother _____ the documents.

① print – send　　② to print – send
③ printed – to send　　④ print – to send
⑤ printed – sent

[07-08] 빈칸에 공통으로 들어갈 알맞은 말을 고르시오.

07
> · I got my hair _____ for the dinner party.
> · I had all the work _____ to go home early.

① do　　② did　　③ to do
④ doing　　⑤ done

08
> · My hobby is _____ puzzles.
> · I asked him _____ the problem.
> · It was easy for him _____ the math questions.

① solve　　② solving　　③ to solve
④ solved　　⑤ to be solved

09 밑줄 친 to부정사의 쓰임이 나머지와 <u>다른</u> 하나는?

① I'm surprised <u>to run into</u> you here.
② This historical report is difficult <u>to read</u>.
③ Do you have anything <u>to say</u>?
④ He must be busy not <u>to answer</u> your phone.
⑤ She set the alarm <u>to get up</u> early the next morning.

[10-11] 두 문장의 의미가 통하도록 빈칸에 알맞은 말을 고르시오.

10
> I can make a kite.
> → I know _____ to make a kite.

① where　② when　③ how
④ who　⑤ what

11
> She seems to have been very pretty when she was young.
> → _____ seems that she _____ very pretty when she was young.

① She – is　② She – was
③ It – is　④ It – was
⑤ That – had been

[12-13] 다음 중 어법상 어색한 문장을 고르시오.

12
① I felt someone to look at me.
② You need to get your bag packed.
③ They didn't let him follow his dream.
④ You can't force a person to do anything.
⑤ Mom always tells me to be careful on the road.

13
① It is too hot to walk on the street.
② He was too busy to travel abroad.
③ He played soccer so well that he could be the MVP.
④ The water is enough clean for people to drink.
⑤ I walked fast so that I could get home before dark.

[14-15] 글을 읽고, 물음에 답하시오.

When I was little, I wanted ❶ to be a writer. My father also had me ❷ to keep a diary. One day I told him I would be a writer in the future. Surprisingly, my father told me ❸ not to become a writer because it is not a good-paying job. I was very disappointed and decided ❹ to listen to him. Several years later, I was traveling in India, and I met a street painter. He said that he used to be a doctor. He quit his job, although everyone advised him not to, because he wanted to follow his dream. At that moment, I realized that it was not my father who forced me ❺ to give up on my dream. (A) 사실을 말하자면, I gave up because of myself.

14 밑줄 친 ❶~❺ 중 어법상 어색한 것은?

15 밑줄 친 (A)를 바르게 영작한 것은?
① To make a long story short
② So to speak
③ Needless to say
④ To tell the truth
⑤ To begin with

[01-02] 우리말과 같은 뜻이 되도록 주어진 단어를 이용하여 문장을 완성하시오.

01 그녀는 한국에서 처음으로 나를 도와준 학생이었다.
(the first student, help)

→ She was _____ _____ _____

_____ _____ me in Korea.

02 내게 있어 이번 시험에서 좋은 성적을 얻는 것은 매우 중요하다. (get)

→ It is very important _____ _____

_____ _____ good grades on

this test.

[03-04] 우리말과 같은 뜻이 되도록 주어진 단어를 이용하여 두 문장을 완성하시오.

03 나는 너무 배가 불러서 더는 먹을 수가 없다. (full, eat)

→ I'm _____ _____ _____ _____
anymore.

→ I'm _____ _____ that I _____
_____ anymore.

04 그는 매우 화가 났었던 것 같아 보인다. (seem, be)

→ He _____ _____ _____ _____
upset.

→ It _____ that _____ _____ upset.

[05-06] 조건에 맞게 대화를 완성하시오.

05 A Have you decided _____ _____
_____ for this summer vacation?

B Yes. I'm going to Singapore.

조건 「의문사+to부정사」를 사용할 것

06 A My brother always does his homework late at night and goes to bed late.

B You shouldn't _____ _____
_____ his homework too late.

조건 let을 사용할 것

[07-08] 글을 읽고, 밑줄 친 부분을 자연스럽게 고쳐 쓰시오.

My name is James. I'm happy (A) to have chosen as a soccer team member. I would like to know (B) how to bring in the first meeting. Please let me know.

07 (A) _____

08 (B) _____

[09-10] 대화를 읽고, 물음에 답하시오.

A Hi, Jake. Are you going to be in the singing contest in the school festival?

B No. I don't sing (A) (do, enough, to, well) that.

A Last time I heard you sing, (B) 너는 노래를 매우 잘 하는 것 같았어.

B Thanks. But instead, my class is going in a soccer match. We are practicing hard so that we can win.

09 밑줄 친 (A)의 주어진 단어를 알맞게 배열하시오.

→ _____

10 밑줄 친 (B)의 우리말과 같은 뜻이 되도록 영작하시오.

→ you _____ _____ _____ very well

Chapter 2

동명사

UNIT 01 동명사의 쓰임

1. 동명사: 「동사원형+-ing」의 형태로, 명사처럼 문장에서 주어, 보어, 목적어 역할을 한다.

   ☆ 동명사 주어는 단수 취급하며, 동명사를 목적어로 취하는 동사에는 enjoy, keep, mind, avoid, finish, quit, stop, give up, consider 등이 있다.

   Introducing oneself <u>is</u> not easy. [주어] 자신을 소개하는 것은 쉽지 않다.

   The worst thing <u>is</u> **losing** your best friend. [보어] 최악은 가장 친한 친구를 잃는 것이다.

   Do you <u>mind</u> **opening** the window? [동사의 목적어] 창문 좀 열어 주시겠어요?

   He was proud <u>of</u> **winning** first prize. [전치사의 목적어] 그는 1등을 한 것이 자랑스러웠다.

2. 동명사의 부정: 동명사 앞에 not이나 never를 쓴다.

   Not having close friends is a sad thing. 친한 친구가 없다는 것은 슬픈 일이다.

3. 의미상 주어: 동명사의 행위자가 문장의 주어와 다를 경우, 동명사 앞에 소유격으로 나타낸다.

   Would you mind **my taking** pictures here? 여기서 제가 사진을 찍어도 될까요?

   I don't like **his staying** at my place. 나는 그가 우리 집에 머무는 것이 싫다.

4. 동명사의 시제

   (1) 「**동사원형+-ing**」: 동명사의 시제가 문장의 동사와 같을 때 쓰고, '단순동명사'라고 부른다.

      He is famous for **making** wonderful jewelry. 그는 멋진 장신구를 만드는 것으로 유명하다.

      ➡ He is famous because he **makes** wonderful jewelry.

   (2) 「**having p.p.**」: 동명사의 시제가 문장의 동사보다 먼저 일어난 일일 때 쓰고, '완료동명사'라고 부른다.

      I am ashamed of **having given up** on my dream. 나는 꿈을 포기했던 것이 부끄럽다.

      ➡ I **am** ashamed that I **gave up** on my dream.

5. 동명사의 수동태: 「being p.p.」, 「having been p.p.」

   Needless to say, people hate **being ignored**. 말할 필요도 없이, 사람들은 무시당하는 것을 싫어한다.

   I remember **having been treated** well as a child. 어렸을 때 대우를 잘 받았던 것이 기억난다.

> **Tips**
> 동명사의 의미상 주어는 소유격 대신 목적격을 쓰기도 한다.
> I don't like **him staying** at my place.

Check-up   ☐ 안에서 알맞은 말을 고르시오.

1 I like he / his coming to the party.

2 Be / Being honest is the best policy.

3 Not doing / Doing not your best will fail you.

4 Forgive me for have hurt / having hurt you before.

5 I am tired of telling / being told what to do by others.

: EXERCISES

A 주어진 단어를 어법에 맞게 바꿔 문장을 완성하시오.

1 I don't like _____ late for the appointment. (be)

2 He is very excited about _____ abroad. (travel)

3 I am ashamed of _____ what to do next. (not, know)

4 My hobby is _____ people on the street. (watch)

5 _____ friends from other countries is interesting. (make)

appointment 명 약속

be ashamed of
~을 부끄러워하다

B [보기]에서 알맞은 동사를 골라 어법에 맞게 바꿔 문장을 완성하시오.

| 보기 | speak | keep | drink | bake |

1 _____ a pet is exciting.

2 She is good at _____ cookies and bread.

3 My greatest fear is _____ in public.

4 People love _____ coffee these days.

pet 명 애완동물

fear 명 두려움, 공포

in public 대중 앞에서

C 두 문장의 의미가 통하도록 문장을 완성하시오.

1 Would you mind if I take this seat?

→ Would you mind _____ this seat?

2 She admitted that she had been told to do that.

→ She admitted _____ to do that.

3 I apologize that I kept you waiting so long.

→ I apologize for _____ you waiting so long.

4 I am so happy that I was accepted into college.

→ I am so happy about _____ into college.

take a seat 자리에 앉다
admit 동 인정하다
apologize 동 사과하다
be accepted into
~에 입학하다

D 우리말과 같은 뜻이 되도록 주어진 단어를 이용하여 문장을 완성하시오.

1 당신을 도와드릴 수 없어서 미안합니다. (be able to, not)

→ I'm sorry for _____ _____ _____ _____ help you.

2 그녀는 그가 자신을 방해하는 것을 참을 수가 없었다. (he, interrupt)

→ She couldn't stand _____ _____ her.

3 그 소식을 알려 주서서 감사합니다. (inform)

→ I am grateful for _____ _____ of the news.

동명사 vs. to부정사

1. 동명사를 목적어로 취하는 동사: admit, avoid, consider, delay, deny, dislike, enjoy, finish, give up, keep, mind, practice, put off, quit, stop, suggest 등

He seems to **avoid talking** to me. 그는 나와 말하는 것을 피하는 것 같다.
She's **considering getting** a part-time job. 그녀는 파트타임 일자리를 얻는 것을 고려하고 있다.

2. to부정사를 목적어로 취하는 동사: agree, ask, choose, decide, expect, hope, learn, plan, promise, refuse, want, wish 등

I **expect to finish** the work by 10 pm. 나는 밤 10시까지 일을 끝낼 거라고 생각한다.
He **decided to go** jogging every morning. 그는 매일 아침 달리기를 하기로 결심했다.

3. 동명사와 to부정사 둘 다 목적어로 취하는 동사

(1) 뜻이 달라지지 않는 동사: like, love, hate, begin, start, continue 등

It **started raining[to rain].** 비가 오기 시작했다.

(2) 뜻이 달라지는 동사: forget, remember, try, regret 등

forget+to부정사 ~할 일을 잊다(아직 하지 않음)	remember+to부정사 ~할 일을 기억하다(아직 하지 않음)
forget+동명사 ~한 일을 잊다(이미 했음)	remember+동명사 ~한 일을 기억하다(이미 했음)
try+to부정사 ~하려고 노력하다[애쓰다]	regret+to부정사 ~하게 되어 유감이다
try+동명사 시험 삼아 (한번) ~하다	regret+동명사 ~한 것을 후회하다

I'm sorry that I **forgot to call** you. I won't forget tonight.
미안해. 너한테 전화하는 걸 잊었어. 오늘 밤에는 잊지 않을게.

I **forgot calling** him and called him again. 나는 그에게 전화했던 것을 잊고 다시 전화를 했다.

Please **remember to close** the window before you leave the house.
집을 떠나기 전에 창문 닫는 것을 기억해 주세요.

I **remember closing** the window this morning. 나는 오늘 아침에 창문을 닫은 것을 기억한다.

I **tried to stay** up all night, but I fell asleep. 나는 밤을 새려고 노력했지만, 잠이 들었다.
If your computer is not working, why don't you **try restarting** it?
네 컴퓨터가 작동하지 않으면 다시 시작해 보는 게 어때?

I **regret to inform** you that you failed the test. 시험에 통과하지 못했음을 알리게 되어 유감입니다.
I don't **regret taking** this job. 나는 이 일을 택한 것을 후회하지 않는다.

Tips

「stop+동명사」 ~하는 것을 멈추다 vs. 「stop+to부정사」 ~하기 위해 멈추다

stop 뒤에 온 to부정사는 stop의 목적어가 아니라 '~하기 위해'라는 의미의 부사로 쓰인 것이다.

I stopped reading a newspaper.
나는 신문을 읽던 것을 멈췄다.

I stopped to read a newspaper.
나는 신문을 읽기 위해 멈췄다.

Check-up [ ] 안에서 알맞은 말을 고르시오.

1 He gave up [driving / to drive] a car to work.

2 She agrees [having / to have] another cup of coffee.

3 Do you remember [meeting / to meet] me at the camp last year?

: EXERCISES

A [　] 안에서 알맞은 것을 고르시오.

donate ⑧ 기부하다
avoid ⑧ 피하다

1 He [decided / stopped] donating money.

2 She's [avoiding / hoping] to see her son.

3 I forgot [buying / to buy] some milk. I need to go to the market again.

4 I forgot [buying / to buy] some milk and bought it again. Now I have too much milk.

B 주어진 단어를 어법에 맞게 바꿔 문장을 완성하시오.

mind ⑧ 신경 쓰다,
　　싫어하다
turn A down A를 낮추다
deny ⑧ 거부하다; 부정하다
accept ⑧ 받아들이다

1 Do you mind _____ the volume down? (turn)

2 She promised _____ me clean the house. (help)

3 He denied _____ the money. (accept)

4 They planned _____ to Italy. (travel)

C 두 문장의 의미가 통하도록 문장을 완성하시오.

pick up A
A를 찾아오다, 데려오다
used to ~하곤 했다
yell at
~에게 소리를 지르다

1 Mom told me to pick up my sister at two, but I forgot.

→ I forgot _____ at two.

2 My dad used to take me to the park, and I remember that.

→ I remember _____ to the park.

3 I wanted to pass the test, so I tried so hard.

→ I tried so hard _____.

4 I yelled at my sister, and now I regret it.

→ I regret _____.

D 우리말과 같은 뜻이 되도록 주어진 단어를 이용하여 문장을 완성하시오.

1 당신을 곧 다시 뵙게 되길 바랍니다. (hope, see)

→ I _____ _____ _____ you again soon.

2 나는 새로운 사람들을 만나는 것을 즐긴다. (enjoy, meet)

→ I _____ _____ new people.

3 이 편지를 John에게 주는 것을 잊지 말아라. (forget, give)

→ Don't _____ _____ _____ this letter to John.

4 나는 살을 빼기 위해 저녁 6시 이후에 안 먹으려고 노력했다. (try, eat, not)

→ I _____ _____ _____ _____ after 6 pm to lose weight.

여러 가지 동명사 표현

go –ing ~하러 가다	I **went shopping** with my grandma. 나는 할머니와 쇼핑을 갔다.
be busy –ing ~하느라 바쁘다	He **is busy looking** after his daughter. 그는 딸을 돌보느라 바쁘다.
be worth –ing ~할 가치가 있다	The book **is worth reading**. 그 책은 읽을 가치가 있다.
cannot help –ing ~하지 않을 수 없다 [cannot but + 동사원형]	I **cannot help looking**[**cannot but look**] at the girl. 나는 그 소녀를 쳐다보지 않을 수 없다.
feel like –ing ~하고 싶다	I **feel like going** for a walk. 나는 산책을 가고 싶다.
have difficulty[trouble] –ing ~하는 데 곤란을 겪다	She **had difficulty**[**trouble**] **finding** a good nanny. 그녀는 좋은 보모를 찾는 데 어려움을 겪었다.
look forward to –ing ~을 고대하다	I'm **looking forward to going** to Hawaii this summer. 나는 이번 여름에 하와이 가는 것을 기대하고 있다.
keep[prevent] + 목적어 + from + –ing ~가 …하는 것을 막다	Mom **keeps**[**prevents**] **me from eating** too many sweets. 엄마는 내가 너무 많은 사탕을 먹지 못하게 한다.
What[How] about –ing ~하는 게 어때?	**What**[**How**] **about taking** a short break? 잠깐 휴식을 하는 것이 어때?
spend + 시간[돈] 등 + –ing ~에 시간[돈] 등을 소비하다	You shouldn't **spend your life chasing** after money. 너는 인생을 돈을 쫓는 데 써서는 안 된다.
be[get] used to –ing ~하는 데 익숙하다	I **am used to getting** up early. 나는 일찍 일어나는 데 익숙하다. cf.) 「used to + 동사원형」 ~하곤 했다 I **used to get** up early when I was young. 나는 어렸을 때 일찍 일어나곤 했다.
On –ing ~하자마자	**On seeing** me, he ran away. 그는 나를 보자마자 도망갔다.
there is no –ing ~할 수 없다	**There is no going** back to the past. 과거로 돌아갈 수 없다.
it is no use –ing ~해도 소용없다	**It is no use complaining**. 불평해도 소용없다.
contribute to –ing ~하는 데 기여하다	They **contributed to making** the world a better place. 그들은 세상을 더 살기 좋은 곳으로 만드는 데 기여했다.
devote ... to –ing ~하는 데 …을 바치다	She **devoted** her time **to curing** the disease. 그녀는 자신의 시간을 그 병을 치료하는 데 바쳤다.

Check-up 　□ 안에서 알맞은 말을 고르시오.

1 I want to go danced / dancing .

2 I feel like take / taking a shower.

3 I couldn't help cry / crying at the scene.

4 She has difficulty read / reading small letters.

: EXERCISES

A [   ] 안에서 알맞은 것을 고르시오.

1 Spend your money [helping / to help] the kids in Africa.

2 She used to [blame / blaming] others for everything.

3 David hasn't got used to [eat / eating] with chopsticks yet.

4 He had trouble [finding / to finding] the way to the hospital.

blame A for B
B에 대해 A를 탓하다

chopsticks 젓가락

B [보기]에서 알맞은 단어를 골라 어법에 맞게 바꿔 문장을 완성하시오.

보기	deny	worry	watch	play

1 I enjoyed the movie a lot. It is worth _____.

2 There is no _____ that he was a great person.

3 He keeps his son from _____ computer games too much.

4 She has never traveled by herself. I cannot help _____ about her.

deny ⑧ 부인하다
worth ⑲ ~할 가치가 있는
keep A from B
A가 B하는 것을 막다
by oneself 혼자서

C 밑줄 친 부분에 유의하여 해석을 완성하시오.

1 It is no use trying to escape.
   → 탈출하려고 _____.

2 I couldn't help bursting into tears.
   → 나는 울음을 _____.

3 He is used to spending time alone.
   → 그는 혼자 시간을 _____.

4 She was very busy preparing for the finals.
   → 그녀는 기말고사를 _____.

D 우리말과 같은 뜻이 되도록 주어진 단어를 이용하여 문장을 완성하시오.

1 고양이를 보자마자 그 개는 크게 짖기 시작했다. (on, see)
   → _____ _____ a cat, the dog started barking loudly.

2 많은 사람들은 필요하지 않은 옷을 사는 데 돈을 쓴다. (spend, buy)
   → Many people _____ _____ _____ unnecessary clothes.

3 나는 스노보드 타는 법을 배우는 것을 매우 기대하고 있다. (look forward to, learn)
   → I _____ _____ _____ _____ _____ how to snowboard.

4 그 소음이 그녀가 공부에 집중하는 것을 방해했다. (keep, from, concentrate)
   → The noise _____ _____ _____ _____ on her studies.

: Review Test

[01-03] 빈칸에 들어갈 알맞은 말을 고르시오.

01

> You shouldn't keep _____ breakfast if you want to be successful at school.

① skip
② skipping
③ to skip
④ have skipped
⑤ to have skipped

02

> My mom is looking forward to _____ her brother in Spain.

① see
② seeing
③ be seen
④ having seen
⑤ having been seen

03

> I apologize for _____ bad words to you yesterday.

① say
② have said
③ to say
④ having said
⑤ having been said

[04-05] 빈칸에 들어갈 수 <u>없는</u> 말을 고르시오.

04

> He _____ persuading his boss.

① gave up
② considered
③ suggested
④ promised
⑤ kept

05

> She _____ to volunteer for the cleaning work.

① enjoys
② wants
③ refuses
④ decides
⑤ starts

06 빈칸에 들어갈 말이 바르게 짝지어진 것은?

> · He devoted his lifetime to _____ young kids.
> · I expect to _____ high school students from March.

① teach – teach
② teaching – teaching
③ teach – teaching
④ teaching – teach
⑤ teach – have taught

07 밑줄 친 <u>to</u>의 성격이 나머지와 <u>다른</u> 하나는?

① It is not good <u>to</u> judge others.
② I'm not used <u>to</u> dancing in public.
③ My weakness is <u>to</u> put things off.
④ She decided <u>to</u> study abroad.
⑤ I want to learn how <u>to</u> live a happy life.

08 다음 중 어법상 <u>어색한</u> 문장은?

① It suddenly started snowing.
② I wish to visit Australia someday.
③ I forgot to take the medicine last night.
④ I remember to watch the movie as a child.
⑤ I tried to understand your feelings.

09 짝지어진 두 문장의 의미가 같지 <u>않은</u> 것은?

① He forgot to do the laundry last night.
 → He didn't do the laundry last night.
② Suddenly, he stopped talking.
 → Suddenly, he stopped to talk.
③ Learning foreign languages is hard.
 → It is hard to learn foreign languages.
④ Would you mind if I turn off the air conditioner?
 → Would you mind my turning off the air conditioner?
⑤ She remembered leaving her phone at home.
 → She remembered that she left her phone at home.

10 우리말을 영어로 옮긴 것 중 바르지 않은 것은?

① 나는 당신을 만나기를 고대하고 있어요.
　→ I'm looking forward to meeting you.
② 그는 그녀가 새집으로 이사하는 것을 도와주기를 꺼리지 않는다.
　→ He doesn't mind helping her move to a new house.
③ 너는 역사 보고서 쓰는 것을 끝마쳤니?
　→ Did you finish writing a history report?
④ 그녀는 얼룩을 제거하려고 애를 쓰고 있었다.
　→ She was trying removing the stain.
⑤ 당신은 지난달에 그녀를 보았던 것을 기억하나요?
　→ Do you remember seeing her last month?

11 빈칸에 들어갈 말이 바르게 짝지어진 것은?

· She enjoys _____ foreign countries.
· He expected _____ good scores.
· The poem is worth _____.

① to visit – to get – memorizing
② visiting – to get – memorizing
③ visiting – getting – memorizing
④ to visit – getting – to memorize
⑤ visiting – getting – to memorize

12 다음 중 어법상 옳은 문장은?

① Have you finished to eating dinner?
② I gave up buying a laptop computer.
③ Could you stop to making noise, please?
④ Instead of take a bus, he took the train.
⑤ I cannot help run away from the scene.

13 우리말을 영어로 바르게 옮긴 것은?

나는 밤늦게 간식을 먹지 않으려고 노력하고 있다.

① I'm trying to not eat snacks late at night.
② I'm trying not to eat snacks late at night.
③ I'm trying not eating snacks late at night.
④ I'm not trying to eat snacks late at night.
⑤ I'm not trying eating snacks late at night.

[14-15] 글을 읽고, 물음에 답하시오.

Last weekend, my friends and I went ❶ hiking. Less than 30 minutes after I began walking, I found myself tired already. I wasn't used to ❷ walk uphill. I started ❸ to feel breathless. When I thought (A) 더 멀리는 갈 수 없다 (no, there, going, further, was), one of my friends suggested ❹ taking a rest. After a short break, we went up to the top. Frankly speaking, I couldn't say I enjoyed the climbing very much, but it was definitely worth ❺ trying.

14 밑줄 친 ❶~❺ 중 어법상 어색한 것은?

15 밑줄 친 (A)의 우리말과 같은 뜻이 되도록 단어를 바르게 배열한 것은?

① no going further was there
② there was no going further
③ no going further there was
④ there was no further going
⑤ no further going was there

[01-02] 우리말과 같은 뜻이 되도록 주어진 단어를 이용하여 문장을 완성하시오.

01 그녀는 여동생과 여행 가는 것을 아주 좋아한다. (love, travel)

→ She _____ with her sister.

02 그는 딸에게 책 읽어 주는 것을 즐거워한다. (enjoy, read)

→ He _____ books to his daughter.

[03-04] 우리말과 같은 뜻이 되도록 주어진 단어를 배열하시오.

03 그 노인은 결국 일주일 전에 불을 냈던 것을 인정했다.
(set, admitted, the fire, having)

→ The old man finally _____
_____ a week ago.

04 그녀는 3년 전에 경찰에 체포되었던 것을 부인했다.
(arrested, having, denied, been)

→ She _____
by the police three years ago.

05 밑줄 친 부분 중, 어법상 <u>어색한</u> 문장을 <u>두 개</u> 찾아 고쳐 쓰시오.

> My Canadian friend, Cathy, is coming to see me next month. In Canada, she and I went shopping together. We spent time to do fun things. I remember to visit wonderful places with her. I look forward to seeing her again.

(1) _____

(2) _____

06 우리말과 같은 뜻이 되도록 주어진 단어를 사용하여 영작 하시오.

(1) 나 숙제 하느라 바빠. (busy, do one's homework)

→ _____

(2) 내일 하이킹하러 가는 게 어때? (what about, go)

→ _____

[07-08] [보기]에서 알맞은 단어를 골라 어법에 맞게 바꿔 대화를 완성하시오.

| 보기 | do | watch | drink | reward |

07 A It's hard for me to fall asleep at night. What do you suggest?

B I suggest _____ some warm milk before going to bed. Also, avoid _____ TV too late.

08 A If you agree to cancel the plan, I promise _____ you later.

B I'm sorry, but I refuse _____ so.

[09-10] 대화를 읽고, 물음에 답하시오.

> A What do you want to be when you grow up?
> B I'm not sure what I enjoy doing. How about you?
> A (A) <u>나는 수의사가 되려고 생각 중이야.</u>
> B I remember you fed a street cat the other day.
> A Yes. I love animals. I hope you have a goal, too. (B) <u>네가 좋아하는 일을 찾도록 노력해 봐.</u>
> B I'll try. Thanks. Good luck with your dream.

09 밑줄 친 (A)를 주어진 단어를 이용하여 영작하시오.

→ I'm _____ a vet.
(consider, become)

10 밑줄 친 (B)를 주어진 단어를 이용하여 영작하시오.

→ _____ what you
_____.
(try, find, like, do)

Chapter 3

분사

분사의 종류

1. 분사의 종류

(1) 현재분사 「동사+-ing」 능동(~하는, ~시키는), 진행(~하고 있는)

a **barking** dog 짖고 있는 개   a **crying** girl 울고 있는 소녀

(2) 과거분사 「동사+-ed」 수동(~되는, ~당하는), 완료(~해진)

a **broken** window 깨진 창문   **fallen** leaves 떨어진 잎(낙엽)

2. 분사의 역할

(1) 명사 수식: 단독으로 쓰인 분사는 명사 앞에서, 수식어와 함께 쓰인 분사는 명사 뒤에서 명사를 수식한다.

Be careful of the **broken glass**. 깨진 유리를 조심해라.

I know **the girl playing** the violin. 나는 바이올린을 연주하는 그 소녀를 안다.

(2) 보어 역할

You look **tired**. [주격보어] 너 피곤해 보여.

I saw my grandmother **knitting**. [목적격보어] 나는 할머니가 뜨개질하는 것을 보았다.

(3) 동사로 쓰인 분사

The baby is **taking** a nap now. [진행형: be+-ing] 아기는 지금 낮잠을 자고 있다.

I have **completed** the task successfully. [완료형: have+p.p.] 나는 그 일을 성공적으로 완수했다.

A lot of products are **sold** on the online market. [수동형: be+p.p.]
온라인 시장에서 많은 제품이 팔린다.

3. 감정을 나타내는 분사: '~한 감정을 느끼게 하는'이라는 의미일 경우 '현재분사'를, '~한 감정을 느끼는'이라는 의미일 경우 '과거분사'를 쓴다.

The movie was very **boring**. [영화가 지루하게 느끼게 하는] 그 영화는 매우 지루했다.

I was very **bored** of the movie. [내가 싫증을 느끼는] 나는 그 영화에 싫증이 났다.

Check-up ☐ 안에서 알맞은 말을 고르시오.

1 This show is interesting / interested .

2 I haven't seeing / seen her for a while.

3 I heard my name calling / called .

: EXERCISES

A   [   ] 안에서 알맞은 것을 고르시오.

1 The lecture on philosophy is so [boring / bored].

2 That was a [surprising / surprised] proposal.

3 I am [satisfying / satisfied] with the results.

4 He seemed [amusing / amused] at the national team's game.

philosophy 몡 철학
proposal 몡 제안
amuse
동 (사람을) 즐겁게 하다

B   [보기]에서 알맞은 단어를 골라 어법에 맞게 바꿔 대화를 완성하시오.

보기	steal	excite	interest	stand

1 A You look _____.
   B Yeah, I'm going to Disneyland!

2 A Is there something wrong?
   B Yes. I think my wallet was _____.

3 A Do you know the boy _____ over there?
   B Yes. He lives next door.

4 A What school subjects do you find _____?
   B Math and English interest me most.

steal 동 훔치다
wallet 몡 지갑
next door 옆집
subject 몡 과목

C   [보기]와 같이 문장을 완성하시오.

보기	The girl is my best friend. She is standing at the bus stop. → The girl <u>standing at the bus stop</u> is my best friend.

1 I saw a dog. The dog was running after a boy.
   → I saw a dog _____.

2 I read a comic book. It was written in English.
   → I read a comic book _____.

3 My sister and I went to the museum. It is located in New York.
   → My sister and I went to the museum _____.

run after ~을 뒤쫓다
comic book 몡 만화책
museum 몡 박물관
be located in
~에 위치해 있다

D   우리말과 같은 뜻이 되도록 주어진 단어를 이용하여 문장을 완성하시오.

1 나는 새 차보다 중고차를 선호한다. (use, car)
   → I prefer _____ _____ _____ to a new car.

2 나는 그 경기가 흥미롭다는 것을 알았다. (find, the game, excite)
   → I _____ _____ _____ _____.

3 나는 누군가 나를 바라보고 있는 것을 느꼈다. (feel, someone, look at)
   → I _____ _____ _____ me.

UNIT 02 분사구문

1. 종속절을 분사구문으로 만들기

~~As he~~ had a cold, ~~he~~ couldn't do anything.
　　① ② ③　　　② ③

➡ **Having** a cold, he couldn't do anything. 그는 감기에 걸려서 아무것도 할 수 없었다.

① 의미 파악에 어려움이 없는 경우, 접속사를 생략한다.

② 주절과 종속절의 주어가 같을 경우, 주어를 생략한다.

③ 주절과 종속절의 시제가 같을 경우, 동사를 −ing 형태로 바꾼다.

2. 분사구문의 부정은 분사 앞에 부정어(not, never)를 붙인다.

Not realizing his own mistake, he blamed others. 그는 자신의 잘못은 모르고 다른 사람들을 탓했다.

3. 분사구문의 여러 가지 의미

(1) 부대상황 ～하면서 (while; 동시 동작), 그리고 ～하다 (and; 연속 동작)

He jogs **listening** to music.
⬅ He jogs **while he listens** to music. 그는 음악을 들으면서 조깅을 한다.

The train left Seoul at 2:00, **arriving** in Busan at 4:30.
⬅ The train left Seoul at 2:00, **and it arrived** in Busan at 4:30.
　　기차는 두 시에 서울을 떠났고, 네 시 삼십 분에 부산에 도착했다.

(2) 시간 ～때, ～동안, ～전에, ～후에 (as, while, when, before, after, as soon as)

Being young, she would spend time outdoors.
⬅ **When she was** young, she would spend time outdoors. 어렸을 때 그녀는 야외에서 시간을 보내곤 했다.

(3) 이유 때문에 (as, because, since)

Wearing it already, I couldn't return the shirt.
⬅ **As I wore** it already, I couldn't return the shirt. 나는 이미 그 셔츠를 입었기 때문에 반품할 수 없었다.

(4) 조건 ～하면 (if)

Looking closely, you will see what the problem is.
⬅ **If you look** closely, you will see what the problem is. 자세히 보면 문제가 무엇인지 알 수 있을 것이다.

(5) 양보 ～이지만, ～임에도 (although, even though, though)

Struggling with the question for hours, he still couldn't solve it.
⬅ **Although he struggled** with the question for hours, he still couldn't solve it.
　　몇 시간 동안 그 문제와 씨름을 했지만 그는 여전히 그것을 풀 수 없었다.

Check-up　　☐ 안에서 알맞은 말을 고르시오.

1 ☐ Ate / Eating ☐ too much, I felt uncomfortable.

2 ☐ Listening not / Not listening ☐ to my mom, I went out.

3 ☐ Go / Going ☐ home, I bought some fruit.

: EXERCISES

A   [   ] 안에서 알맞은 것을 고르시오.

1   [Have / Having] no money, he had to walk home.

2   [To forget / Forgetting] to bring an umbrella, she got wet.

3   [Looked / Looking] upset, he kicked the door.

4   [Having not / Not having] lunch, I was very hungry.

bring ⑧ ~을 가져오다
upset ⑲ 화난

B   두 문장이 같은 의미가 되도록 분사구문을 이용하여 문장을 완성하시오.

1   When he sleeps, he snores loudly.

   → _____, he snores loudly.

2   As I was so tired, I wanted to take a nap.

   → _____, I wanted to take a nap.

3   Because she woke up late, she was late for school.

   → _____, she was late for school.

4   Although they did their best, they still couldn't make it.

   → _____, they still couldn't make it.

snore ⑧ 코를 골다
loudly ⑨ 크게
take a nap 낮잠 자다
wake up 일어나다
do one's best
최선을 다하다
make it 해내다, 성공하다

C   [보기]에서 알맞은 접속사를 골라 두 문장이 같은 의미가 되도록 부사절을 완성하시오.

보기	because	even though	if

1   Seeing me, he will give me a big smile.

   → _____, he will give me a big smile.

2   Studying hard, he still got low grades.

   → _____, he still got low grades.

3   Growing up in the countryside, she knew a lot about plants.

   → _____, she knew a lot about plants.

countryside 시골 지역
plant ⑲ 식물

D   우리말과 같은 뜻이 되도록 주어진 단어를 이용하여 문장을 완성하시오.

1   그녀는 그 아름다운 경치를 보면서 행복했다. (watch, the beautiful scenery)

   → She felt happy, _____ _____ _____ _____.

2   신중히 생각해 보면 해결책을 찾을 수 있을 것이다. (think, carefully)

   → _____ _____, you will find the solution.

3   그녀는 책을 많이 샀지만 다 읽을 수 없었다. (buy, a lot of)

   → _____ _____ _____ _____ _____, she
     couldn't read them all.

UNIT 03 여러 가지 분사구문

1. 완료분사구문 「Having p.p.」: 종속절의 일이 주절보다 먼저 일어난 일일 때 사용한다.

Having slept enough last night, she feels great now.

← As she **slept** enough last night, she feels great now.

그녀는 어젯밤에 잠을 충분히 자서 지금 기분이 좋다.

2. 수동분사구문 「Being p.p.」, 「Having been p.p.」: Being과 Having been은 생략할 수 있다.

(Being) Informed of the danger, he decided not to go there.

← As he **was informed** of the danger, he decided not to go there.

그는 위험에 대해 알게 되어 그곳에 가지 않기로 결정했다.

(Having been) Painted by Vincent Van Gogh, the picture is priceless.

← As it **was painted** by Vincent Van Gogh, the picture is priceless.

그 그림은 Vincent Van Gogh에 의해 그려졌기 때문에 매우 귀중하다.

3. 「접속사+분사구문」: 뜻을 명확하게 하기 위해 접속사를 쓰기도 한다.

Before criticizing me, you should listen to my story.

나를 비난하기 전에 당신은 내 이야기를 들어 봐야 한다.

Although badly hurt, he refused to go to see a doctor.

그는 심하게 다쳤음에도 병원에 가기를 거부했다.

4. 독립분사구문: 종속절의 주어가 주절의 주어와 다른 경우 분사구문 앞에 주어를 쓴다.

The road being so slippery, **you** should walk carefully. 길이 미끄러우니 조심해서 걸어야 한다.

It being rainy, **I** stayed home. 비가 와서 나는 집에 있었다.

5. 비인칭 독립분사구문: 종속절의 주어가 일반인인 경우 주절의 주어와 달라도 생략할 수 있다.

frankly speaking 솔직히 말해서	strictly speaking 엄밀히 말해서
roughly speaking 대략적으로 말해서	generally speaking 일반적으로 말해서
considering ~을 고려하자면	judging from ~로 판단하건대
speaking of ~에 대해 이야기하면	

6. 「with+명사+분사」: ~가 …한 채로 (명사와 분사의 관계가 능동이면 현재분사, 수동이면 과거분사)

I can't focus **with** <u>you</u> **watching** me. 나는 당신이 지켜보고 있는 채로 집중할 수 없다.

She looked at me **with** <u>her eyes</u> **filled** with tears. 그녀는 눈에 눈물이 가득한 채로 나를 바라보았다.

> **Tips**
>
> 「with+명사+분사」에서 분사 자리에 형용사나 부사, 전치사구 등이 올 수도 있다.
>
> He left the room **with the lights on.**
> 그는 불을 켜 둔 채 방을 나섰다.

Check-up   □ 안에서 알맞은 말을 고르시오.

1 Had lived / Having lived in Russia as a child, she can speak Russian.

2 Being / The weather being nice, we can go windsurfing.

3 It's a bad habit to sit with your legs crossing / crossed .

: EXERCISES

A [ ] 안에서 알맞은 말을 고르시오.

bark ⑧ 짖다
fall over 넘어지다

1 I cannot sleep with the dog [barking / barked].

2 [Was told / Being told] to stay indoors, I didn't go out.

3 [Surprising / Surprised] at the news, she almost fell over.

4 [Having gone / Going] to bed so late last night, she is very tired now.

B 두 문장이 같은 의미가 되도록 분사구문을 이용하여 문장을 완성하시오.

sold out 품절의, 매진된
be impressed with
~에 감명 받다
raise ⑧ 기르다, 양육하다

1 As the tickets were sold out, I couldn't buy any.

→ _____, I couldn't buy any.

2 As he spent all his money, he can't buy the jeans now.

→ _____, he can't buy the jeans now.

3 As she was impressed with music, she became a musician.

→ _____, she became a musician.

4 As she was born and raised in Quebec, she speaks English and French.

→ _____, she speaks English and French.

C 두 문장이 같은 의미가 되도록 「with+명사+분사」 형태를 이용하여 문장을 완성하시오.

crossed ⑱ 교차한
fall down 떨어지다

1 She was looking at the fire, and her arms were crossed.

→ She was looking at the fire _____.

2 He was listening to music, and his eyes were closed.

→ He was listening to music _____.

3 She was looking at the picture and tears were falling down.

→ She was looking at the picture _____.

D 우리말과 같은 뜻이 되도록 주어진 단어를 이용하여 문장을 완성하시오.

1 엄밀히 말하자면, 두 단어의 뜻은 같지 않다. (speak)

→ _____ _____, the meanings of the two words are not the same.

2 주어진 상황을 고려하면, 지금은 네가 참을성을 발휘할 때이다. (consider)

→ _____ the situation, it's time for you to be patient.

3 Tom에 대해서 말하자면, 그는 믿을 만한 사람이 아니다. (speak)

→ _____ _____ Tom, he is not a trustworthy man.

4 그녀의 발음으로 판단하건대, 그녀는 영국 사람인 것 같다. (judge)

→ _____ _____ her pronunciation, she seems to be English.

: Review **Test**

[01-03] 빈칸에 들어갈 알맞은 말을 고르시오.

01

A man _____ William called you.

① name   ② naming   ③ named
④ to name   ⑤ having named

02

In the picture, the girl _____ sunglasses is my sister.

① wear   ② wearing   ③ worn
④ to wear   ⑤ being worn

03

She can't go swimming now, _____ her leg last week.

① broken   ② breaking
③ having been broken   ④ having broken
⑤ have broken

[04-05] 빈칸에 들어갈 말이 바르게 짝지어진 것을 고르시오.

04

· The lecture was so _____. I couldn't help falling asleep.
· I did the same job all morning, and I got very _____.

① bored - bored   ② bore - boring
③ boring - bore   ④ bored - boring
⑤ boring - bored

05

· I am _____ in her making excuses constantly.
· The game was canceled because of rain. It was really _____.

① disappoint - disappointing
② disappointing - disappointed
③ disappointed - disappoint
④ disappointing - disappoint
⑤ disappointed - disappointing

06 [보기]의 밑줄 친 부분과 쓰임이 같은 것은?

> 보기   I saw you <u>wandering</u> around the house in the middle of the night.

① You seem to enjoy <u>making</u> fun of others.
② <u>Helping</u> others will make you happy as well.
③ We need to buy a new <u>washing</u> machine.
④ She was <u>asking</u> for help desperately.
⑤ My hope is <u>making</u> enough money for my family.

07 우리말을 영어로 옮긴 것 중 바르지 <u>않은</u> 것은?

① 그녀는 노래를 부르면서 운전을 했다.
   → She drove a car, sang a song.
② 그녀는 장학금을 받아서 대학에 다닐 수 있었다.
   → Receiving a scholarship, she could go to college.
③ 모퉁이를 돌면 주유소가 보일 거예요.
   → Turning around the corner, you will see the gas station.
④ 날씨가 너무 더워서 나는 에어컨을 켰다.
   → The weather being so hot, I turned on the air conditioner.
⑤ 그녀는 두 번째 기회를 얻게 되어 기뻤다.
   → Given a second chance, she was pleased.

[08-09] 두 문장이 같은 뜻이 되도록 빈칸에 들어갈 알맞은 말을 고르시오.

08

My dog follows me everywhere, waving its tail.
   → My dog follows me everywhere _____ it waves its tail.

① if   ② as   ③ since
④ because   ⑤ although

09

I had a hairdresser trim my hair.
   → I had my hair _____ by a hairdresser.

① trim   ② trimming   ③ trimmed
④ to trim   ⑤ having trimmed

[10-11] 다음 중 어법상 <u>어색한</u> 문장을 고르시오.

10 ① Reading the letter, she burst into tears.
② Following his father, he became a lawyer.
③ Been sick in bed, he couldn't go to school.
④ Bored from the book, he turned on the TV.
⑤ After leaving his hometown, he never came back.

11 ① Please don't speak with your mouth full.
② Exciting at the concert, the audience shouted loudly.
③ Interviewed by the CEO, she found herself a little nervous.
④ Having graduated a long time ago, he found the campus unfamiliar.
⑤ The windows being painted in blue, the white house looked really pretty.

12 밑줄 친 분사구문을 부사절로 옮긴 것 중 어법상 <u>어색한</u> 것은?
① He sang a song, <u>taking a shower</u>.
→ He sang a song while he was taking a shower.
② <u>Praised for his actions</u>, he felt proud of himself.
→ As he was praising for his actions, he felt proud of himself.
③ <u>Reducing what I ate</u>, I still didn't lose weight.
→ Even though I reduced what I ate, I still didn't lose weight.
④ He won first place in the contest, <u>becoming a celebrity</u>.
→ He won first place in the contest and became a celebrity.
⑤ I went jogging this morning with my dog <u>running beside me</u>.
→ I went jogging this morning, and my dog was running beside me.

13 다음 중 어법상 옳은 문장은?
① Not have money, they couldn't buy food.
② Left my wallet at home, I had to go back.
③ Putting not sunscreen, I got sunburn.
④ The plane departed late, and arriving late as well.
⑤ Exhausted from the workout, she had no energy left.

[14-15] 글을 읽고, 물음에 답하시오.

I volunteered at the local hospital this summer. One day, I saw a little girl ____ⓐ____ brightly to everyone. She liked helping patients and listening to their stories. Soon we became friends, and I asked her why she was wearing a hat (A) 그녀가 일을 하는 동안. She smiled once again, and instead of answering my question, she brought her hand to her hat. When she took the hat off, I saw she had no hair. I was ____ⓑ____. She had a cancer. I was so ____ⓒ____ with her bravery. She is the bravest person I've ever known.

14 밑줄 친 ⓐ, ⓑ, ⓒ에 들어갈 말이 바르게 짝지어진 것은?
	ⓐ	ⓑ	ⓒ
①	smiled	shocking	impressed
②	smiled	shocked	impressing
③	smiling	shocking	impressing
④	smiling	shocked	impressed
⑤	smiling	shocked	impressing

15 밑줄 친 (A)의 우리말을 분사구문으로 바르게 옮긴 것은?
① while working
② she having worked
③ she worked
④ having worked
⑤ while she working

[01-02] 주어진 단어를 현재분사나 과거분사로 바꿔 문장을 완성하시오.

01 Long ago, there was a great conqueror _____ Chingiz Khan. (call)

02 The man _____ with the elderly is my father. (help)

[03-04] 두 문장의 의미가 통하도록 문장을 완성하시오.

03 Look at the man. He is writing something on the wall.
→ Look at the man _____
_____ .

04 The kindergarten students are really cute. They are guided by a teacher.
→ The kindergarten students _____
_____ are really cute.

[05-06] 우리말과 같은 뜻이 되도록 주어진 단어를 이용하여 문장을 완성하시오.

05 그는 노를 저으면서 혼잣말을 했다. (row a boat)
→ He talked to himself, _____
_____ _____ .

06 그는 노래를 부르면서 나를 응시했다. (sing a song)
→ He stared at me, _____ _____
_____ .

07 두 문장이 같은 뜻이 되도록 문장을 완성하시오.

(1) As I don't have money, I can't lend you any.
→ _____ , I can't lend you any.

(2) After I finish this, I'll answer your questions.
→ _____ , I'll answer your questions.

08 [보기]에서 단어를 골라 우리말과 같은 뜻이 되도록 어법에 맞게 바꿔 문장을 완성하시오.

| 보기 | wave | finish | smile | write |

(1) 완성된 작품은 오른쪽 상단에 이름을 써서 제출하세요.
→ Submit your _____ work with your name _____ at the top right corner.

(2) 그녀는 미소를 짓고 손을 흔들며 비행기에 올랐다.
→ She got on the airplane, _____ and _____ her hand.

[09-10] 우리말과 같은 뜻이 되도록 주어진 단어를 배열하시오.

09 그녀는 팔짱을 낀 채 깊은 생각에 잠겨 있었다.
(folded, her arms, with)
→ She was deep in thought _____
_____ .

10 그 건물은 튼튼한 자재로 지어져서 지금도 사용된다.
(built, been, having)
→ _____ with strong materials, the building is still used.

Chapter 4

시제

현재완료와 현재완료진행

1. 현재완료 「have[has]+p.p.」: 과거 어느 시점에서 일어난 일이나 상태가 현재에도 영향을 미칠 때 사용하며, 명백한 과거를 나타내는 말(yesterday, a year ago 등)과는 함께 쓸 수 없다.

(1) 경험 ~한 적이 있다 (ever, never, once, often, before와 주로 쓰임)

Have you ever **been** to Europe? 유럽에 가 본 적이 있니?

(2) 계속 ~해 왔다 (for, since, so far와 주로 쓰임)

I **have lived** in this house for three years. 나는 이 집에서 3년 동안 살아 왔다.

(3) 완료 (이제) 막 ~했다 (just, yet, already와 주로 쓰임)

I **have** just **finished** my homework. 나는 숙제를 막 끝마쳤다.

(4) 결과 ~해 버렸다

I **have lost** my locker key. 나는 사물함 열쇠를 잃어 버렸다. (지금은 열쇠를 가지고 있지 않다.)

> **Tips**
> 「for+기간」
> I have studied English **for ten years.**
> 나는 영어를 10년 동안 공부해 왔다.
>
> 「since+기준 시점」
> I have studied English **since 2010.**
> 나는 2010년 이후로 영어를 공부해 왔다.

2. 현재완료진행 「have[has] been+-ing」: 과거 어느 시점에서 일어난 일이나 상태가 현재까지 진행되고 있음을 강조할 때 사용한다.

He **has been teaching** math for 10 years. 그는 10년 동안 수학을 가르쳐 오고 있다.

She **has been studying** yoga since 2012. 그녀는 2012년 이후로 요가를 배우고 있다.

> **Tips**
> 현재완료 vs. 현재완료진행
> 현재완료(완료, 결과)는 행위의 '완료'나 '결과'에 초점을 두는 반면, 현재완료(계속)와 현재완료진행은 '행위 자체'에 초점을 둔다.
> I **have mowed** the lawn this morning. 나는 오늘 아침에 잔디를 깎았다. [행위의 완료, 결과 강조]
> I **have mowed** the lawn since this morning. 나는 오늘 아침부터 잔디를 깎고 있다. [행위 자체, 잔디를 깎고 있음]
> I **have been mowing** the lawn since this morning. 나는 오늘 아침부터 잔디를 깎고 있다.

Check-up ☐ 안에서 알맞은 말을 고르시오.

1 I'm not hungry. I ☐ eat / have eaten ☐ dinner.

2 We have been walking ☐ since / for ☐ hours, but we're not there yet.

: EXERCISES

A [   ] 안에서 알맞은 것을 고르시오.

1 [Have you / Did you] ever been to Japan?

2 We [went / have been] to this school five years ago.

3 He's not here. He [has been / has gone] to Canada.

4 I have been thinking about the question [for / since] an hour.

B 밑줄 친 부분을 어법에 맞게 고쳐 쓰시오.

1 I <u>have lost</u> my bag yesterday.

2 She <u>works</u> as a computer programmer since last year.

3 Hailey and I <u>know</u> each other for 10 years.

4 The elevator <u>has been</u> out of order two hours ago, but it's working now.

work as ~로서 일하다
programmer
명 프로그래머
elevator 명 승강기
out of order 고장 난
work 동 작동하다

C for나 since를 활용하여 두 문장을 한 문장으로 바꿔 쓰시오.

1 I started to study French two years ago. I am still studying it.

→ I ＿＿＿＿＿ ＿＿＿＿＿ French ＿＿＿＿＿ two years.

2 He started to wait for his girlfriend at 6 pm. He's still waiting for her.

→ He ＿＿＿＿ ＿＿＿＿ ＿＿＿＿ for his girlfriend ＿＿＿＿ 6 pm.

3 Brian and I became friends when we were kids. We are still best friends.

→ Brian and I ＿＿＿＿ ＿＿＿＿ best friends ＿＿＿＿ we were kids.

4 We started to watch a movie one hour ago. We're still watching the movie.

→ We ＿＿＿＿ ＿＿＿＿ ＿＿＿＿ the movie ＿＿＿＿ one hour.

study 동 ~을 공부하다
wait for ~을 기다리다

D 우리말과 같은 뜻이 되도록 주어진 단어를 이용하여 문장을 완성하시오.

1 너는 내 휴대 전화를 본 적이 있니? (ever, see)

→ ＿＿＿＿＿ ＿＿＿＿＿ ＿＿＿＿＿ ＿＿＿＿＿ my cell phone?

2 나는 한 번도 Kelly와 이야기를 해 본 적이 없다. (never, talk to)

→ I ＿＿＿＿＿ ＿＿＿＿＿ ＿＿＿＿＿ ＿＿＿＿＿ Kelly.

3 그녀는 두 시간 동안 피아노를 치고 있다. (play, two hours)

→ She ＿＿＿＿＿ ＿＿＿＿＿ ＿＿＿＿＿ the piano ＿＿＿＿＿

＿＿＿＿＿ ＿＿＿＿＿ .

UNIT 02 과거완료와 과거완료진행

1. 과거완료「had+p.p.」: 과거의 한 시점을 기준으로 그보다 더 이전부터 그 기준이 되는 시점까지 일어난 일을 나타낼 때 사용한다.

(1) 경험 ~한 적이 있었다

I **had** never **lived** alone before I entered college.
나는 대학에 가기 전에 한 번도 혼자 산 적이 없었다.

(2) 계속 (과거 한 시점까지) 계속 ~해 왔었다

The students **had stayed** in the classroom until their teacher came back.
학생들은 선생님이 돌아올 때까지 교실에 머물렀다.

(3) 완료 (이미) ~해 버렸다, 했었다

When we arrived at the party, they **had** already **eaten** all the cake.
우리가 파티에 도착했을 때 그들은 이미 케이크를 다 먹어 버렸다.

(4) 결과 ~했었다 (그 결과가 과거 기준 시점에 영향을 미침)

Lily **had lost** too much weight, so she had to buy new clothes.
Lily는 살이 너무 많이 빠져서 옷을 새로 사야 했다.

2. 과거완료와 과거: 과거완료는 대과거라고 하고, 과거에 일어난 일의 선후 관계를 나타낼 때 사용한다.

When I **came** home, my mother **had** already **made** delicious snacks.
내가 집에 왔을 때 어머니가 이미 맛있는 간식을 만들어 놓으셨다.
[어머니가 간식을 만드신 것이 먼저 일어난 일, 내가 집에 온 것이 나중에 일어난 일]

3. 과거완료진행「had been+－ing」: 과거 한 시점을 기준으로 그보다 더 이전부터 그 기준이 되는 시점까지 행위나 상태가 계속됨을 나타낼 때 사용한다.

When my sister came home, I **had been playing** the guitar.
내 여동생이 집에 왔을 때 나는 기타를 치고 있었다.

☆ 그림으로 이해하는 과거, 과거완료, 과거완료진행 시제

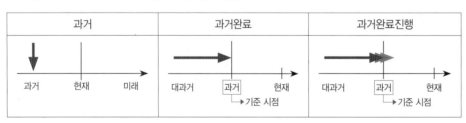

> **Plus α**
>
> **1 미래완료**
> 「will have+p.p.」:
> 현재 또는 과거에 시작된 일이 미래의 한 시점에 완료될 것으로 예측할 때 쓴다. 현재완료와 마찬가지로 경험, 계속, 완료, 결과의 의미로 사용된다.
>
> He'll **have gone** to New York <u>by this time next year.</u>
> 내년 이맘때면 그는 뉴욕에 가고 없을 것이다.
>
> **2 미래완료진행**
> 「will have been+－ing」:
> 현재 또는 과거에 시작된 일이 미래의 한 시점에 진행 중임을 강조할 때 사용한다.
>
> By next year, I **will have been working** for three years.
> 내년이면 나는 3년 동안 일을 해온 것이 된다.

Check-up ☐ 안에서 알맞은 말을 고르시오.

1 He ｜ has lived / had lived ｜ a normal life before he became a singer.

2 Mom ｜ has been working / had been working ｜ as a nurse before I was born.

: EXERCISES

A [   ] 안에서 알맞은 것을 고르시오.

1 When I got home, my sister [has been sleeping / had been sleeping].

2 When I woke up, my parents [have already gone / had already gone] out.

3 He had never caused trouble before he [entered / had entered] high school.

4 By the time he moves to Italy, he [has saved / will have saved] enough money.

5 He [has been / had been] in the hospital for a year, and he left the hospital yesterday.

> wake up 잠에서 깨다
> go out 외출하다
> cause
> 동 일으키다, 야기하다
> enter
> 동 입학하다, 들어가다
> save 동 저축하다

B 밑줄 친 부분을 어법에 맞게 고쳐 쓰시오.

1 By next year, you <u>have become</u> a manager.

2 When I saw her, it was clear that she <u>has been</u> crying.

3 She had never seen snow before she <u>moves</u> to this country.

4 When I found my lost wallet, all the money <u>has already gone</u>.

5 He <u>had told</u> the police that he had never heard of that name before.

> manager 명 관리자, 팀장
> clear 형 분명한, 명백한
> wallet 명 지갑

C [보기]에서 알맞은 동사를 골라 과거완료형으로 바꿔 문장을 완성하시오.

보기	leave	tell	steal	go

1 She said that somebody _____ her watch.

2 By the time the police arrived there, he _____ already _____.

3 When I came home, I found I _____ my textbook at school.

4 Kenny _____ me what time to meet, but I forgot about it.

> steal 동 훔치다
> arrive 동 도착하다
> forget 동 잊다

D 우리말과 같은 뜻이 되도록 주어진 단어를 이용하여 문장을 완성하시오.

1 그가 내게 전화를 했을 때 나는 이미 그를 용서한 상태였다. (already, forgive)

→ I _____ _____ _____ him when he called me.

2 전화가 울렸을 때 그녀는 한 시간째 TV를 보고 있던 중이었다. (watch, an hour)

→ She _____ _____ _____ TV _____ _____ _____ when the phone rang.

3 내년이면 그들은 결혼한 지 20년이 된다. (be married, next year)

→ They _____ _____ _____ _____ for 20 years _____ _____ _____.

: Review Test

[01-04] 빈칸에 들어갈 알맞은 말을 고르시오.

01

I _____ schools more than four times so far.

① transfer
② have transferred
③ am transferring
④ had transferred
⑤ will have transferred

02

He _____ a gold medal in the Olympics last year.

① wins
② has won
③ won
④ had won
⑤ will win

03

I _____ in the same house for ten years. But I want to move to a new place.

① have been living
② had been living
③ will have lived
④ lived
⑤ had lived

04

We were very tired. We _____ hard for a month.

① work
② have worked
③ have been working
④ had been working
⑤ will have been working

05 다음 중 어법상 옳은 문장은?

① How long have you stay in the U.S.A.?
② We haven't heard anything since she left.
③ How many times had you been here so far?
④ I have been there twice when I was young.
⑤ Recently I had been forgetting things a lot.

06 대화의 빈칸에 들어갈 알맞은 말은?

A Do you know where Catherine is?
I _____ her since this morning.
B I saw her in the library a while ago.

① look for
② had looked for
③ have been looking for
④ had been looking for
⑤ will have looked for

[07-08] [보기]의 밑줄 친 부분과 쓰임이 같은 것을 고르시오.

07

보기 They have lived in this country since 2002.

① I have never met a famous person.
② The train has just arrived.
③ I have studied Chinese for two years.
④ She has already seen the movie.
⑤ He has lost his wallet.

08

보기 He has never traveled abroad.

① He has eaten all the bananas.
② He has stayed in the hotel for two days.
③ They have already finished packing.
④ She has just arrived at the airport.
⑤ Have you ever been to Costa Rica?

09 밑줄 친 부분이 어법상 어색한 것은?

① I <u>have forgotten</u> my password, so I can't log in.

② I found somebody <u>had broken</u> a window.

③ I realized I <u>had forgotten</u> to save the file.

④ I'm sorry to <u>have kept</u> you waiting.

⑤ His grandfather <u>had passed away</u> two years ago.

10 두 문장의 의미가 통하도록 할 때, 빈칸에 들어갈 가장 알맞은 말은?

> Lisa left for Paris last month, so I can't see her now.
> → Lisa _____ to Paris.

① has been

② has gone

③ went

④ will have been

⑤ will have gone

11 우리말을 영어로 옮길 때, 빈칸에 들어갈 알맞은 말은?

> 영화가 끝날 때쯤이면 비가 그쳐 있을 거야.
> → By the time the movie is over, the rain _____.

① stops

② stopped

③ has stopped

④ had stopped

⑤ will have stopped

12 다음 중 어법상 옳은 문장은 모두 몇 개인가?

> · He has never lost a game so far.
> · She had had a bad cold since last week.
> · Nobody had found mistakes in the paper until then.
> · He has never apologized to me first until now.
> · By next year, I will have graduated from middle school.

① 1개   ② 2개   ③ 3개

④ 4개   ⑤ 5개

13 빈칸에 공통으로 들어갈 알맞은 말은?

> · He has been coaching the national soccer team _____ last year.
> · Two years had passed _____ the accident happened.

① since   ② for

③ during   ④ by the time

⑤ when

[14-15] 글을 읽고, 물음에 답하시오.

> Last Saturday, my dog died. At first, ❶ I couldn't believe that he had gone. I haven't slept well ⓐ _____ my dog died. ❷ Last night, I haven't slept at all. My father was really worried about me. ❸ So he told me that he would buy me a new dog. ❹ And he asked me which dog I would like to have. But it won't be the same. ❺ I had spent so much time with him before he died. I don't think I can get over it.

14 밑줄 친 ❶~❺ 중 어법상 옳지 않은 것은?

15 빈칸 ⓐ에 들어갈 가장 알맞은 것은?

① for   ② since   ③ yet

④ with   ⑤ until

[01-02] 우리말과 같은 뜻이 되도록 문장을 완성하시오.

01 나는 그 편지를 누가 나에게 보냈는지 궁금했다.
→ I wondered who _____ _____ me the letter.

02 그는 그때까지 누군가를 위해 요리를 해 본 적이 없었다.
→ He _____ _____ _____ for someone until then.

03 두 문장이 같은 뜻이 되도록 문장을 완성하시오.

I started to wait in line to enter the building 30 minutes ago. I am still waiting outside.
→ I _____ in line for 30 minutes to enter the building.

04 주어진 동사를 이용하여 대화를 완성하시오.

A Is your grandmother still staying in the hospital?

B Yes. She _____ in the hospital for a month. (stay)

05 그림을 보고, 주어진 단어를 이용하여 문장을 완성하시오.

Do not sit on the bench. I _____ just _____ it. (paint)

[06-08] 글을 읽고, 물음에 답하시오.

> When I got back home last night, I got very scared. The house was a total mess. I realized somebody **(A)** (break) into my house. **(B)** I was upset because the thief has stolen my brand-new camera. I reported it to the police immediately, but they said it would be hard to get my camera back. But I've just got a phone call from the police. **(C)** (arrested, been, the thief, has). I guess I'll be able to get my camera back.

06 밑줄 친 (A)를 어법에 맞게 바꿔 쓰시오.

_____

07 밑줄 친 (B)에서 어법상 어색한 부분을 찾아 고쳐 쓰시오.

_____

08 밑줄 친 (C)의 주어진 단어를 알맞게 배열하시오.

_____

09 두 문장을 완료 시제와 for를 이용하여 한 개의 문장으로 바꿔 쓰시오.

I moved to this house two years ago. I'm still living here.
→ _____

10 밑줄 친 부분을 바르게 고쳐 문장을 다시 쓰시오.

By the time you are 20, the world had changed a lot.
→ _____
_____

Chapter 5

조동사

01

can, must, may, should

1. can

I **can** play the guitar. [가능, 능력] (= be able to) 나는 기타를 칠 수 있다.

Can I go to the bathroom? [허가, 부탁] (= May) 화장실에 가도 될까요?

It **can't** be true. [강한 추측] 그것은 사실일 리가 없다.

She **could** memorize long poems when she was young. [가능, 능력]
그녀는 젊었을 때 긴 시들을 외울 수 있었다.

2. must

We **must** obey the laws. [의무] (= have to) 우리는 법에 복종해야 한다.

She **must** be upset to have lost her wallet. [강한 추측] 그녀는 지갑을 잃어 버려서 당황했음이 틀림없다.

He **had to** finish his report by today. [의무] 그는 오늘까지 보고서를 끝내야 했다.

He **didn't have to** finish his report by yesterday. The due date had been postponed.
[불필요] 그는 어제까지 보고서를 끝낼 필요가 없었어. 마감일이 연기되었거든.

3. may

You **may** go now. [허가] (= can) 너는 이제 가도 좋다.

It **may** sound strange, but it's true. [약한 추측] 이상하게 들릴지 모르지만, 그것은 사실이다.

He warned me that it **might** be dangerous. [약한 추측]
그는 나에게 그것이 위험할지도 모른다고 경고했다.

4. should

You **should** eat breakfast. [의무, 충고] (= ought to) 너는 아침을 먹어야 한다.
You **shouldn't** cross the street here. [의무, 충고] (= ought not to) 여기서 길을 건너면 안 된다.

> **Plus α**
>
> 「insist, demand, require, suggest, order, command (that)+주어(+should)+동사원형」:
> 주장, 요구, 제안, 명령 등을 나타내는 동사 뒤에 온 that절이 '~해야 한다'는 의미일 경우 「should+동사원형」을
> 쓰고, 이때 should는 생략하고 동사원형만 쓰기도 한다.
> They insisted that he **(should) leave** the country. 그들은 그가 나라를 떠나야 한다고 주장했다.

> **Plus α**
>
> It **will** rain tomorrow.
> [미래에 대한 추측]
> (= be going to)
> 내일 비가 올 것이다.
>
> I **will** help you.
> [화자의 의지]
> 내가 너를 도와줄게.

> **Tips**
>
> 조동사의 과거형 would, could, might는 독립적인 뜻을 지닌 다른 조동사로 쓰일 때가 많다.
>
> He **would** sit here and spend hours watching stars. [과거의 습관]
> 그는 여기 앉아 별을 보며 몇 시간씩 보내곤 했다.
>
> It **could** be a possibility.
> [약한 추측]
> 그것은 가능할 수도 있다.
>
> I **might** be wrong.
> [약한 추측]
> 내가 틀릴지도 모른다.

Check-up 　　 안에서 알맞은 말을 고르시오.

1 Can / May you speak Japanese?

2 I can not run / run not a full marathon.

3 I must join / had to join the army last year.

: EXERCISES

A [ ] 안에서 알맞은 것을 고르시오.

1 I'm not sure, but it [should / might] rain today.

2 She will [can / be able to] make her dream come true.

3 He got up late and [must / had to] take a taxi this morning.

4 You [have to / don't have to] bring your own pen and paper. We'll give them to you.

sure (형) 확신하는

come true 실현되다

own (형) 자신의

B 두 문장의 의미가 통하도록 문장을 완성하시오.

1 Can I use your calculator?

→ _____ your calculator?

2 You should follow the traffic rules.

→ You _____ the traffic rules.

3 I am able to play several musical instruments.

→ I _____ several musical instruments.

4 He has to study hard to be the top in his school.

→ He _____ hard to be the top in his school.

calculator (명) 계산기

follow the rules
규칙을 따르다

musical instrument
악기

C 밑줄 친 부분에 유의하여 해석을 완성하시오.

1 It <u>cannot be true</u> that he is a criminal.

→ 그가 범죄자라는 것은 _____.

2 You <u>don't have to come</u> here every day.

→ 당신은 매일 여기에 _____.

3 You <u>may be surprised</u> to hear the news.

→ 당신은 그 소식을 듣고 _____.

4 He <u>must be tired</u> because he went to bed late last night.

→ 그는 어젯밤에 늦게 잤기 때문에 _____.

D 우리말과 같은 뜻이 되도록 주어진 단어를 이용하여 문장을 완성하시오.

1 당신은 여기서 기다릴 필요가 없습니다. (wait)

→ You _____ _____ _____ _____ here.

2 그는 손가락을 베지 않기 위해서 조심해야 했다. (be)

→ He _____ _____ _____ careful not to cut his finger.

3 그녀가 그 퍼즐을 풀었다. 그녀는 천재임이 틀림없다. (be)

→ She solved the puzzle. She _____ _____ a genius.

UNIT 02
had better, used to,
would rather, may as well

1. 「had better+동사원형」 ~하는 것이 좋겠다

You **had better tell** me the truth. 너는 나한테 사실을 말하는 것이 좋을 거야.
You**'d better not lie** to me. 너는 나한테 거짓말을 안 하는 것이 좋을 거야.

2. 「used to+동사원형」 ~하곤 했다

☆ used to는 과거의 반복되는 행동이나 상태를 나타낼 때 쓴다. would 역시 비슷한 의미인데 과거의 상태를 나타낼 때는 쓸 수 없다.

I **used to[would] practice** soccer here. [동작] 나는 이곳에서 축구 연습을 하곤 했다.

There **used to be** a white house on the hill. [상태] (would로 바꿔 쓸 수 없음)
언덕 위에 하얀 집이 있었다.

I **didn't use to get** up early in the morning. [부정문] (= used not to get)
나는 아침 일찍 일어나지 않았다.

Did you **use to come** and spend time here? [의문문] 당신은 여기 와서 시간을 보내곤 했나요?

3. 「would rather+동사원형」 차라리 ~하는 편이 낫겠다

I **would rather talk** to him in person. 차라리 그와 직접 얘기하는 것이 낫겠다.
I**'d rather not sleep** tonight. 오늘 밤에는 잠을 안 자는 것이 낫겠다.

4. 「may as well+동사원형」 (더 나은 할 일이 없으니) ~하는 편이 낫겠다

If we don't have anything else to do, we **may as well go** to sleep.
다른 할 일이 없으면 우리는 잠자러 가는 것이 낫겠다.

There isn't anything interesting to do, so I **may as well go** home.
재미있는 일이 없으니 집에 가는 게 낫겠다.

Plus α
「may well+동사원형」 ~하는 것도 당연하다
You **may well be** proud of your son. 당신의 아들을 자랑스러워하는 건 당연하다.

Plus α
1 「get use to+-ing」
~하는 데 익숙해지다
I **got used to sharing** the room with my sister.
나는 여동생과 방을 함께 쓰는 것에 익숙해졌다.

2 「be used to+동사원형」
~하는 데 사용되다
The Internet **is used to search** for information.
인터넷은 정보를 찾는 데 사용된다.

Tips
「would rather A than B」
B하느니 차라리 A하겠다
I **would rather** die **than** follow your order.
네 명령을 따르느니 차라리 죽는 것이 낫겠다.

Check-up 안에서 알맞은 말을 고르시오.

1 You would / had better stay silent.

2 He used to spend / spending time in an old bookstore.

3 I would rather not / would not rather deliver the message.

: EXERCISES

A [   ] 안에서 알맞은 것을 고르시오.

shy ⑱ 수줍어하는
get sick 병이 나다

1 She [would / used to] be a shy girl.

2 I [had / would] rather be hungry than eat that.

3 You had [rather / better] quit smoking, or you will get sick.

4 It is raining outside. I [may as well / may well] stay home.

B [보기]에서 알맞은 말을 골라 어법에 맞게 바꿔 문장을 완성하시오. [한 번씩만 사용할 것]

countryside ⑲ 시골
graduate ⑧ 졸업하다
go fishing 낚시 가다

보기	used to	get used to	would	had better

1 I _____ living in the countryside.

2 You _____ study hard, or you won't graduate.

3 There _____ be a beautiful lake on the mountain.

4 My father and I _____ go fishing when I was young.

C 우리말과 같은 뜻이 되도록 어법상 <u>어색한</u> 곳을 찾아 바르게 고쳐 쓰시오.

1 우리 엄마는 매일 쇼핑을 하곤 했다.

→ My mom used to shopping every day.

2 해안가에서 3마일 떨어진 곳에 섬 하나가 있었다.

→ There would be a small island 3 miles offshore.

3 너는 텔레비전을 너무 많이 보지 않는 것이 좋겠다.

→ You had not better watch too much TV.

D 우리말과 같은 뜻이 되도록 주어진 단어를 이용하여 문장을 완성하시오.

1 춤을 추느니 차라리 노래를 하겠다. (sing, dance, than)

→ I _____ _____ _____ _____ _____.

2 내가 어렸을 땐 이곳에 동물원이 있었다. (be, zoo)

→ There _____ _____ _____ _____

here when I was a child.

3 너는 내가 말하는 것을 적는 것이 좋겠다. (write down)

→ You _____ _____ _____ _____ what I'm saying.

4 우리 엄마는 나에게 케이크를 구워주시곤 했다. (bake, cake)

→ My mom _____ _____ _____ for me.

03 조동사+have+p.p.

☆ 「조동사+have+p.p.」: 과거의 일에 대한 가정, 추측, 후회나 유감 등의 의미를 나타낸다.

1. 「must have p.p.」 ~했음이 틀림없다 [강한 추측]

Her eyes are swollen. She **must have cried** a lot. 그녀의 눈이 부었어. 많이 울었음이 틀림없어.

He is not here. He **must have left** early. 그는 여기 없어. 일찍 떠났음이 틀림없어.

2. 「cannot[can't] have p.p.」 ~했을 리가 없다 [강한 추측]

He **cannot have been** sick. I saw him at the theater.
그가 아팠을 리가 없어. 나는 극장에서 그를 봤어.

He **can't have won** the game. He is too young. 그가 게임에서 이겼을 리가 없어. 그는 너무 어려.

3. 「may[might] have p.p.」 ~했을지도 모른다 [약한 추측]

He was limping. He **might have fallen** down the stairs.
그가 발을 절고 있었어. 계단에서 넘어졌을지도 몰라.

I don't know if he has my phone number. He **may not have called** me.
그가 내 전화번호를 갖고 있는지 모르겠어. 나에게 전화를 하지 않았을지도 몰라.

4. 「should have p.p.」 ~했어야 했다 (하지 않았다) [후회, 유감]

I'm sorry I couldn't help you last time. I **should have helped** you.
지난번에 도와주지 못해서 미안해. 너를 도와 줬어야 했는데.

I **shouldn't have stayed** up all night. I fell asleep in class.
나는 밤을 새지 않았어야 했어. 수업 시간에 잠이 들었어.

> **Plus α**
> **가정법**
> 「could have p.p.」
> ~할 수 있었을 것이다 (못했다)
>
> We **could have won** the game.
> 우리가 게임에서 이길 수 있었을 텐데. (우리가 졌다.)
>
> 「couldn't have p.p.」
> 할 수 없었을 것이다 (했다)
>
> We **couldn't have won** the game without him.
> 우리는 그가 없었다면 게임에서 이길 수 없었을 것이다. (우리가 이겼다.)

Check-up 우리말과 같은 뜻이 되도록 □ 안에서 알맞은 말을 고르시오.

---

1 그가 그들에게 그 사고에 대해 말했음이 틀림없어.

→ He │ may / must │ have told them about the accident.

2 그가 그런 실수를 했을 리가 없다.

→ He │ can / cannot │ have made a mistake like that.

3 그는 그 문제에 대해 알지 못했을지도 몰라.

→ He │ may not have known / may have not known │ about the problem.

: EXERCISES

A [   ] 안에서 알맞은 것을 고르시오.

say hello 인사하다

miss ⑧ 그리워하다

1 I failed the test. I [should / must] have studied hard.

2 He [must / can't] have seen me yesterday. He didn't say hello to me.

3 I miss her very much. I [should / shouldn't] have let her go ten years ago.

4 I heard Charlie saw her at the party. She [may / must] have gone to the party last night.

B 두 문장의 의미가 통하도록 문장을 완성하시오.

appointment
⑲ 약속, 예약

regret ⑧ 후회하다

keep ⑧ 보관하다, 가지다

1 I am sure that he forgot the appointment.

→ He _____ the appointment.

2 She didn't listen to her mom. Now she regrets it.

→ She _____ to her mom.

3 I'm not sure, but it was possible that she kept my book.

→ She _____ my book.

C 우리말과 같은 뜻이 되도록 어법상 <u>어색한</u> 곳을 찾아 바르게 고쳐 쓰시오.

1 그는 이미 점심을 먹었을지도 몰라. 벌써 12시 30분이야.

→ He might eat lunch. It's already 12:30.

2 나는 너의 도움 없이는 그 일을 끝낼 수 없었을 거야. 고마워.

→ I couldn't finish it without your help. Thank you.

3 그가 지갑을 훔쳤을 리가 없어. 그는 정직한 사람이야.

→ He may not have stolen the wallet. He is an honest man.

4 그녀는 그 회의에 참석했어야 했어. 그녀는 두 번째 기회를 놓쳤어.

→ She must have attended the meeting. She lost her second chance.

D 우리말과 같은 뜻이 되도록 주어진 단어를 이용하여 문장을 완성하시오.

1 그녀는 마지막 버스를 놓치지 않았어야 했어. (miss)

→ She _____ _____ _____ the last bus.

2 네가 내게 말했다면 내가 도울 수 있었을 텐데. (help)

→ I _____ _____ _____ you if you had told me.

3 그는 전에 그녀를 만난 적이 있음이 틀림없어. 그녀의 이름을 알고 있었어. (meet)

→ He _____ _____ _____ _____ before.
He knew her name.

: Review Test

[01-02] 빈칸에 들어갈 알맞은 말을 고르시오.

01

He hasn't eaten anything all day. He _____ hungry.

① can't be   ② must be   ③ could be
④ might be   ⑤ shouldn't be

02

Mike _____ be at home. I've just seen him in the gym.

① can't   ② could   ③ should
④ might not   ⑤ ought not to

[03-05] 대화의 빈칸에 들어갈 알맞은 말을 고르시오.

03

A Can you do it by yourself?
B Sure. You _____ worry about me.

① may   ② can't   ③ must
④ couldn't   ⑤ don't have to

04

A Do you have any plans for the vacation?
B I haven't decided yet, but I _____ to Hawaii.

① may go   ② must go   ③ should go
④ had to go   ⑤ ought to go

05

A How was the party? Was it fun?
B You _____. It was awesome.

① must have come
② can't have come
③ should have come
④ might have come
⑤ shouldn't have come

[06-07] 빈칸에 들어갈 수 <u>없는</u> 말을 고르시오.

06

She will _____ be there tomorrow.

① not   ② must   ③ have to
④ certainly   ⑤ be able to

07

They _____ that nature be protected.

① insist   ② order   ③ demand
④ suggest   ⑤ understand

08 빈칸에 들어갈 말이 바르게 짝지어진 것은?

· You _____ call me every day. Once a week is enough.
· There _____ be a big drugstore on the corner.
· He _____ study for the test last week.

① must not – would – had to
② must not – would – must
③ don't have to – used to – must
④ don't have to – would – had to
⑤ don't have to – used to – had to

09 다음 중 어법상 <u>어색한</u> 문장은?

① You had not better cheat on tests.
② You don't have to worry about the weather.
③ Don't you think you should apologize to me?
④ He should have saved money. He doesn't have money to pay the bill.
⑤ She plays the guitar very well. She must have practiced a lot.

[10-11] 다음 중 어법상 옳은 문장을 고르시오.

10　① She used to dancing when she was young.
　　② I would rather live poor than cheating others.
　　③ No one will be able to master a foreign language in a day.
　　④ You have better turn off the fan before going to bed.
　　⑤ I must return to Seoul yesterday.

11　① I have to cleaning my room and do my homework.
　　② You will can hear your mom calling.
　　③ I cut my finger. I must have been careful.
　　④ You should look around before you cross the road.
　　⑤ He would be a rude boy, but not anymore.

12　두 문장의 의미가 통하도록 할 때 잘못 연결된 것은?

　　① I should have visited my grandparents.
　　　→ I had to visit my grandparents, but I didn't.
　　② She must have gotten a scholarship.
　　　→ I'm sorry she didn't get a scholarship.
　　③ You shouldn't have played games all night.
　　　→ I'm sorry you played games all night.
　　④ He may not have eaten breakfast.
　　　→ It was possible that he didn't eat breakfast.
　　⑤ He could have won first prize.
　　　→ I'm sorry he couldn't win first prize.

13　두 문장의 의미가 통하도록 할 때 빈칸에 들어갈 말은?

> I was afraid of swimming, but now I like it.
> → I _____ be afraid of swimming.

　　① use to　　　　　② used to
　　③ was used　　　　④ was used to
　　⑤ was using to

[14-15] 글을 읽고, 물음에 답하시오.

> What do you think about using cell phones in class? Some people strongly suggest that it ❶ be stopped while others don't think that way. Some people say cell phones (A) 허용되지 않았어야 했다 in the first place. On the other hand, others argue that using cell phones in class ❷ might be disturbing sometimes but ❸ can be helpful as well: for instance, searching the Internet for information, looking up unknown words on an online dictionary, and reaching parents in emergencies. In short, answering the question ❹ can't be easy, but there is a solution: you ❺ had better not to use it too often.

14　밑줄 친 (A)를 바르게 영작한 것은?

　　① couldn't have allowed
　　② couldn't have been allowed
　　③ shouldn't have been allowed
　　④ mustn't have been allowed
　　⑤ shouldn't have allowed

15　밑줄 친 ❶~❺ 중 쓰임이 어색한 것은?

01 두 문장에 공통으로 들어갈 조동사를 쓰시오.

· You _____ save your file before you turn the computer off.

· He _____ be very hungry after skipping two meals.

02 주어진 글과 의미가 통하도록 문장을 완성하시오.

I rode a bike every weekend. But now I don't do it anymore.

→ I _____ a bike.

[03-06] 우리말과 같은 뜻이 되도록 주어진 단어를 이용하여 문장을 완성하시오.

03 그는 원하는 것은 무엇이든 할 수 있었다. (do)

→ He _____ whatever he wanted.

04 우리는 미래에는 더 빨리 여행할 수 있을 것이다. (travel)

→ We _____ faster in the future.

05 그녀는 아들에게 예의 바르게 행동하는 법을 가르쳐야 했다. (teach)

→ She _____ her son how to behave politely.

06 전쟁 전에는 강가에 초등학교가 있었다. (be)

→ There _____ an elementary school by the river before the war.

07 [보기]에서 알맞은 말을 골라 문장을 완성하시오.

보기   don't have to   had better   used to

(1) You _____ do as I say.

(2) He _____ be a teacher.

(3) You _____ answer every question. Just choose three of them.

08 주어진 단어를 이용하여 대화를 완성하시오.

(1) A Look at this total mess. There _____ _____ a thief in the house. (be)

B I'll call the police.

(2) A You are all wet.

B It's raining outside, and I didn't carry my umbrella this morning.

A You _____ it. (bring)

[09-10] 도서관에서 볼 수 있는 안내문이다. 주어진 단어를 이용하여 문장을 완성하시오.

조건 should나 shouldn't를 사용할 것

09 Books _____ by the due date. (return)
(책은 반납일까지 반납되어야 합니다.)

10 Food _____ at the desk. (eat)
(책상에 앉아서 음식을 먹지 않아야 합니다.)

Chapter 6

수동태

UNIT 01 수동태의 의미와 형태

1. 「주어+be+p.p.(+by+행위자(목적격))」: 주어가 동작을 당하는 대상이 되어 '~되다, 하여지다'라는 의미로 쓰인 문장을 '수동태'라고 한다.

The building **was built** in 1990 (by them). 그 건물은 1990년에 (그들에 의해) 지어졌다.

☆ 능동태를 수동태로 전환할 경우 시제와 수 일치에 주의해야 한다.

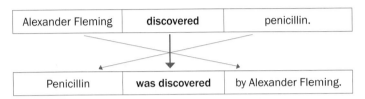

[능동태] Alexander Fleming이 페니실린을 발견했다.
→ [수동태] 페니실린은 Alexander Fleming에 의해 발견되었다.

2. 수동태의 여러 형태

(1) 미래 「will+be+p.p.」
The 2022 World Cup **will be held** in Qatar. 2022년 월드컵은 카타르에서 열릴 것이다.

(2) 진행 「be+being+p.p.」
So much energy **is being wasted** worldwide. 전 세계적으로 너무 많은 에너지가 낭비되고 있다.

(3) 완료 「have/has/had+been+p.p.」
The appointment **has** just **been canceled**. 약속이 방금 취소되었다.

(4) 조동사 「조동사+be+p.p.」
The patient **must be treated** with medication. 그 환자는 약물 치료를 받아야 한다.
The schedule **can be changed** if necessary. 필요한 경우 일정은 변경될 수 있습니다.

> **Plus α**
> 수동태로 쓰지 않는 동사: 목적어를 갖지 않는 동사(appear, disappear, happen, become 등),
> 소유동사(have, belong to), cost(비용이 ~가 들다), resemble(닮다) 등
> He **resembles** his father. 그는 아버지를 닮았다.
> He ~~is resembled by~~ his father. (X)

Check-up ☐ 안에서 알맞은 말을 고르시오.

1 We [warmly welcomed / were warmly welcomed] by them.

2 She [bought / be bought] some food on her way home.

: EXERCISES

A   [   ] 안에서 알맞은 것을 고르시오.

1   More than 100 people [injured / were injured] in the accident.

2   You must [follow / be followed] the rules at school.

3   Politicians [influence / are influenced] by public opinion.

4   Historic sites must [protect / be protected].

5   My mom [was preparing / was prepared] a special dinner for my birthday.

injure
⑧ 다치게 하다, 상처 입히다
follow ⑧ 지키다, 따르다
politician ⑲ 정치인
influence
⑧ 영향을 미치다
public opinion 여론
historic site 유적지

B   주어진 문장을 수동태 문장으로 바꿔 쓰시오.

1   The bad weather delayed the flight.

    → The flight _____ .

2   We can recycle paper and cans.

    → Paper and cans _____ .

3   In the future, robots might replace many jobs.

    → In the future, many jobs _____ .

4   Someone buried treasures across the island.

    → Treasures _____ .

delay ⑧ 지연시키다
replace ⑧ 대체하다
bury ⑧ 묻다, 매장하다
treasure ⑲ 보물

C   [보기]에서 알맞은 단어를 골라 어법에 맞게 바꿔 문장을 완성하시오.

보기	resemble	reach	release	finish

1   His new movie will _____ tomorrow.

2   The project must _____ by this weekend.

3   We finally _____ an agreement last week.

4   These days, Sally often hears that she _____ her father.

reach ⑧ 이르다, 도달하다
release
⑧ 개봉하다, 출시하다
agreement ⑲ 합의, 일치

D   우리말과 같은 뜻이 되도록 주어진 단어를 이용하여 문장을 완성하시오.

1   흡연은 건물 전체에서 허용되지 않습니다. (allow)

    → Smoking _____ _____ _____ anywhere in the building.

2   그는 자신의 행동으로 인해 비난을 받았다. (criticize for)

    → He _____ _____ _____ his behavior.

3   그것은 무료로 배송될 것입니다. (deliver)

    → It _____ _____ _____ free of charge.

UNIT 02 4문형, 5문형 수동태

1. 4문형의 수동태: 목적어가 두 개인 문장은 보통 두 개의 수동태 문장을 만들 수 있다.

He gave <u>me</u> <u>a second chance</u>. 그는 내게 두 번째 기회를 주었다.
　　　　　간·목　　　직·목

➡ <u>I</u> **was given** a second chance by him. [간접목적어를 주어로]

➡ <u>A second chance</u> **was given** <u>to me</u> by him. [직접목적어를 주어로]

☆ 직접목적어가 주어 자리에 오면 간접목적어 앞에 전치사 to, for, of 등을 붙여 준다.

Tips

• to를 쓰는 동사: bring, give, lend, pass, show, offer, send, tell, teach, pay 등

• for를 쓰는 동사: buy, get, make, cook, find, build 등

• of를 쓰는 동사: ask 등

2. 5문형의 수동태

(1) 일반적인 5문형의 수동태: 목적격보어를 그대로 쓴다.

They elected <u>him</u> <u>mayor</u>. 그들은 그를 시장으로 선출하였다.
　　　　　목적어 목적격보어

➡ <u>He</u> **was elected** <u>mayor</u> (by them).

He asked <u>me</u> to go with him. 그는 나에게 함께 가자고 부탁했다.

➡ <u>I</u> **was asked** <u>to go with him</u>.

Plus α
잘 쓰이는 5문형의 수동태

• be allowed to
～하도록 허락 받다
(사역동사 let의 수동태 개념)

• be told to
～하라는 말을 듣다

• be asked to
～해 달라고 부탁 받다

• be expected to
～할 것으로 예상되다

• be required to
～할 것으로 요구되다

• be forced to
～하도록 강요받다

> **Plus α** 4문형 vs. 5문형
>
> Her mother gave <u>her</u> <u>a skirt</u>. [4문형] 그녀의 어머니가 그녀에게 치마를 주셨다.
> (her ≠ a skirt: '그녀에게 치마를'이라고 해석되며, 간접목적어와 직접목적어는 동일한 것이 아니다.)
> ➡ (O) <u>She</u> was given a skirt by her mother.
> ➡ (O) <u>A skirt</u> was given <u>to her</u> by her mother.
>
> Her mother made <u>her</u> <u>president</u>. [5문형] 그녀의 어머니가 그녀를 대통령으로 만들었다.
> (her = president: '그녀를 대통령으로'라고 해석되며, 목적어와 목적격보어는 동일한 것이다.)
> ➡ (O) <u>She</u> was made president by her mother.
> ➡ (X) ~~President was made her by her mother.~~ (목적격보어는 수동태 문장의 주어가 될 수 없다.)

(2) 지각동사와 사역동사가 있는 문장의 수동태: 목적격보어가 분사인 경우는 그대로 써 주고, 동사원형인 경우는 to부정사로 바꾼다.

She **heard** a dog **barking**. 그녀는 개가 짖는 소리를 들었다.

➡ A dog **was heard barking** by her.

He **made** me **cancel** the meeting. 그는 나로 하여금 회의를 취소하게 만들었다.

➡ I **was made to cancel** the meeting by him.

Tips

지각동사의 목적격보어로 동사원형이 온 경우 수동태 전환 시에는 to부정사보다는 '-ing'가 자연스럽다.

I **watched** him **enter** his room.

➡ He **was watched entering** his room.
나는 그가 방에 들어가는 것을 지켜보았다.

Check-up　☐ 안에서 알맞은 말을 고르시오.

1 Rules of the game were told ☐ for / to ☐ him.

2 The thief was seen ☐ entering / enter ☐ the shop.

: EXERCISES

A   [   ] 안에서 알맞은 것을 고르시오.

1   A free gift will be given [for / to] everyone after the show.

2   The concert tickets were bought [for / to] us by my uncle.

3   He was seen [leave / leaving] the classroom late at night.

4   Jake was made [vacuum / to vacuum] the house by his mother.

5   They are expected [move / to move] out of the building next week.

free ⑱ 무료의

leave ⑧ 떠나다

vacuum
⑧ 진공청소기로 청소하다

expect
⑧ 예상하다, 기대하다

B   주어진 문장을 수동태 문장으로 바꿔 쓰시오.

1   They gave the waiter a tip.

→ The waiter _____ .

→ A tip _____ .

2   Her mother made Jenny her wedding dress.

→ Jenny's wedding dress _____ .

3   I heard my brother playing the violin.

→ My brother _____ .

4   My mother told me to pick him up at the airport.

→ I _____ .

5   Ms. Johnson made me erase the blackboard.

→ I _____ .

pick up
⑧ (차로) 마중 나가다

erase ⑧ 지우다

C   우리말과 같은 뜻이 되도록 주어진 단어를 이용하여 문장을 완성하시오.

1   나는 아이들에게 이상한 질문을 받았다. (ask)

→ I _____ _____ awkward questions by the kids.

2   Harry에게 잔디를 깎도록 시켰다. (make, mow)

→ Harry _____ _____ _____ _____ the lawn.

3   그 장미는 그녀의 남편이 그녀에게 사준 것이다. (buy)

→ The roses _____ _____ _____ _____ by her husband.

4   어젯밤에 Greg이 그 버스에 타는 것이 목격되었다. (see, get on)

→ Greg _____ _____ _____ _____ the bus last night.

5   나는 다음 월요일까지 그 프로젝트를 완성하라고 들었다. (tell, complete)

→ I _____ _____ _____ _____ the project by next Monday.

주의해야 할 수동태

1. 「It+be+p.p.+that ~」: 목적어가 절인 문장의 수동태 (주로 say, believe, think, expect, know 등의 동사에 해당함)

People **say that** tomatoes are very good for health. 토마토가 건강에 매우 좋다고들 말한다.

➡ **It is said that** tomatoes are very good for health. [가주어 it을 사용하고 that절을 뒤로 보낸다.]

➡ Tomatoes **are said to be** very good for health.
[that절의 주어를 주어로 사용한 경우 that절의 동사는 「to+동사원형」이 된다.]

2. 동사구의 수동태: 동사구를 하나의 단어처럼 생각하여 분리하지 않는다.

put off ~을 연기하다	look after ~을 돌보다	deal with ~을 다루다
turn off ~을 끄다	throw away ~을 버리다	hand out ~을 나눠주다
take away ~을 가져가다	run over ~을 (차로) 치다	clean up ~을 깨끗이 치우다
take out ~을 가지고 (나)가다		

The school **put off** the test for a week. 학교가 시험을 일주일 연기했다.

➡ The test **was put off** for a week by the school.

3. 여러 가지 전치사를 쓰는 수동태

be known to+명사 ~에게 알려져 있다	be surprised[astonished] at[by] ~에 놀라다
be known to+동사원형 ~로 알려져 있다	be worried[concerned] about ~에 대해 걱정하다
be known as ~로서 알려져 있다	be filled with ~로 가득 차다(= be full of)
be known for ~로 유명하다	be covered with[in] ~로 덮이다
be known by ~로 알 수 있다	be crowded with ~로 붐비다
be tired of ~에 싫증나다	be pleased with ~로 기뻐하다
be tired from ~ 때문에 지치다	be satisfied with ~에 만족하다
be made of ~로 만들어지다(재료의 물리적 변화)	be bored with[by] ~을 지겨워하다
be made from ~로 만들어지다(재료의 화학적 변화)	be disappointed with[in] ~에 실망하다
be interested in ~에 흥미 있다	

The mountains **are covered with** snow and ice. 산이 눈과 얼음으로 덮여 있다.

I **am satisfied with** the test results. 나는 시험 결과에 만족한다.

Cheese **is made from** milk. 치즈는 우유로 만들어진다.

Check-up ☐ 안에서 알맞은 말을 고르시오.

1 She is said [that is / to be] one of the richest women in the world.

2 The airport was crowded [with / in] people going on vacation.

: EXERCISES

A [   ] 안에서 알맞은 것을 고르시오.

1 This ring is made [of / from] pure gold.

2 The Amazon is known [as / to] the lungs of our planet.

3 We were disappointed [to / with] the ending of the movie.

4 My complaint [was dealt / was dealt with] by the manager.

5 The light [has been turned off / has been turned off by] him.

pure
휑 불순물이 없는, 순수한
lung 몡 폐, 허파
planet 몡 행성, 지구
deal with ~을 다루다
turn off 끄다

B 밑줄 친 부분을 어법에 맞게 고쳐 쓰시오.

1 They were pleased <u>to</u> their son's progress.

2 Old clothes and shoes <u>were thrown away</u> her.

3 <u>He</u> is said that he owns more than half of the area.

4 This is known <u>that</u> be the most difficult puzzle in the world.

progress 몡 진전
throw away 버리다
own 동 소유하다

C 주어진 문장을 수동태 문장으로 바꿔 쓰시오. [by+행위자 생략]

1 People say that he is a piano genius.

→ It _____.

→ He _____.

2 A boy is handing out the leaflets to the classmates.

→ The leaflets _____.

3 Somebody took away my watch on the train.

→ My watch _____.

genius 몡 천재
hand out ~을 제출하다

D 우리말과 같은 뜻이 되도록 주어진 단어를 이용하여 문장을 완성하시오.

1 사슴 한 마리가 차에 치었다. (run over)

→ A deer _____ _____ _____ _____ a car.

2 플라스틱은 석유로 만들어진다. (make)

→ Plastic _____ _____ _____ oil.

3 대통령은 국가의 미래에 대해 걱정한다. (worry)

→ The president _____ _____ _____ the future of the country.

4 한국에서 숫자 4는 불행을 가져 온다고 여겨진다. (think)

→ In Korea, it _____ _____ _____ the number 4 brings bad luck.

[01-05] 빈칸에 들어갈 알맞은 말을 고르시오.

01

My life _____ by this movie.

① changes
② was changing
③ was changed
④ was been changed
⑤ has changed

02

The new cell phone _____ at the beginning of next year.

① released
② be released
③ will be releasing
④ will be released
⑤ is releasing

03

Tim was made _____ the whiteboard after class.

① erase
② erasing
③ erased
④ to erasing
⑤ to erase

04

A bicycle was bought _____ me by my grandfather. It was my birthday gift.

① by
② for
③ of
④ as
⑤ to

05

My husband _____ starting his own business.

① interests
② is interested in by
③ is interested
④ is interested by
⑤ is interested in

[06-07] 두 문장이 같은 의미가 되도록 할 때 빈칸에 알맞은 것을 고르시오.

06

The store owner should clean up the street.
→ The street _____ the store owner.

① should be cleaned
② should be cleaned by
③ should be cleaned up
④ should be cleaned up by
⑤ should clean up by

07

My brother made me wear silly pants.
→ I _____ silly pants.

① made to wear
② was made wear
③ was made to wear
④ was made to wearing
⑤ was made to wear by

[08-09] 다음 중 어법상 어색한 문장을 고르시오.

08 ① English is spoken in many countries.
② He was impressed by her passion.
③ The robber has been arrested.
④ I was forced to leave early.
⑤ My ID was shown the police officer.

09 ① You are not allowed to smoke here.
② Your garbage bin must be taken out after 6 pm.
③ My brother was made to do his homework.
④ Your donation will be given to the poor.
⑤ He was seen cheat on the exam.

10 빈칸에 공통으로 들어갈 알맞은 말은?

> · We were disappointed _____ the result of the match.
> · My teacher was not satisfied _____ my presentation.

① to   ② for   ③ with
④ by   ⑤ on

[11-12] 우리말과 같은 뜻이 되도록 빈칸에 들어갈 알맞은 말을 고르시오.

11 월스트리트를 세계 금융의 중심지라고 한다.
> → It _____ Wall Street is the financial center of the world.

① said   ② be said   ③ is saying
④ is said to   ⑤ is said that

12 그 남자가 병원에서 노인들을 돕는 것이 목격되었다.
> → The man _____ the elderly in the hospital.

① was watched help
② was watched helping
③ was watching helping
④ watch helping
⑤ watch help

13 수동태 문장으로 바꾼 것 중 올바른 것은?

① Students elected him class president.
  → Class president was elected him by students.
② People spoke well of her.
  → She was spoken well by people.
③ I saw beautiful butterflies.
  → Beautiful butterflies was seen by me.
④ He was writing a new book.
  → A new book was writing by him.
⑤ I will pay the money tomorrow.
  → The money will be paid by me tomorrow.

[14-15] 글을 읽고, 물음에 답하시오.

> Do you know who took the first-ever photograph? The first photograph _____ⓐ_____ in 1827 by Joseph Niépce. Then, in the late 1800s, camera film _____ⓑ_____ by a man named George Eastman. And lots of developments had been made, but it was still far from modern. Today, the most popular type of photography is digital. Digital cameras (A) were introduced the mass market in the 1990s.

14 빈칸 ⓐ와 ⓑ에 들어갈 말이 바르게 짝지어진 것은?

	ⓐ		ⓑ
①	took	–	invented
②	was taken	–	was invented
③	took	–	was invented
④	was taken	–	invented
⑤	is taken	–	is invented

15 밑줄 친 (A)를 바르게 고친 것은?

① were introduced to the mass market
② were introduced by the mass market
③ were introduced of the mass market
④ were introduced with the mass market
⑤ were introduced for the mass market

[01-02] 우리말과 같은 뜻이 되도록 주어진 단어를 이용하여 문장을 완성하시오.

01 나는 작년에 오븐을 샀지만 그것은 지금까지 한 번도 사용된 적이 없다. (never, use)

→ I bought an oven last year, but until now it

_____ .

02 여름 보너스가 모든 직원에게 제공될 것입니다. (will, give)

→ The summer bonus _____

every employee.

[03-04] 두 문장이 같은 뜻이 되도록 문장을 완성하시오.

03 She told me to have dinner before going out.

→ I _____ before

going out.

04 I saw the man cross the street.

→ The man _____

the street.

05 그림을 보고, 주어진 단어를 이용하여 문장을 완성하시오.

The beach _____ people. (fill)

06 [보기]와 같이 문장을 바꿔 쓰시오.

> 보기
> People believe that he is an honest seller.
> → He is believed to be an honest seller.

People think that the U.S. is one of the strongest nations in the world.

→ _____

_____

07 대화를 읽고, 주어진 단어를 이용하여 밑줄 친 우리말과 같은 뜻이 되도록 영작하시오.

> A Who was chosen to be the president of the student council?
> B Me! 내가 학생회 회장에 선출되었어.
> A Wow! Congratulations!

→ _____

(elect, the president of the student council)

[08-10] 글을 읽고, 물음에 답하시오.

> Do you know about Agnes Gonxha Bojaxhiu? She (A) (as, is, Mother Teresa, known). She is famous for spending her life helping the poor. Due to her efforts and devotion, (B) 1979년에 그녀에게 노벨평화상이 수여되었다. She passed away in 1997. (C) She will remember forever.

08 밑줄 친 (A)의 주어진 단어를 알맞게 배열하시오.

→ _____

09 밑줄 친 (B)를 주어진 단어를 이용하여 영작하시오.

→ the Nobel Peace Prize _____

in 1979 (award)

10 밑줄 친 (C)에서 어법상 어색한 부분을 찾아 고쳐 쓰시오.

조건 주어는 변화시키지 말 것

→ _____

Chapter 7

가정법

가정법 과거, 과거완료, 혼합가정

1. 가정법 과거: 현재 사실을 반대로 가정하거나 실현 가능성이 없는 일을 말할 때 쓴다.

☆ 「If+주어+동사의 과거형, 주어+조동사의 과거형+동사원형」 만약 ~라면, ~할 텐데

If we **went** by plane, we **could save** time. 우리가 비행기로 간다면, 시간을 절약할 수 있을 텐데.

➡ As we **don't go** by plane, we **can't save** time.

　　우리는 비행기로 가지 않기 때문에 시간을 절약할 수 없다.

> **Plus α**
>
> 1　단순조건: 실현 가능성이 있음
>
> 　**If** you **send** the letter today, it **will** arrive tomorrow.
> 　네가 그 편지를 오늘 보낸다면, 그것은 내일 도착할 것이다.
>
> 2　가정법 과거: 실현 가능성이 없거나 현재 사실의 반대 상황을 가정
>
> 　**If** you **sent** the letter today, it **would** arrive tomorrow.
> 　(오늘 편지를 보낼 수 없는 상황임을 암시) 네가 그 편지를 오늘 보낸다면, 그것은 내일 도착할 텐데.

Tips

가정법 과거의 조건절에서 be동사는 인칭에 관계없이 were를 쓰지만, 구어체에서는 was를 쓰기도 한다.

If I **were[was]** you, I wouldn't act like that.
내가 너라면 그렇게 행동하지는 않을 텐데.

2. 가정법 과거완료: 과거 사실을 반대로 가정할 때 쓴다.

☆ 「If+주어+had p.p., 주어+조동사의 과거형+have p.p.」 만약 ~였다면, ~했을 텐데

If I **had studied** harder, I **would have done** well on the exam.

만약 내가 더 열심히 공부했다면, 시험을 잘 봤을 텐데.

➡ As I **didn't study** harder, I **didn't do** well on the exam.

　　공부를 더 열심히 하지 않았기 때문에, 나는 시험을 잘 보지 못했다.

3. 혼합가정법: 과거에 실현되지 못한 일이 현재에 영향을 미칠 때 쓴다.

☆ 「If+주어+had p.p., 주어+조동사의 과거형+동사원형」 만약 ~였다면, ~할 텐데

If it **hadn't rained** a lot, we **would be** at the beach now.

만약 비가 많이 오지 않았다면, 우리는 지금 해변에 있을 텐데.

➡ As it **rained** a lot, we **are not** at the beach now.

　　비가 많이 왔기 때문에, 우리는 지금 해변에 있지 않다.

Check-up　　안에서 알맞은 말을 고르시오.

1 If I were rich, I [will / would] buy the house.

2 If you [came / had come] earlier, you could have eaten pizza.

: EXERCISES

A [   ] 안에서 알맞은 것을 고르시오.

1 If it rains tomorrow, we [will / would] stay home.

2 If I [am not / weren't] tired, I would go to the concert.

3 If she [weren't / hadn't been] sick, she would have passed the test.

4 If I had eaten breakfast this morning, I wouldn't [be / have been] hungry now.

stay (동) 머무르다

tired (형) 피곤한

B 주어진 단어를 이용하여 가정법 문장을 완성하시오.

1 If Cindy were at home now, I would _____ her. (visit)

2 If the weather _____ fine, we would go on a picnic. (be)

3 If he _____ enough last night, he wouldn't be tired now. (sleep)

4 If my grandparents _____ far from my house, I would have visited them often. (move)

visit (동) 방문하다

weather (명) 날씨

go on a picnic
소풍을 가다

C 두 문장의 의미가 통하도록 문장을 완성하시오.

1 As I am not tall, I can't reach the shelf.

  → If I _____, I _____.

2 As it rained, it is humid now.

  → If it _____, it _____.

3 As she didn't finish her homework, she could not watch the game.

  → If she _____, she _____.

reach (동) ~에 닿다

shelf (명) 선반

humid (형) 습한

D 우리말과 같은 뜻이 되도록 주어진 단어를 이용하여 문장을 완성하시오.

1 만약 그녀가 진실을 알았다면, 속상해 했을 텐데. (know, be)

  → If she _____ _____ the truth, she _____
  _____ _____ upset.

2 만약 그 배우를 만나면, 그와 악수를 할 텐데. (meet, shake)

  → If I _____ the actor, I _____ _____ hands with him.

3 만약 내가 영어 공부를 열심히 했다면, 지금 저 외국인과 말할 수 있을 텐데. (study, talk with)

  → If I _____ _____ English hard, I _____ _____
  _____ that foreigner now.

I wish, as if, but for, without 가정법

1. I wish 가정법

(1) 「**I wish+가정법 과거**」 ~하면 좋을 텐데

(실현 불가능한 일에 대한 소망이나 현재 사실에 대한 유감을 표현)

I wish I **were** taller. 내 키가 더 크면 좋을 텐데.

➡ **I'm sorry** I**'m not** taller. 내 키가 더 크지 않아서 유감이다.

(2) 「**I wish+가정법 과거완료**」 ~했다면 좋을 텐데 (과거에 이루지 못한 일에 대한 유감을 표현)

I wish I **had won** the game. 내가 그 경기에서 이겼다면 좋을 텐데.

➡ **I'm sorry** I **didn't win** the game. 내가 그 경기에서 이기지 못해서 아쉽다.

2. as if[as though] 가정법

(1) 「**as if[as though]+가정법 과거**」 마치 ~인 것처럼

He acts **as if[as though]** he **knew** the answer. 그는 마치 정답을 아는 것처럼 행동한다.

➡ In fact, he **doesn't know** the answer. 사실 그는 정답을 모른다.

(2) 「**as if[as though]+가정법 과거완료**」 마치 ~였던 것처럼

She talks **as if[as though]** she **had traveled** around Europe.

그녀는 마치 유럽을 여행했던 것처럼 이야기한다.

➡ In fact, she **didn't travel** around Europe. 사실 그녀는 유럽을 여행하지 않았다.

3. without, but for 가정법

(1) 「**without[but for] ~, 가정법 과거**」 ~이 없다면

Without[But for] your help, I **couldn't pass** the exam.

➡ **If it were not for** your help, I **couldn't pass** the exam.

네 도움이 없다면, 나는 시험에 합격할 수 없을 거야.

(2) 「**without[but for] ~, 가정법 과거완료**」 ~이 없었다면

Without[But for] his advice, we **would have made** a big mistake.

➡ **If it had not been for** his advice, we **would have made** a big mistake.

그의 충고가 없었다면, 우리는 큰 실수를 저질렀을 것이다.

Plus α

1 if절에 were, had, should 등이 오면 if를 생략할 수 있다. 이때 주어, 동사의 위치를 바꿔 주어야 한다.

If it were not for your help, I couldn't finish this on time.

➡ **Were it** not for your help, I couldn't finish this on time.

네 도움이 없다면, 나는 이 것을 제시간에 끝낼 수 없을 거야.

2 「It's time+주어+동사의 과거형」 ~할 시간이다

It's time you **went** to bed.

자야 할 시간이야. (안 자는 것에 대한 유감을 표현)

Check-up   안에서 알맞은 말을 고르시오.

1 I wish she lives / lived next door.

2 Brian acts as if he is / were my father.

: EXERCISES

A [   ] 안에서 알맞은 것을 고르시오.

1 I wish she [is / were] here now.

2 I wish I [said / had said] sorry to her first at that time.

3 I think I'm old enough. But he treats me as if I [were / had been] a child.

4 [Without / But] for the seat belt, I would have got badly hurt in the accident.

treat (동) 다루다
seat belt (명) 안전벨트
badly (부) 심하게
hurt (형) 다친 (동) 다치다
accident (명) 사고

B 주어진 단어를 이용하여 가정법 문장을 완성하시오. [축약형을 사용할 것]

1 He is not a prince. He acts as if he _____ a prince. (be)

2 If it _____ for your umbrella, I would have been all wet. (be, not)

3 I'm a middle school student. I wish I _____ a college student now. (be)

4 She acts as if she _____ the truth. But she knew it. (know, not)

wet (형) 젖은
college (명) 대학

C 두 문장의 의미가 통하도록 문장을 완성하시오.

1 I'm sorry you don't remember me.

→ I wish _____ _____ _____.

2 In fact, she is very nervous.

→ She talks as if _____ _____ _____ _____.

3 If it were not for her help, I couldn't write a report.

→ _____ _____ _____ _____, I couldn't write a report.

4 If it had not been for your effort, we couldn't have finished this project.

→ _____ _____ _____, we couldn't have finished this project.

remember (동) 기억하다
nervous (형) 긴장되는
effort (명) 노력

D 우리말과 같은 뜻이 되도록 주어진 이용하여 문장을 완성하시오.

1 그녀가 우리 반 친구라면 좋을 텐데. (be, my classmate)

→ I wish she _____ _____ _____.

2 그는 나를 잘 아는 것처럼 행동한다. (as if, know)

→ He acts _____ _____ _____ _____ me well.

3 지도가 없었다면, 나는 그 장소를 찾을 수 없었을 것이다. (the map)

→ _____ _____ _____, I couldn't have found the place.

4 너무 늦었어. 잠자리에 들 시간이야. (go to bed)

→ It's very late. It's time you _____ _____ _____.

: Review Test

[01-05] 빈칸에 들어갈 알맞은 말을 고르시오.

01

If I _____ you, I would go to the concert.

① be ② am
③ were ④ had been
⑤ would have been

02

If I _____ my cell phone, I wouldn't have been late.

① lost ② don't lose
③ didn't lose ④ hadn't lost
⑤ would have lost

03

I'm sorry he can't come with us. I wish he _____ with us.

① come ② came
③ can come ④ could come
⑤ could have come

04

Emily isn't sick, but she is acting as if she _____ sick.

① is ② be ③ were
④ will be ⑤ would be

05

Without your encouragement, I _____ in the contest last year.

① don't participate
② didn't participate
③ wouldn't participate
④ haven't participated
⑤ wouldn't have participated

[06-07] 다음 중 어법상 어색한 문장을 고르시오.

06 ① If she asked me for help, I would do anything for her.
② If we had hurried, we would have got there on time.
③ I wish I have more time to think it over.
④ If I had finished the history report, I would be in the theater now.
⑤ They're crying as if the world would end soon.

07 ① It's time you studied for the tests.
② Should you have any questions, please contact me.
③ If it hadn't been for her idea, we couldn't have finished the project.
④ Without electricity, we couldn't live.
⑤ But you, I couldn't go to university.

08 빈칸에 들어갈 수 없는 말은?

_____ the bridge, we couldn't cross the river.

① Without ② But for
③ If it were not for ④ Had it not been for
⑤ Were it not for

[09-11] 두 문장의 의미가 통하도록 빈칸에 들어갈 알맞은 말을 고르시오.

09

I'm sorry tomorrow is Monday.
→ I wish tomorrow _____ Monday.

① is ② was ③ isn't
④ were ⑤ weren't

10

In fact, I'm not a troublemaker.
→ She talks as if I _____ a troublemaker.

① am
② were
③ am not
④ were not
⑤ had been

11

As he hurt his leg, he couldn't go hiking.
→ If he hadn't hurt his leg, he _____ hiking.

① went
② can go
③ could go
④ had gone
⑤ could have gone

[12-13] 우리말과 같은 뜻이 되도록 빈칸에 들어갈 알맞은 말을 고르시오.

12

내가 돈이 많다면, 가난한 사람들을 도울 텐데.
→ If I _____ plenty of money, I would help the poor.

① have
② had
③ will have
④ would have
⑤ had had

13

내가 어렸을 때 시골에 살았다면 좋을 텐데.
→ I wish I _____ in the countryside when I was young.

① live
② would live
③ lived
④ had lived
⑤ have lived

[14-15] 글을 읽고, 물음에 답하시오.

Yesterday my brother and I went swimming in the sea. Before going into the sea, he said, "If you _____ⓐ_____ a jellyfish, you have to get away from it as quickly as possible. It's very dangerous." But I didn't care. (A) 그는 언제나 모든 걸 다 아는 것처럼 이야기한다. I just wanted to jump into the water. While I was swimming, I saw a round clear thing. Out of curiosity, I touched it, and it hurt me badly. If I _____ⓑ_____ to him, I wouldn't have been hurt.

14 빈칸 ⓐ와 ⓑ에 들어갈 말이 바르게 짝지어진 것은?

	ⓐ		ⓑ
①	saw	–	listened
②	saw	–	had listened
③	had seen	–	listen
④	see	–	had listened
⑤	see	–	listened

15 밑줄 친 (A)를 바르게 영작한 것은?

① He always talks as if he knows everything.
② He always talks as if he would know everything.
③ He always talks as if he knew everything.
④ He always talks as if he had known everything.
⑤ He always talks as if he would have known everything.

[01-02] 우리말과 같은 뜻이 되도록 주어진 단어를 이용하여 문장을 완성하시오.

01 만약 내가 조종사라면, 세계를 여행할 텐데. (be, travel)

→ If I _____ a pilot,

I _____ around the world.

02 그의 도움이 아니었다면, 나는 길을 잃었을 것이다. (get)

→ Without his help, I _____ lost.

[03-04] 두 문장의 뜻이 통하도록 빈칸에 알맞은 말을 쓰시오.

03 I'm sorry I don't live near my school.

→ _____ near my school.

04 As it snowed a lot, the road was very slippery.

→ If it hadn't snowed a lot, the road _____

_____ very slippery.

[05-06] 주어진 문장을 [보기]와 같이 바꾸어 쓰시오.

> 보기
> In fact, he doesn't know the answer.
> → He acts as if he knew the answer.

05 In fact, she isn't good at dancing.

→ She acts _____.

06 In fact, he didn't see a ghost.

→ He acts _____.

07 주어진 단어를 이용하여 대화를 완성하시오.

(1) A Do you have a brother?

B No, I don't. I'm sorry that I don't have a brother. _____ a brother. (wish)

(2) A You don't look good. What happened?

B I failed the test.

A I'm sorry to hear that.

B If I _____ harder, I would have passed the test. (study)

[08-10] 글을 읽고, 물음에 답하시오.

Last night, a fire broke out in the forest near my school. I heard that it was caused by a cigarette butt. The fire spread quickly. If the weather (A) (not, be) dry, it wouldn't have spread that fast. The forest was the place I went hiking with my family for the first time. So I was very sad. The forest had always been green but now, it looks as black (B) (had, nothing, there, as if, lived). (C) I'm sorry I can't see the green forest again.

08 밑줄 친 (A)를 어법에 맞게 바꿔 쓰시오.

_____

09 밑줄 친 (B)의 주어진 단어를 알맞게 배열하시오.

_____

10 밑줄 친 (C)를 I wish 가정법 문장으로 바꿔 쓰시오.

→ _____

Chapter 8

관계대명사

☆ 관계대명사는 「접속사+대명사」 역할을 하고, 관계대명사가 이끄는 절은 형용사처럼 선행사를 수식한다.

선행사	주격	목적격	소유격
사람	who/that	who(m)/that	whose
동물, 사물	which/that	which/that	whose
사람, 동물, 사물	that	that	X
선행사를 포함할 때	what	what	X

1. 주격 관계대명사 who, which, that

Mrs. Gordon is **a teacher**. + **She** is strict but kind.

➡ Mrs. Gordon is **a teacher who** is strict but kind. Gordon 씨는 엄격하지만 친절한 선생님이다.

　　　　　　　　선행사　　주격 관계대명사 [관계사절 내에서 주어 역할]

2. 목적격 관계대명사 who(m), which, that

This is **the present**. + I got **it** on my birthday.

➡ This is **the present which** I got on my birthday. 이것은 내가 생일날 받은 선물이다.

　　　　　　선행사　　　목적격 관계대명사 [관계사절 내에서 목적어 역할]

3. 소유격 관계대명사 whose

I want to buy **the house**. + The walls **of the house** are white.

➡ I want to buy **the house whose** walls are white. 나는 벽이 흰색인 그 집을 사고 싶다.

　　　　　　　　선행사　　　소유격 관계대명사 [관계사 뒤에 나오는 명사의 소유격 역할]

4. 선행사를 포함하는 관계대명사 what (= the thing that/which)

What you know is not everything. [주어] 네가 아는 것이 전부는 아니다.

Keep in mind **what** I said today. [목적어] 오늘 내가 한 말을 명심해라.

This is **what** you shouldn't forget. [보어] 이것이 네가 잊지 말아야 할 것이다.

Plus α

1 최상급, the first, the only, the very, every, all 등의 표현이 쓰인 선행사를 수식할 때 주로 that을 쓴다.

He is **the only person that** I know here.
그는 내가 여기에서 유일하게 아는 사람이다.

2 관계대명사 that vs. 접속사 that

관계대명사 that 뒤에는 불완전한 문장이, 접속사 that 뒤에는 완전한 문장이 온다.

This is a girl **that lives next door.**
[관계대명사+주어가 없는 불완전한 문장] 이 사람이 옆집에 사는 소녀이다.

People know **that exercise is good for their health.**
[접속사+완전한 문장] 사람들은 운동이 건강에 좋다는 것을 안다.

Check-up ☐ 안에서 알맞은 말을 고르시오.

1 She is a person ☐ who / which ☐ is warm-hearted.

2 Give me the book ☐ who / which ☐ you borrowed from me last week.

3 I have a friend ☐ who / whose ☐ brother is a movie star.

4 The stem cell is ☐ that / what ☐ she's been studying for decades.

: EXERCISES

A [ ] 안에서 알맞은 것을 고르시오.

1 Pay close attention to [which / what] I am saying.

2 This shirt is the one [which / what] I was looking for.

3 The book [which / whose] cover is red looks interesting.

4 Every person [which / that] came for the contest did great.

pay attention to
~에 주의를 기울이다

look for ~을 찾다

cover 몡 표지

B 두 문장을 관계대명사를 이용하여 한 문장으로 만드시오.

1 This is the only chance. The chance is given to you.

   → This is the only chance _____ .

2 My mom often bakes cookies. The cookies have a lot of nuts.

   → My mom often bakes cookies _____ .

3 Tell me the words. You've had the words on your mind for a long time.

   → Tell me the words _____ .

4 Santorini is famous for white houses. The windows of the houses are blue.

   → Santorini is famous for white houses _____ .

chance 몡 기회

have A on one's mind
A를 ~의 마음에 담아 두다

C 밑줄 친 부분을 어법에 맞게 고쳐 쓰시오.

1 I've written down that you should do.

2 She is the student which all teachers like.

3 My mom has a friend which daughter is a supermodel.

4 There are many people and animals who suffer from hunger.

suffer from
~로 고통받다

hunger 몡 굶주림

D 우리말과 같은 뜻이 되도록 주어진 단어를 배열하시오.

1 나는 대회에서 일등을 한 그 가수를 안다. (first prize, the singer, won, who)

   → I know _____ in the contest.

2 그가 점심으로 만들어 준 음식은 맛이 있었다. (made, was, for lunch, which, tasty, he)

   → The dish _____ .

3 내 여동생은 내가 지닌 습관과 똑같은 습관을 지녔다. (that, have, the same, I, habit)

   → My sister has _____ .

4 내가 말하려는 것이 너를 화나게 할지도 몰라. (I'm going to, might, say, upset, what)

   → _____ you.

☆ 관계부사는 「접속사+부사」 역할을 하고, 관계부사가 이끄는 절은 형용사처럼 선행사를 수식한다. 관계부사는 「전치사+관계대명사」로 바꿔 쓸 수 있다.

Tell me **the date**. You met him **on that day**.

➡ Tell me **the date when** you met him. 네가 그를 만난 날을 나에게 말해 줘.
　　　　　선행사　　관계부사(=on which)

	선행사	관계부사	전치사+관계대명사
장소	the place, the town, the house	where	in / at / on + which
시간	the year, the time, the day	when	in / at / on + which
이유	the reason	why	for + which
방법	the way	how	in + which

Plus α

선행사가 the place, the time, the reason과 같이 일반적인 표현인 경우 관계대명사 또는 선행사를 생략할 수 있다.

This is **the place where** I keep my letters.

➡ This is **where** I keep my letters.

➡ This is **the place** I keep my letters. 이곳이 내가 편지를 보관하는 장소이다.

1. where: 선행사가 장소를 나타내는 표현인 경우

This is <u>the house</u> **where** I was born. 이곳이 내가 태어난 집이다.
　　　　　선행사　　　관계부사

➡ This is <u>the house</u> **in which** I was born.
➡ This is <u>the house</u> **which** I was born **in**.

2. when: 선행사가 시간을 나타내는 표현인 경우

I still remember <u>the day</u> **when** I turned twenty. 나는 스무 살이 되던 날을 아직 기억한다.
　　　　　　　　　선행사　　= on which

3. why: 선행사가 이유를 나타내는 표현인 경우

I don't understand <u>the reason</u> **why** she didn't go there. 그녀가 그곳에 가지 않은 이유를 모르겠다.
　　　　　　　　　선행사　　= for which

4. how: 선행사가 방법을 나타내는 표현인 경우

I want to learn **how** he passed the test. 나는 그가 시험에 합격한 방법을 배우고 싶다.
　　　　　= the way[in which]

(X) I want to learn ~~the way how~~ he passed the test. [the way와 how는 함께 쓸 수 없다.]

Check-up 　☐ 안에서 알맞은 말을 고르시오.

1 I forgot the place | when / where | I put my bag.

2 Tell me the time | when / where | you arrived here.

3 Do you know the reason | how / why | he didn't come?

4 I will show you | how / the way how | you borrow books from the library.

: EXERCISES

A [   ] 안에서 알맞은 것을 고르시오.

1 We need to learn [which / how] we can save the Earth.

2 Do you know the reason [which / why] he didn't give it to me?

3 I bought this scarf at the market [how / where] I went last weekend.

4 This book was written in the year [when / where] World War II broke out.

save ⑧ 구하다
scarf ⑲ 목도리
break out
(전쟁이) 발발하다

B 빈칸에 알맞은 관계부사를 넣어 문장을 완성하시오.

1 I go to school by bike. This is _____ I go to school.

2 My daughter is the only reason _____ I live to this day.

3 Renaissance is the period _____ art and architecture bloomed.

4 The Amazon Rainforest is the place _____ many tropical species are found.

to this day 오늘날까지
Renaissance
⑲ 르네상스(문예부흥기)
architecture ⑲ 건축
bloom ⑧ 꽃을 피우다
rainforest ⑲ 열대 우림
tropical ⑲ 열대의
species ⑲ 종(種)

C 두 문장을 관계부사를 이용하여 한 문장으로 만드시오.

1 This is the book. I found a lot of lessons about life in that book.

→ This is the book _____.

2 I still remember the day. I first met her on that day.

→ I still remember the day _____.

3 I know the reason. She changed her mind for that reason.

→ I know the reason _____.

4 I'll show you the way. I fixed your laptop computer in that way.

→ I'll show you _____.

lesson ⑲ 교훈
still ⑨ 여전히
change one's mind
생각, 결심을 바꾸다

D 우리말과 같은 뜻이 되도록 주어진 단어를 배열하시오.

1 기말고사가 내가 지금 열심히 공부하는 이유다. (the reason, hard, I, why, am studying)

→ The finals are _____ right now.

2 나는 사자를 처음 본 순간을 잊을 수가 없다. (I, a lion, when, first saw, the moment)

→ I can't forget _____.

3 나는 어떻게 그가 그 일을 시간 안에 끝냈는지 궁금하다. (the work, how, finished, in time, he)

→ I wonder _____.

4 이곳은 아버지와 내가 낚시를 하던 곳이다. (my father and I, where, fish, the place, used to)

→ This is _____.

주의해야 할 관계사의 쓰임

1. 제한적 용법 vs. 계속적 용법

(1) 제한적 용법: 관계사절이 형용사처럼 선행사를 수식하여 선행사의 의미를 제한한다.

I am wearing **a coat which[that]** my sister gave me. 나는 언니가 준 코트를 입고 있다.

(2) 계속적 용법: 관계사 앞에 콤마(,)가 있으며, 관계사절은 선행사에 추가적인 정보를 제공한다.

관계대명사절은 「접속사+대명사」로 바꿔 쓸 수 있고, 관계부사절은 「접속사+부사」로 바꿔 쓸 수 있다.

Ryu, who throws a fast ball, is playing on our team. [관계대명사절]

➡ Ryu is playing on our team, **and he** throws a fast ball.
류는 우리 팀에서 뛰고 있고 빠른 공을 던진다.

(X) ~~Ryu, that~~ throws a fast ball, is playing on our team. [that은 계속적 용법으로 쓸 수 없음]

I visited Thailand, **where** the food was fantastic. [관계부사절]

➡ I visited Thailand, **and there** the food was fantastic.
나는 태국을 방문했는데, 그곳은 음식이 환상적이었다.

> **Plus α**
>
> 계속적 용법으로 쓰인 관계대명사 which는 단어, 구, 앞문장 전체를 선행사로 받을 수 있다.
>
> He told me that he stayed at home last night, **which** wasn't true.
> 그는 어젯밤에 집에 있었다고 말했는데, 그것은 사실이 아니었다.

2. 관계사의 생략

(1) 목적격 관계대명사는 생략 가능하다.

This is the watch **(that[which])** I want to buy. 이것이 내가 사고 싶어 하는 시계이다.

(2) 「관계대명사+be동사」는 생략 가능하다.

Is the boy **(who is)** sitting over there your classmate? 저기 앉아 있는 남자 아이가 너의 반이니?

3. 「전치사+관계대명사」: 관계대명사가 전치사의 목적어로 쓰인 경우, 전치사는 관계대명사의 앞이나 관계사절의 맨 마지막에 온다.

I know the girl **to whom** my mom is talking. 나는 우리 엄마와 말하고 있는 소녀를 안다.

I know the girl **(who(m)[that])** my mom is talking **to**.
[전치사가 관계사절 뒤에 온 경우 관계대명사 생략 가능]

(X) I know the girl ~~to that~~ my mom is talking. [전치사 바로 뒤에는 관계대명사 that을 쓸 수 없음]

(X) I know the girl ~~to (whom)~~ my mom is talking. [전치사 바로 뒤에 온 관계대명사는 생략할 수 없음]

(X) I know the girl ~~to who~~ my mom is talking. [전치사 뒤에는 주격 관계대명사 who를 쓸 수 없음]

> **Tips**
>
> in that ~라는 점에서
> It is a delicate matter **in that** it involves many people.
> 그것은 많은 사람들을 포함한다는 점에서 매우 민감한 문제이다.

Check-up ☐ 안에서 알맞은 말을 고르시오.

1 There was heavy rain, | that / which | flooded the village.

2 This is the ball on | that / which | the famous player Chu signed his name.

: EXERCISES

A [   ] 안에서 알맞은 것을 고르시오.

1 That's the girl for [who / whom] the song was written.

2 She lost her wallet, in [that / which] she had 100 dollars in cash.

3 The young man offered me a seat, [that / which] was very kind of him.

4 The lecture was about a theme [in which / which] I am very interested.

wallet 몡 지갑
in cash 현금으로
offer 동 권하다, 제공하다
seat 몡 좌석, 자리
theme 몡 주제

B 밑줄 친 부분이 생략 가능하면 O, 불가능하면 X표를 하시오.

1 I have news at <u>which</u> you'll be surprised.

2 This is the moment <u>that</u> I've been waiting for.

3 The man <u>who is</u> reading newspapers is my father.

4 The girl <u>who</u> you saw in front of my house is my little sister.

C 두 문장의 의미가 통하도록 관계사를 이용하여 문장을 완성하시오.

1 They sent an ambulance, and it saved my life.

→ They sent an ambulance, _____.

2 This morning, I met Laura, and she came from England

→ This morning, I met Laura, _____.

3 He started working in the food industry, and there he had a great success.

→ He started working in the food industry, _____.

4 I turned 13 last year, and then I started learning to draw pictures.

→ I turned 13 last year, _____.

ambulance 몡 구급차
industry 몡 산업
success 몡 성공
turn 동 ~이 되다

D 우리말과 같은 뜻이 되도록 주어진 단어를 배열하시오.

1 공상과학 소설은 내가 가장 흥미를 느끼는 장르이다. (that, most interest, find, in, I, the genre)

→ The sci-fi novel is _____.

2 나중에 후회할 말은 하지 않는 것이 좋다. (you, be, will, which, sorry for, words)

→ You'd better not say _____ later.

3 저 소녀는 Susan인데, 그녀는 자신의 할머니를 따라 이름 지어졌다.
(was named after, her grandma, who)

→ That girl is Susan, _____.

4 Ben은 어제 Jane을 우연히 마주쳤는데, 그녀는 초등학교 동창인 옛 친구이다.
(is, elementary school, who, his old friend, from)

→ Yesterday Ben ran into Jane, _____.

복합관계사

1. 복합관계대명사: 「관계대명사+ever」의 형태로, 선행사를 포함하며 명사절과 양보의 부사절을 이끈다.

복합관계사	양보의 부사절	명사절
whoever	no matter who 누가 ~해도	anyone who ~하는 사람은 누구든지
whomever	no matter whom 누구를 ~해도	anyone whom ~하는 사람은 누구든지
whatever	no matter what 무엇을 ~해도	anything that ~하는 것은 무엇이든지
whichever	no matter which 어떤 것을 ~해도	anything which ~하는 것은 어느 것이나

Whoever asks me, I won't do anything. [양보의 부사절] 누가 부탁해도, 나는 어떤 것도 하지 않을 것이다.
= No matter who

Whoever comes first will get the present. [명사절] 맨 먼저 오는 사람은 누구든지 선물을 갖게 될 것이다.
= Anyone who

Whatever happens, I'll support you. [양보의 부사절] 무슨 일이 생겨도, 나는 너를 지지할 것이다.
= No matter what

Whatever he touched turned into gold. [명사절] 그가 만지는 것은 무엇이든 금으로 변했다.
= Anything that

Whichever you choose, you'll be satisfied. [양보의 부사절] 너는 어떤 것을 선택해도 만족할 것이다.
= No matter which

Here are three colors. Pick **whichever** you like. [명사절] 여기 세 가지 색이 있어. 네가 좋은 것 어느 것이든 골라.
= anything which

2. 복합관계부사: 「관계부사+ever」의 형태로 시간, 장소, 양보의 부사절을 이끈다.

복합관계부사	양보의 부사절	시간·장소의 부사절
whenever	no matter when 언제 ~해도	at any time when[that], every time ~할 때면 언제나
wherever	no matter where 어디서 ~해도	at any place where[that] ~하는 곳은 어디든지
however	no matter how 아무리 ~해도	-

Whenever you come, you are always welcome. [양보의 부사절] 언제 오든 너는 항상 환영이다.
= No matter when

Whenever I see him, he seems an inch taller. [시간의 부사절]
= Every time   그는 볼 때마다 1인치씩 더 자란 것 같아 보인다.

Wherever I go, my cat follows me. [양보의 부사절] 내가 어디를 가든지 우리 고양이는 날 따라다닌다.
= No matter where

Have a seat **wherever** you like. [장소의 부사절] 네가 좋은 대로 아무 데나 앉으렴.
= at any place where

However easy the task seems, you should do your best. [양보의 부사절]
= No matter how   아무리 과제가 쉬워 보여도, 최선을 다해야 한다.

Check-up 　　　 안에서 알맞은 말을 고르시오.

1 　Whoever / However　 made this, he must be a genius.

2 　Whatever / Whenever　 I hear a siren, it reminds me of a war.

: EXERCISES

A [ ] 안에서 알맞은 것을 고르시오.

1 I'll accept [whomever / whatever] is offered.

2 Tell the news to [whomever / whatever] you meet first.

3 [However / Whatever] poor you are, you shouldn't give up your hope.

4 [Whatever / Whenever] I hear this song, it reminds me of my grandma.

accept ⑤ 받아들이다
offer ⑤ 제공하다
give up 포기하다
remind A of B
A에게 B를 상기시키다

B 두 문장의 의미가 통하도록 문장을 완성하시오.

1 I won't betray you whatever happens.

→ I won't betray you _____ happens.

2 You can bring whoever wants to join the project.

→ You can bring _____ wants to join the project.

3 Whatever goes into the black hole will disappear.

→ _____ goes into the black hole will disappear.

4 Wherever I hide, my sister finds me.

→ _____ I hide, my sister finds me.

betray ⑤ 배신하다
black hole
〈천문〉 블랙홀(초고밀도에
의해 생기는 중력장의 구멍)
disappear ⑤ 사라지다
hide ⑤ 숨다

C [보기]에서 알맞은 단어를 골라 문장을 완성하시오. [한 번씩만 쓸 것]

| 보기 | whoever | whenever | wherever | however |

1 I hope you are happy _____ you go.

2 _____ fast he ran, he couldn't beat his brother.

3 _____ loves plays is welcome in this theater.

4 _____ I ask her questions, she kindly answers them.

beat ⑤ 이기다
play ⑲ 연극
kindly ⑨ 친절하게

D 우리말과 같은 뜻이 되도록 주어진 단어를 배열하시오.

1 나는 그가 무슨 말을 하든 믿을 수가 없다. (says, he, whatever)

→ _____, I can't believe it.

2 네가 편할 때 아무 때나 우리 집에 놀러 와. (is, you, it, for, whenever, convenient)

→ Come to my place _____.

3 그 빛을 바라보는 사람은 누구든 눈이 멀었다. (saw, the light, whoever)

→ _____ went blind.

4 아무리 애를 써도 그는 그 바위를 들어 올릴 수 없었다. (hard, he, however, tried)

→ _____, he couldn't lift the rock.

: Review Test

[01-04] 빈칸에 들어갈 알맞은 말을 고르시오.

01
> She does yoga every day, _____ is really good for her health.

① who ② which ③ that
④ whose ⑤ what

02
> On my birthday, I got a dress _____ color is my favorite, pink.

① who ② that ③ which
④ whose ⑤ what

03
> There are more than 100 people and animals in the school building _____ were rescued from the flood.

① whom ② which ③ that
④ whose ⑤ what

04
> Tell me _____ you were doing in my office.

① who ② that ③ which
④ whose ⑤ what

[05-06] 빈칸에 공통으로 들어갈 알맞은 말을 고르시오.

05
> · You are the only one _____ I trust.
> · She is the kind of person _____ will never tell a lie.

① whom ② which ③ that
④ whose ⑤ what

06
> · Mom bought a tie _____ goes really well with my father's suit.
> · Dad bought flowers for Mom, _____ made Mom really happy.

① who ② that ③ which
④ whose ⑤ what

07 밑줄 친 부분 중 생략할 수 없는 것은?

① The girl who you saw in school is my twin sister.
② There is a well which you can get clean water from.
③ The thief stole all the money that I had at home.
④ This is the neighborhood in which I spent my childhood.
⑤ A camel is an animal which is used in transportation on the desert.

[08-09] 두 문장이 같은 뜻이 되도록 빈칸에 들어갈 알맞은 말을 고르시오.

08
> I will pay for anything that you choose.
> → I will pay for _____ you choose.

① whichever ② whatever
③ however ④ wherever
⑤ whenever

09
> No matter how difficult the problem is, there is always an answer.
> → _____ difficult the problem is, there is always an answer.

① Whenever ② However
③ Whichever ④ Whatever
⑤ Wherever

10 다음 중 어법상 어색한 문장은?

① Take this ticket for which I paid.

② That's the place where everything started.

③ This is the tunnel that I go through every morning and night.

④ Follow the career where you can find interest in.

⑤ This is the conclusion I gave a lot of thought to.

11 [보기]의 두 문장을 한 문장으로 바꿔 쓴 것 중 어법상 어색한 것을 모두 고르시오.

보기	Marlow is a small town. + I lived in the town for 30 years.

① Marlow is a small town in I lived for 30 years.

② Marlow is a small town in which I lived for 30 years.

③ Marlow is a small town which I lived in for 30 years.

④ Marlow is a small town where I lived for 30 years.

⑤ Marlow is a small town where I lived in for 30 years.

12 밑줄 친 부분의 쓰임이 올바른 것은?

① A knife is a tool with which we cut things.

② However it gets dark, don't turn on the lights.

③ Forgive me for the things what I did.

④ Please teach me the way how you succeed.

⑤ The playground in that I used to play disappeared.

[13-15] 글을 읽고, 물음에 답하시오.

Today is the day ⓐ when I realized that there are still good people out there. ⓑ When I was walking into a coffee shop, I saw a sign that said, "We have five suspended coffees now." I was curious to know what a "suspended" coffee was, so I asked the coffee shop owner. She said, "A suspended coffee is (A) what people have paid in advance for other people. So, (B) 따뜻한 커피 한 잔이 필요한 사람이라면 누구나 들어올 수 있다 and enjoy it for free." I was touched. I think it is a great idea because there's a time for everyone ⓒ when they need warmth from society.

13 밑줄 친 ⓐ, ⓑ, ⓒ 중 관계부사로 쓰인 것을 모두 고르시오.

① ⓐ   ② ⓐ, ⓑ   ③ ⓐ, ⓒ

④ ⓑ, ⓒ   ⑤ ⓐ, ⓑ, ⓒ

14 밑줄 친 (A)와 바꿔 쓸 수 있는 말은?

① that   ② which

③ whatever   ④ the coffee which

⑤ the coffee what

15 밑줄 친 (B)를 바르게 영작한 것은?

① who can come in needs a hot cup of coffee

② who needs a hot cup of coffee can come in

③ whoever can come in needs a hot cup of coffee

④ whoever needs a hot cup of coffee can come in

⑤ whomever needs a hot cup of coffee can come in

[01-03] [보기]에서 알맞은 말을 골라 대화를 완성하시오.

보기	where	when	why
	how	whatever	whichever
	whenever	wherever	however

01 A What would you like to have for lunch?

 B You choose. I'll have _____ you like.

02 A Why are we here, Mom?

 B I want to show you the place _____ I grew up.

03 A I don't think I can do this anymore.

 B _____ bad the situation is, you shouldn't give up.

[04-05] 두 문장을 한 문장으로 바꿔 쓸 때 빈칸에 알맞은 관계사를 써 넣으시오.

04 I decided to buy the book. The design of the book attracted me.

 → I decided to buy the book _____ design attracted me.

05 Don't postpone the things. You can do the things today.

 → Don't postpone _____ you can do today.

[06-07] 두 문장을 관계사를 이용하여 한 문장으로 바꿔 쓰시오.

06 They made some changes in the original plan.

 + Those changes produced better results.

 → They made some changes in the original plan, _____ .

07 Our family went to Busan last summer.

 + We made a lot of good memories there.

 → Our family went to Busan last summer, _____ .

[08-10] 우리말과 같은 뜻이 되도록 주어진 단어를 이용하여 문장을 완성하시오.

08 다른 사람들이 너에 대해 하는 말에 주의를 기울여라.
(other people, say)

 → Pay attention to _____ _____ _____ _____ about you.

09 그 의견은 한 회사가 기금을 기증한 1990년에 실현되었다.
(a company, donate, funds)

 → The idea became a reality in 1990, _____ _____ _____ _____ _____ .

10 이 책은 한국이 인쇄술이 발명된 최초의 국가라고 주장한다.
(the printing press, invent)

 → This book argues that Korea is the first country _____ _____ _____ _____ _____ _____ .

Chapter 9

접속사

간접의문문, 상관접속사

1. **간접의문문:** 의문문이 문장의 일부로 들어간 문장

(1) 의문사가 있는 문장의 간접의문문: 의문사가 접속사 역할을 하며, 「의문사+주어+동사」의 어순으로 쓴다.

Can you tell me? + <u>What</u> did <u>they</u> <u>say</u>?

➡ Can you tell me **what they said**? 그들이 무슨 말을 했는지 말해 줄 수 있니?

(2) 의문사가 없는 문장의 간접의문문: 접속사 if나 whether를 이용하고, 「if/whether+주어+동사」의 어순으로 쓴다.

I wonder. + <u>Will</u> <u>she</u> <u>come</u>?

➡ I wonder **if[whether]** <u>she</u> <u>will</u> <u>come</u>. 나는 그녀가 올 것인지 궁금하다.

2. **상관접속사**

(1) not only A but also B A뿐만 아니라 B도(= B as well as A)

Not only I **but also** <u>my sister</u> <u>likes</u> classical music. [B에 수 일치]

➡ <u>My sister</u> **as well as** I <u>likes</u> classical music. 나뿐 아니라 나의 여동생도 고전음악을 좋아한다.

(2) both A and B A와 B 둘 다

Both <u>students</u> **and** <u>parents</u> <u>were</u> satisfied with the program. [복수 동사]
학생과 학부모 모두 그 프로그램에 만족했다.

(3) either A or B A와 B 둘 중 하나

Either you **or** <u>he</u> <u>has</u> to do it. [B에 수 일치] 너와 그 둘 중 하나가 그것을 해야 한다.

(4) neither A nor B A와 B 둘 다 아닌

Neither I **nor** <u>she</u> <u>wants</u> to do it. [B에 수 일치] 나도 그녀도 그것을 하고 싶어 하지 않는다.

Check-up ☐ 안에서 알맞은 말을 고르시오.

1 Show me what | do you have / you have | in your hand.

2 Neither Mom | and / nor | Dad likes eating out.

: EXERCISES

A [   ] 안에서 알맞은 것을 고르시오.

comedies
(명) 코미디 (영화, 드라마)

horror movie 공포 영화

1 Do you know where [did he go / he went]?

2 Please tell me [if you saw / did you see] my brother.

3 Either Tom [or / and] Jim broke the window.

4 I like both comedies [or / and] horror movies.

B 두 문장을 한 문장의 간접의문문으로 바꿔 쓰시오.

treasure (명) 보물

bury (동) 묻다

draw (동) 그리다

1 Do you think? + What does she want?

→ _____ do you think _____?

2 Do you know? + Where is the treasure buried?

→ Do you know _____?

3 Can you tell me? + Is the concert starting soon?

→ Can you tell me _____ soon?

4 I wonder. + Who drew this picture?

→ I wonder _____.

C 두 문장의 의미가 통하도록 주어진 상관접속사를 이용하여 문장을 완성하시오.

tasty (형) 맛있는

performance (명) 공연

audience (명) 청중

join (동) ~에 합류하다

1 Fruit is tasty and good for your health, too. (not only ~ but also)

→ Fruit is _____.

2 The singer enjoyed the performance, and the audience did, too. (both ~ and)

→ _____ enjoyed the performance.

3 I didn't join the soccer club, and my brother didn't, either. (neither ~ nor)

→ _____ joined the soccer club.

4 We should take a taxi or we should walk fast. (either ~ or)

→ We should _____.

D 우리말과 같은 뜻이 되도록 주어진 단어를 이용하여 문장을 완성하시오.

1 당신이 언제 떠날지 저에게 말해 주세요. (will, leave)

→ Please tell me _____ _____ _____ _____.

2 그는 잘 생겼을 뿐만 아니라 친절하다. (handsome, gentle)

→ He is _____ _____ _____ _____ _____.

3 우리는 그가 회의에 나타날 것인지 궁금하다. (show up)

→ We wonder _____ _____ _____ _____ _____ at the meeting.

UNIT 02 종속접속사

1. 시간을 나타내는 접속사: as, after, as soon as, before, every time, since, until, when, while

Can you answer the phone **while** I am away? 내가 없는 동안 전화 좀 받아줄래?

We have 30 minutes **until** the show begins. 쇼가 시작할 때까지 30분이 남았다.

Wash your hands **as soon as** you come home. 집에 오자마자 손을 씻어라.

Plus α as의 여러 가지 의미

① ~할 때 [접속사]

As I was walking down the road, I ran into an old friend of mine.
길을 가다가 오랜 친구 한 명을 우연히 마주쳤다.

② ~ 때문에 [접속사]

As he was extremely thirsty, he drank some water. 그는 목이 몹시 말라서 물을 약간 마셨다.

③ ~함에 따라 [접속사]

People tend to get wiser **as** they grow older. 사람들은 나이가 들어감에 따라 더욱 현명해진다.

④ ~하는 대로, ~처럼 [접속사]

When in Rome, do **as** Romans do.
로마에 있을 때는 로마 사람들이 하는 대로 하라. [로마에서는 로마법을 따르라.]

⑤ ~로(서) [전치사]

He took the theory **as** an example. 그는 그 이론을 예로 들었다.

---

2. 이유를 나타내는 접속사: as, because, since

Since you don't want to see him, I will go alone. 네가 그를 보고 싶어 하지 않으니, 나 혼자 갈게.

As it is getting dark, let's hurry home. 어두워지고 있으니 서둘러 집에 가자.

3. 양보를 나타내는 접속사: although, even if, even though, though

Although I called her name loudly, she didn't hear me.
내가 큰 소리로 그녀의 이름을 불렀지만 그녀는 듣지 못했다.

Even though you fail, you shouldn't stop trying. 실패한다 할지라도 시도를 멈춰서는 안 된다.

4. 조건을 나타내는 접속사: if, unless(= if ~ not)

If you arrive at the station by 11, you can catch the last train.
11시까지 역에 도착하면 막차를 탈 수 있어.

Let me go **unless** you have anything to tell me. 할 말이 없으면 저를 보내 주세요.

➡ Let me go **if** you don't have anything to tell me.

Tips

while 반면

My sister loves spicy food **while** I hate it.
나는 매운 음식을 싫어하는 반면 우리 언니는 매우 좋아한다.

Plus α

so that ~하기 위하여, ~할 수 있도록 [목적]

Take vitamins **so that** you get better soon.
빨리 나을 수 있도록 비타민을 먹어라.

so ~ that 너무 ~해서 ~하다 [결과]

I was **so** worried **that** I couldn't sleep.
너무 걱정이 되어 잠을 잘 수 없었다.

Plus α

시간, 조건 부사절에서는 현재 시제가 미래 시제를 대신한다.

If the weather **permits**, I will go on a picnic tomorrow.
날씨가 허락한다면 나는 내일 소풍을 갈 것이다.

When I **get** home, I will call you.
내가 집에 도착하면 전화할게.

Check-up ☐ 안에서 알맞은 말을 고르시오.

1 Press this button | when / because | you need any help.

2 | As soon as / Although | I was very tired, I got up early.

: EXERCISES

A [   ] 안에서 알맞은 것을 고르시오.

1 Give me a call [if / unless] something happens.

2 You shouldn't waste money [if / even if] you are rich.

3 You have to do it [because / although] you don't like it.

4 I will take a driving test when I [turn / will turn] nineteen.

give A a call
A에게 전화하다

waste 동 낭비하다

a driving test
운전면허 시험

turn 동 ~가 되다

B [보기]에서 알맞은 말을 골라 문장을 완성하시오.

보기	as soon as	because	although	if

1 _____ I was full, I ate more.

2 _____ you don't leave now, you will miss the train.

3 She kept calling him _____ she was so worried about him.

4 _____ he saw the police officer, the suspect began to run.

keep -ing 계속 ~하다

be worried about
~에 대하여 걱정하다

police officer 경찰관

suspect 명 용의자

C 주어진 접속사를 이용하여 두 문장의 의미가 통하도록 문장을 완성하시오.

1 If you don't try, you never know what you can do. (unless)

→ _____, you never know what you can do.

2 On seeing the picture, she burst out laughing. (as soon as)

→ _____, she burst out laughing.

3 The task was difficult, but we completed it on time. (although)

→ _____, we completed it on time.

try 동 시도하다

on -ing ~하자마자

burst out laughing
웃음을 터뜨리다

complete 동 완성하다

on time 정각에

D 우리말과 같은 뜻이 되도록 주어진 단어를 이용하여 문장을 완성하시오.

1 시간이 지남에 따라, 나의 기억은 흐려진다. (pass by)

→ _____ _____ _____, my memory becomes
   unclear.

2 그가 잠자리에 들자마자, 누군가가 문을 두드렸다. (go to bed)

→ Someone knocked on the door _____ _____ _____
   _____ _____ _____ _____.

3 만약 네가 원하지 않는다면, 너는 그곳에 갈 필요 없어. (want to)

→ _____ _____ _____ _____, you don't need to go there.

4 그는 매우 어렸지만, 그 어려운 문제를 풀었다. (very young)

→ _____ _____ _____ _____ _____ _____,
   he solved the difficult question.

[01-04] 빈칸에 들어갈 알맞은 말을 고르시오.

01

He can't swim _____ he lives near the beach.

① as   ② since   ③ when
④ because   ⑤ even though

02

You should _____ eat less or exercise more to lose weight.

① both   ② either   ③ neither
④ not only   ⑤ but also

03

Don't call me on this number _____ it is an emergency.

① that   ② as   ③ while
④ unless   ⑤ as soon as

04

Global warming affects _____ the environment but also the economy.

① both   ② not   ③ not only
④ either   ⑤ neither

05 빈칸에 들어갈 수 없는 동사는?

What do you _____ they want to do for the vacation?

① think   ② know   ③ believe
④ suppose   ⑤ imagine

[06-09] 빈칸에 공통으로 들어갈 말을 고르시오.

06

· _____ I was playing with my cat, Dad took some pictures of us.
· Mom loves dramas _____ I like action movies.

① as   ② since   ③ while
④ though   ⑤ that

07

· _____ we approached the top of the mountain, the air became scarcer.
· I had no knowledge about the world _____ I was just a little girl at that time.

① as   ② since   ③ that
④ if   ⑤ unless

08

· I haven't seen him again _____ I left the village.
· _____ you are here, I can give you this in person instead of mailing it.

① if   ② as   ③ since
④ because   ⑤ although

09

· _____ someone asks me a favor, I can't say no.
· I wonder _____ she is the person I talked to on the phone.

① as   ② if   ③ while
④ whether   ⑤ although

[10-12] 다음 중 어법상 <u>어색한</u> 문장을 고르시오.

10 ① Talk to me if you have something to say.

② Please take off your hat as you enter the room.

③ It's been already 10 years since I saw them last.

④ Unless you are not diligent, you can't succeed in your life.

⑤ Even though you're good at it, you should practice more.

11 ① People want to know who set the fire.

② Could you tell me how I should do it?

③ I wonder whether or not I can make it.

④ Did you find out if he committed a crime?

⑤ I'm not sure where did I put the keys.

12 ① Do you know what the problem is?

② No one knows whether he is a real genius or not.

③ Neither the employer nor employees wasn't able to find the solution.

④ Who do you think is the best person for the job?

⑤ You missed the presentation because you were late.

13 다음 중 나머지와 의미가 <u>다른</u> 하나는?

① Not only you but also I was unsatisfied with the result.

② Both you and I were unsatisfied with the result.

③ Neither you nor I was satisfied with the result.

④ You were unsatisfied with the result and so was I.

⑤ Either you or I was unsatisfied with the result.

[14-15] 글을 읽고, 물음에 답하시오.

David is Michelangelo's famous masterpiece. There is an interesting story about (A) 미켈란젤로가 자신의 다비드 상을 어떻게 조각했는지. To begin with, he ordered a block of marble. _____ ⓐ _____ the marble arrived, however, it was cracked and full of holes. He considered returning it _____ ⓑ _____ he doubted he could create anything good with it. But he _____ ⓒ _____ wanted to return it nor started work on the damaged marble. However, he decided to use it. After five years, he finally finished the masterpiece.

14 빈칸 ⓐ, ⓑ, ⓒ에 들어갈 말이 바르게 짝지어진 것은?

	ⓐ		ⓑ		ⓒ
①	When	–	though	–	neither
②	When	–	because	–	neither
③	When	–	because	–	either
④	While	–	because	–	either
⑤	While	–	though	–	either

15 밑줄 친 (A)를 바르게 영작한 것은?

① how did Michelangelo sculpt his David

② how sculpted Michelangelo his David

③ how Michelangelo sculpted his David

④ Michelangelo how sculpted his David

⑤ how sculpted his David Michelangelo

[01-02] 두 문장이 같은 뜻이 되도록 빈칸에 알맞은 말을 쓰시오.

01 My brother doesn't like cleaning the room, and I don't like it, either.

→ _____ my brother _____ I like cleaning the room.

02 This book is interesting, and it is informative, too.

→ This book is _____ _____ interesting _____ _____ informative.

03 [보기]에서 알맞은 접속사를 골라 문장을 완성하시오.

보기	if	since	while

(1) He didn't want to go out _____ he was tired.

(2) I listened to music _____ I was studying.

(3) _____ you want to buy a new computer, you have to save more money.

[04-05] 어법상 어색한 부분을 찾아 바르게 고쳐 쓰시오.

04 Show me where can I buy the same T-shirt as yours.

_____

05 Do you think what children are interested in these days?

_____

[06-07] 간접의문문을 이용하여 대화를 완성하시오.

06 A Where is the post office?

B Sorry, I don't know _____

_____.

07 A Will Daniel come to the party?

B Umm. I'm not sure _____

_____.

[08-10] 우리말과 같은 뜻이 되도록 주어진 단어를 이용하여 문장을 완성하시오.

08 그는 부자가 아니었음에도 가난한 아이들을 도왔다. (be, rich)

→ _____ _____ _____

_____, he helped poor children.

09 그가 소원을 빌자마자, 그의 소원이 이루어졌다. (make a wish)

→ _____ _____ _____

_____ _____ _____

_____, his wish came true.

10 내일 비가 오지 않으면, 우리는 놀이공원에 갈 것이다. (rain)

→ _____ _____ _____

_____, we will go to the amusement park.

Chapter 10

UNIT 01 원급, 비교급, 최상급

1. 「비교급+than」 ~보다 …한

Alice's hair is **longer than** mine. Alice의 머리카락이 내 머리카락보다 길다.

Doing is **more difficult than** saying. 행동하는 것이 말하는 것보다 어렵다.

I drink **more** water **than** Julia does. 나는 Julia보다 많은 물을 마신다.

Plus α

much, a lot, still, far, even 등은 비교급을 강조하여 '훨씬 더 ~한[하게]'이라는 뜻으로 쓰인다.

I think Tom is **much** more handsome than Brian. 나는 Tom이 Brian보다 훨씬 더 잘생겼다고 생각한다.

---

2. 「as+원급+as」 ~만큼 …한   「not as[so]+원급+as」 ~만큼 …하지 않은

I am **as active as** my brother. 나는 우리 형만큼 활동적이다.

Julia is **not as[so] sensitive as** Cindy. Julia는 Cindy만큼 예민하지 않다.

James reads **as many books as** I do. James는 나만큼 많은 책을 읽는다.

☆ 비교급의 문장 전환

I'm **not as[so] brave as** him. 나는 그만큼 용감하지 않다.

➡ I'm **not braver than** him. 나는 그보다 용감하지 않다.

➡ I'm **less brave than** him. 나는 그보다 덜 용감하다.

➡ He's **braver than** me. 그는 나보다 더 용감하다.

3. 「the+최상급」 가장 ~한

She is **the most famous** actress in my country. 그녀가 우리나라에서 가장 유명한 여배우이다.

He is **the most careful** of all my friends. 그는 내 친구들 중 가장 신중하다.

Tips

「최상급+in+단수명사(장소/집단)」, 「최상급+of+복수명사(비교대상)」

She is **the most popular girl in** our class. 그녀는 우리 반에서 가장 인기 있는 여자아이이다.

She is **the most popular girl of** all the students in our class.
그녀는 우리 반의 학생들 중에서 가장 인기 있는 여자아이이다.

Check-up   안에서 알맞은 말을 고르시오.

1 This chocolate cake is sweet / sweeter than that cheesecake.

2 The black cat is as smart / smarter as the white cat.

3 Russia is the larger / largest country in the world.

: EXERCISES

A [   ] 안에서 알맞은 것을 고르시오.

1 This dictionary is [thick / thicker] than that novel.

2 The moon is [smaller / smallest] than Mars.

3 My grandfather is as [healthy as / healthier than] my father.

4 The price of fruit here is [much / very] lower than that in the department store.

thick 웹 두꺼운
Mars 웹 〈천문〉화성
healthy 웹 건강한

B 우리말과 같은 뜻이 되도록 [보기]에서 알맞은 단어를 골라 어법에 맞게 바꿔 문장을 완성하시오.

보기	early	sour	fancy	pleased

1 이 소스는 식초만큼 시다.

→ This sauce is _____ _____ _____ vinegar.

2 그녀는 나보다 기뻐 보였다.

→ She looked _____ _____ _____ me.

3 그녀는 평상시보다 일찍 일어나야 했다.

→ She had to get up _____ _____ usual.

4 이 식당이 이 동네에서 가장 고급스럽다.

→ This restaurant is _____ _____ one in this town.

C 소파의 가격에 관한 표를 보고, 주어진 단어를 이용하여 문장을 완성하시오.

color	white	black	brown	grey
price ($)	100	120	140	120

1 The grey sofa is _____ _____ the brown one. (cheap)

2 The black sofa is _____ _____ _____ the grey one. (expensive)

3 The brown sofa is _____ _____ _____ among the four of them. (expensive)

D 우리말과 같은 뜻이 되도록 주어진 단어를 이용하여 문장을 완성하시오.

1 Christine은 나만큼 많은 옷을 가지고 있다. (many, clothes)

→ Christine has _____ _____ _____ _____ I do.

2 아프리카가 아시아보다 훨씬 더 덥다. (hot, a lot)

→ Africa is _____ _____ _____ _____ Asia.

3 이 가게에서 가장 편안한 소파는 어떤 것입니까? (comfortable sofa)

→ Which one is _____ _____ _____ _____ _____ the store?

여러 가지 비교급, 최상급 표현

1. 「as+원급+as possible」= 「as+원급+as+주어+can」 가능한 한 ~하게

Please call me **as soon as possible**. 가능한 한 빨리 제게 전화주세요.

➡ Please call me **as soon as you can**.

2. 「배수사+as+원급+as」 ~의 몇 배 …한

This computer is **twice as expensive as** that one. 이 컴퓨터는 저것보다 두 배 더 비싸다.

3. 「비교급+and+비교급」 점점 더 ~한

The exams are getting **more and more** difficult. 시험이 점점 더 어려워지고 있다.

4. 「the+비교급, the+비교급」 ~하면 할수록 더 …하다

The more you have, **the more** you want. 가지면 가질수록 더 원하게 된다.

➡ As you have more, you want more.

5. 「the+비교급+of the two」 둘 중에서 더 ~한

Jack is **the faster of the two**. 둘 중에 Jack이 더 빠르다.

6. 「one of the+최상급+복수 명사」 가장 ~한 것 중 하나

It is **one of the most famous buildings** in my country.

그것은 우리나라에서 가장 유명한 건물 중 하나이다.

7. 「the+최상급(+that)+주어+have ever p.p.」 지금까지 ~한 것 중 가장 …한

He is **the most diligent** boy I **have ever seen**. 그는 내가 지금까지 본 중에 가장 부지런한 아이이다.

8. 원급과 비교급을 이용한 최상급 표현

The Nile is **the longest** river in the world. 나일강은 세계에서 가장 긴 강이다.

➡ **No (other)** river in the world is **as[so] long as** the Nile.

➡ **No (other)** river in the world is **longer than** the Nile.

➡ The Nile is **longer than any other** river in the world.

➡ The Nile is **longer than all the other** rivers in the world.

> **Plus α**
>
> twice와 half를 제외하고, 「배수사+as+원급+as」는 「배수사+비교급+than」으로 바꿔 쓸 수 있다.
>
> This package is **three times as heavy as** that one.
>
> ➡ This package is **three times heavier than** that one.
> 이 소포는 저것보다 세 배 무겁다.

Check-up ☐ 안에서 알맞은 말을 고르시오.

1 The days are getting long and long / longer and longer .

2 The more you practice it, the better / the best you do.

: EXERCISES

A [   ] 안에서 알맞은 것을 고르시오.

try to ~하려고 노력하다
solve ⑧ (문제를) 풀다

1 It is the [funnier / funniest] movie I have ever seen.

2 The weather is getting colder [and / than] colder.

3 I'm trying to solve the questions as soon as I [am / can].

4 This is one of the highest [mountain / mountains] in the country.

B 우리말과 같은 뜻이 되도록 [보기]에서 알맞은 말을 골라 문장을 완성하시오.

보기	the more quickly	as briefly as possible
	as expensive as	slower and slower

1 저에게 가능한 한 간단하게 말해 주세요.

→ Please tell me _____.

2 이 집은 저 집보다 세 배 비싸다.

→ This house is three times _____ that one.

3 내 컴퓨터가 요즘 점점 더 느려지고 있다.

→ My computer is getting _____ these days.

4 날씨가 더워지면 더워질수록 음식이 더 빨리 상한다.

→ The hotter the weather gets, _____ food goes bad.

C 주어진 문장과 의미가 통하도록 문장을 완성하시오.

generous ⑱ 관대한

> James is the most generous man in the world.

→ _____ other _____ in the world is _____ as James.

→ _____ other _____ in the world is _____ than James.

→ James is _____ in the world.

→ James is _____ all the other _____ in the world.

D 우리말과 같은 뜻이 되도록 주어진 단어를 이용하여 문장을 완성하시오.

1 그 책을 가능한 한 빨리 보내 주세요. (soon)

→ Please send me the book _____ _____ _____ _____.

2 나는 점점 더 과학에 흥미를 갖게 되었다. (interested)

→ I became _____ _____ _____ in science.

3 그는 나라에서 가장 유명한 가수 중 한 명이다. (popular, singer)

→ He is _____ _____ _____ _____
_____ in the country.

[01-04] 빈칸에 들어갈 알맞은 말을 고르시오.

01

> I feel that English is much _____ than math.

① easy　　② easier　　③ easyer
④ easiest　　⑤ most easy

02

> My sister draws pictures as _____ as you do.

① well　　　　　② better
③ best　　　　　④ much better
⑤ the best

03

> The global environment is getting _____.

① as bad as　　　② the worst
③ worse and worse　④ as bad as possible
⑤ even more bad

04

> He is _____ teacher in the school.

① more respected
② most respected
③ the most respected
④ as respected as
⑤ the more respected

05 두 문장의 의미가 통하도록 할 때 빈칸에 들어갈 말은?

> Vegetables are healthier than meat.
> → Meat is _____ vegetables.

① less healthy than
② as healthy as
③ not so healthier as
④ less healthier than
⑤ less healthy as

06 다음 중 어법상 어색한 문장은?

① He is the youngest of all my family members.
② That tree is five times as tall as this one.
③ The higher we go, the thinner the air gets.
④ This is one of the best selling toy in the world.
⑤ The market is less crowded than I expected.

07 짝지어진 두 문장의 의미가 같지 <u>않은</u> 것은?

① Nothing is more important than health.
　→ Health is the most important thing.
② Andy is not as tall as Tom.
　→ Tom is shorter than Andy.
③ As you exercise harder, you will lose weight sooner.
　→ The harder you exercise, the sooner you will lose weight.
④ Please come home as soon as possible.
　→ Please come home as soon as you can.
⑤ Mark runs faster than any other student in my class.
　→ No other student runs as fast as Mark in my class.

08 다음 중 나머지와 뜻이 <u>다른</u> 하나는?

① This brown chair is more comfortable than any other chair in the store.
② This brown chair is the most comfortable in the store.
③ No other chair is more comfortable than this brown chair in the store.
④ No other chair is as comfortable as this brown chair in the store.
⑤ This brown chair is as comfortable as all the other chairs in the store.

09 빈칸에 들어갈 수 <u>없는</u> 말은?

> I bought many books, but my friend bought _____ more.

① even   ② still   ③ far
④ much   ⑤ very

10 두 문장의 의미가 통하도록 빈칸에 들어갈 말이 바르게 짝지어진 것은?

> As you are kinder to people, you'll have more friends.
> → _____ you are to people, _____ friends you'll have.

① Kind - many
② The kind - the many
③ The kindest - the most
④ The kinder - the more
⑤ The more kind - the more

[11-12] 우리말과 같은 뜻이 되도록 빈칸에 들어갈 알맞은 말을 고르시오.

11
> 가능한 한 멀리 공을 던져 볼래?
> → Will you throw the ball _____?

① as far as you
② as far as you can
③ farther than you can
④ as farther as possible
⑤ as the farthest as you can

12
> Jena는 Daniel보다 세 배는 빨리 말을 하는 것 같다.
> → It seems that Jena talks _____ Daniel does.

① three as fast as
② three faster than
③ three times as fast as
④ three times as faster as
⑤ as three times as faster than

13 밑줄 친 부분을 가장 바르게 고친 것은?

> <u>The late</u> you stay awake, the more you eat.

① More late   ② Late   ③ Later
④ The later   ⑤ The latest

[14-15] 글을 읽고, 물음에 답하시오.

> Yesterday I made my mom very angry. I know there's no excuse for that, because I lied to her. I skipped an English class and played basketball with my friends. It was the most stupid thing I have ever done. But I don't like English because it is too difficult. (A) <u>나는 영어가 가장 어려운 과목이라고 생각한다.</u> I promised my mom that I wouldn't lie to her again. She asked me what happened to Pinocchio's nose when he lied. And I answered, " ____ⓐ____ he lied, ____ⓑ____ his nose grew."

14 밑줄 친 (A)와 같은 뜻이 되도록 영작한 것이 <u>아닌</u> 것은?

① I think English is the most difficult subject.
② I think no other subject is as difficult as English.
③ I think English is one of the most difficult subjects.
④ I think no other subject is more difficult than English.
⑤ I think English is more difficult than any other subject.

15 빈칸 ⓐ와 ⓑ에 들어갈 말이 바르게 짝지어진 것은?

	ⓐ		ⓑ
①	More	–	longer
②	The more	–	the long
③	Much more	–	the long
④	The more	–	the longer
⑤	The most	–	the longest

[01-03] 우리말과 같은 뜻이 되도록 주어진 단어를 이용하여 문장을 완성하시오.

01 금붕어는 돌고래만큼 지능이 높지 않다. (intelligent)

→ A goldfish is _____

a dolphin.

02 한국 음식이 세계적으로 점점 더 인기를 얻고 있다. (popular)

→ Korean food is becoming _____

_____ around the world.

03 인사동은 한국에서 가장 유명한 관광 명소 중 하나이다. (famous, tourist attraction)

→ Insa-dong is _____

_____ in Korea.

04 표를 보고, 주어진 단어를 이용하여 문장을 완성하시오.

Name	Sarah	Nick	Mark
Height (cm)	155	185	170

조건 최상급, 비교급, 원급 비교를 이용할 것

(1) Sarah is _____ _____ of all.
(short)

(2) Nick is _____ _____
Sarah. (much, tall)

(3) Mark is _____ _____
_____ _____ Nick. (tall)

[05-06] 두 문장이 같은 뜻이 되도록 주어진 단어를 이용하여 문장을 완성하시오.

05 Gold is more expensive than silver.

→ Silver is _____ _____ than
gold. (expensive)

06 I promise I will visit you as often as possible.

→ I promise I will visit you _____

_____ _____
_____. (often)

07 주어진 문장을 [보기]와 같이 바꾸어 쓰시오.

> 보기
> Jake is the bravest boy in the class.
> → No other boy in the class is braver than Jake.

Soccer is the most exciting sport to me.

→ _____

[08-10] 글을 읽고, 물음에 답하시오.

> Do you know what the ⓐ (fast) animal on land is? If you came up with a cheetah, that's right! (A) No other animal on land is faster than the cheetah. A cheetah can run 70 miles per hour. Can you imagine how fast that is? You can imagine a car going 70 miles per hour on the highway. How about other animals? A lion can run 50 miles per hour, and a rabbit can run 35 miles per hour. A cheetah can run ⓑ (fast) than a lion, and (B) 치타는 토끼의 두 배만큼 빨리 달릴 수 있다.

08 밑줄 친 ⓐ와 ⓑ를 어법에 맞게 바꿔 쓰시오.

ⓐ _____ ⓑ _____

09 밑줄 친 (A)와 의미가 통하도록 문장을 완성하시오.

→ The cheetah is _____
on land.

10 밑줄 친 (B)를 주어진 단어를 이용하여 영작하시오.

→ a cheetah can run _____
a rabbit can (twice)

Chapter 11

UNIT 01 수 일치

1. 단수 취급

(1) each/every+단수 명사, -thing, -one, -body

Every student <u>has</u> to follow the rules. 모든 학생은 규칙을 따라야 한다.

Does **anyone** want some more coffee? 누구 커피 더 드실 분 있어요?

(2) 시간, 거리, 가격, 무게 등

Ten years <u>is</u> not a short time. 10년은 짧은 시간이 아니다.

(3) 구 또는 절

Reading books in the dark <u>is</u> not good for your eyes.
어두운 곳에서 책을 읽는 것은 눈에 좋지 않다.

What I want to do <u>is</u> to get some sleep. 내가 하고 싶은 것은 잠을 좀 자는 것이다.

(4) 학문, 질병, 국가명

Mathematics <u>is</u> very difficult and complicated. 수학은 매우 어렵고 복잡하다.

(5) 「one of+한정사+복수 명사」 ~ 중 하나

One of the oldest trees in Korea <u>is</u> over there. 한국에서 가장 오래된 나무들 중 하나가 저기 있다.

2. 복수 취급

(1) 「(Both) A and B」 A와 B는

Jackie and I <u>are</u> best friends. Jackie와 나는 가장 친한 친구 사이다.

(2) 「the+형용사」 = 「형용사+people」 ~한 사람들

The old[Old people] <u>tend</u> to forget things easily. 나이 든 사람들은 쉽게 잊어버리는 경향이 있다.

(3) 「A number of+복수 명사」 많은 ~

A number of people <u>are</u> waiting for the bus. 많은 사람들이 버스를 기다리고 있다.

3. 부분이나 전체를 나타내는 표현의 수 일치: 동사를 of 뒤에 오는 명사의 수에 일치시킨다.

(1) 「some/many/most/half/the rest/분수+of+단수 명사+단수 동사」

Most of his life <u>was</u> spent working for the poor.
그의 인생 대부분은 가난한 사람들을 위해 일하는 데 쓰였다.

(2) 「some/many/most/half/the rest/분수+of+복수 명사+복수 동사」

One third of the students <u>are</u> from other countries.
학생들의 3분의 1은 다른 나라에서 온 학생들이다.

Tips

수식어의 삽입으로 주어, 동사 사이가 멀어진 경우 수 일치에 주의해야 한다.

The boy (who is playing with toy cars) **is** my nephew.
장난감 자동차를 가지고 놀고 있는 소년은 내 조카이다.

Plus α

「A and B」가 단일 개념으로 쓰일 때에는 단수 취급한다.

Bread and butter is my favorite breakfast.
버터 바른 빵은 내가 가장 좋아하는 아침 식사다.

Plus α

Not only A but also B [B as well as A]: B에 수 일치 A뿐만 아니라 B도

Not only I but also **my sister** <u>likes</u> traveling.

My sister as well as I <u>likes</u> traveling.
나뿐만 아니라 나의 언니도 여행하는 것을 좋아한다.

Plus α

「The number of+복수 명사」 ~의 수[단수 취급]

The number of stars in the night sky <u>is</u> countless.
밤하늘에 떠 있는 별의 수는 셀 수 없이 많다.

Check-up ☐ 안에서 알맞은 말을 고르시오.

1 Each answer ☐ is / are ☐ worth five points.

2 A number of people ☐ use / uses ☐ their smartphones to buy things.

: EXERCISES

Answers / p.32

A [   ] 안에서 알맞은 것을 고르시오.

increase
ⓥ 늘다, 증가하다

dramatically
ⓐ 극적으로

take care of ~을 돌보다

1 [Do / Does] anyone have questions?

2 Eating apples in the morning [is / are] better than eating them at night.

3 One of the most popular Korean foods [is / are] bulgogi.

4 The number of tourists from China [has / have] increased dramatically.

5 In every country, the sick [need / needs] to be taken care of.

B 빈칸에 is와 are 중 알맞은 것을 써 넣으시오.

favorite ⓐ 매우 좋아하는

newborn baby 신생아

decrease ⓥ 줄어들다

after-school
ⓐ 방과 후의

1 Curry and rice _____ my favorite food.

2 The number of newborn babies _____ decreasing.

3 The United States _____ one of the biggest countries.

4 The boy who is wearing sunglasses _____ my brother.

5 Two fifths of the students _____ taking after-school classes.

C 주어진 동사를 어법에 맞게 바꿔 문장을 완성하시오. [현재 시제를 사용할 것]

the injured 부상자

critical ⓐ 위태로운

condition ⓝ 상태, 상황

get used to
~에 익숙해지다

fridge ⓝ 냉장고

economics 경제학

major ⓝ 전공

1 What I need _____ a nice hot bath. (be)

2 The injured _____ in critical condition. (be)

3 As each day _____ by, you'll get used to it. (go)

4 The rest of the cake _____ in the fridge for you. (be)

5 Economics _____ one of the most popular majors in college. (be)

D 우리말과 같은 뜻이 되도록 주어진 단어를 이용하여 문장을 완성하시오.

1 요즘 내 옷 중 몇 개가 잘 맞지 않는다. (some, my clothes, fit)

→ _____ _____ _____ _____
_____ me well these days.

2 많은 사람들이 출근할 때 지하철을 이용한다. (number, use)

→ _____ _____ _____ _____ _____ the
subway to go to work.

3 나의 가장 친한 친구 중 한 명은 댄스 동아리에 가입하기를 원한다. (best, want)

→ _____ _____ _____ _____
_____ to join a dance club.

UNIT 02 시제 일치

1. **시제 일치**: 주절의 시제에 따라 종속절의 시제가 달라진다. 주절의 시제가 현재이면 종속절에는 모든 시제가 가능하지만, 주절의 시제가 과거이면 종속절에는 주로 과거와 과거완료가 온다.

주절	종속절
현재	모든 시제
과거	과거/과거완료

I **know** that he **will be** a university student next year.
나는 내년에 그가 대학생이 된다는 것을 안다.

I **know** that he **is** a university student. 나는 그가 대학생이라는 것을 안다.

I **know** that he **was** a university student last year. 나는 그가 작년에 대학생이었다는 것을 안다.

I **knew** that he **told** me a lie. 나는 그가 나에게 거짓말을 했다는 것을 알았다.

I **knew** that he **had told** me a lie. 나는 그가 나에게 거짓말을 했었다는 것을 알았다.

2. **시제 일치의 예외**

(1) **일반적 진리, 격언**: 항상 현재로 쓴다.
The teacher **said** that time **is** gold. 선생님은 시간이 금이라고 하셨다.
I **learned** wood **floats** on water. 나는 나무가 물에 뜬다고 배웠다.

(2) **현재에도 지속되는 일**: 현재 또는 과거로 쓸 수 있다.
She **said** she **goes** jogging in the park every morning.
She **said** she **went** jogging in the park every morning.
그녀는 매일 아침 공원으로 달리기를 하러 간다고 말했다.

(3) **역사적 사실**: 항상 과거로 쓴다.
Do you **know** that the Korean War **broke** out on June 25, 1950?
너는 한국 전쟁이 1950년 6월 25일에 일어났다는 것을 알고 있니?
I **learned** that the Korean Independence Movement **started** on March 1st, 1919.
나는 대한독립운동이 1919년 3월 1일에 시작되었다고 배웠다.

> **Plus α**
> 시간, 조건의 부사절에서는 현재 시제가 미래 시제를 대신한다.
> When I **get** there, I'll **call** you.
> 거기에 도착하면 너에게 전화할게.

Check-up [   ] 안에서 알맞은 말을 고르시오.

1 I thought he [will / would] come to my party last Friday.

2 She said walls [have / had] ears.

: EXERCISES

A [   ] 안에서 알맞은 것을 고르시오.

1 I thought you [have / had] been there.

2 We know that the earth [is / was] round.

3 I found that I [have / had] left my book at home.

4 I'm sure that you [will / would] get over this crisis soon.

5 It seemed that it [will / would] rain this morning. The sky was dark and cloudy.

round (형) 둥근
get over 극복하다
crisis (명) 위기

B 주어진 단어를 어법에 맞게 바꿔 문장을 완성하시오.

1 I thought that she _____ come on time. (will)

2 We learned that light _____ faster than sound. (be)

3 She wondered why he _____ there at that time. (be)

4 She said that a friend in need _____ a friend indeed. (be)

5 Do you know that the Wright Brothers _____ the airplane? (invent)

on time 정각에, 제시간에
wonder
(동) ~을 궁금해하다,
알고 싶어 하다
in need 어려움에 처한
indeed (부) 정말, 사실
invent (동) 발명하다

C 주절의 시제를 과거 시제로 바꿔 문장을 완성하시오.

1 We don't know where she is.
   → We _____.

2 He says that action speaks louder than words.
   → He _____.

3 My teacher says to us that baseball was invented in Britain.
   → My teacher _____.

D 우리말과 같은 뜻이 되도록 주어진 단어를 이용하여 문장을 완성하시오.

1 그는 그녀가 반장이 될 거라고 생각했다. (think, will, be)
   → He _____ that she _____ _____ the class president.

2 나는 Galileo Galilei가 망원경을 발명했다는 것을 몰랐다. (know, invent)
   → I _____ _____ Galileo Galilei _____ telescopes.

3 나는 금성이 우리 태양계에서 가장 더운 행성이라고 배웠다. (learn, be)
   → I _____ Venus _____ the hottest planet in our solar system.

화법 전환

☆ 직접화법은 다른 사람의 말을 큰따옴표를 이용하여 그대로 전달하는 것이고, 간접화법은 다른 사람의 말을 전달자의 입장에서 바꿔 말하는 것이다.

1. 평서문의 화법 전환

He **said to** me, "**I want** to go home **now**."
①   ② ③④   ⑤

➡ He **told** me **that he wanted** to go home **then**. 그는 그때 내게 집에 가고 싶다고 말했다.

① 전달동사를 say ➡ say, say to ➡ say to 또는 tell로 바꾼다.
② 쉼표(,)와 큰따옴표를 삭제하고 접속사 that을 쓴다. (접속사 that은 생략 가능)
③ that절의 인칭대명사를 전달자의 입장에서 적절하게 바꿔 준다.
④ that절의 시제를 적절하게 바꿔 준다.
  (전달동사: 현재는 그대로, 과거는 과거나 과거완료로 바꿔 준다.)
⑤ 부사를 적절하게 바꿔 준다.

2. 의문문의 화법 전환

(1) 의문사 의문문: 전달동사를 ask로 바꾸고, 「의문사+주어+동사」 어순으로 쓴다.

My mother **said to** me, "**When are you** going to do **your** homework?"
➡My mother **asked** me **when I was** going to do **my** homework.
  우리 어머니는 내게 숙제를 언제 할 거냐고 물으셨다.

(2) 의문사가 없는 의문문: 전달동사를 ask로 바꾸고 「if[whether]+주어+동사」 어순으로 쓴다.

She **said to** me, "**Will you go** to the movies with **me**?"
➡She **asked** me **if [whether] I would go** to the movies with **her**.
  그녀는 내게 자기와 영화를 보러 가겠냐고 물었다.

3. 명령문의 화법 전환

전달동사를 tell, ask, order, advise 등으로 바꾸고, 명령문의 동사 앞에 to를 붙여 준다.
부정명령문은 not to를 붙인다.

My mother **said to** me, "**Wash your** hands first."
➡ My mother **told** me **to wash my** hands first. 우리 어머니는 내게 손을 먼저 씻으라고 말했다.

My brother **said to** me "**Don't be** afraid."
➡ My brother **advised** me **not to be** afraid. 우리 형은 내게 겁먹지 말라고 조언했다.

Check-up 화법에 맞게 ☐ 안에서 알맞은 말을 고르시오.

1 She said, "I have to go now."

  → She said that she ⏢ have to / had to ⏣ go then.

2 My dad said to me, "When will you come back home?"

  → My dad asked me when ⏢ will you / I would ⏣ come back home.

: EXERCISES

A [   ] 안에서 알맞은 것을 고르시오.

watch one's step
조심하다, 조심해서 걷다

1 She told me [to watch / watch] my step.

2 I asked her why [was she / she was] crying.

housewarming
(명) 집들이

3 He asked me [if / that] I was coming to the housewarming.

see a doctor
병원에 가다, 진찰을 받다

4 Greg told me that he [will / would] call me the next day.

5 Ann said that she was going to see a doctor [now / then].

B 직접화법을 간접화법으로 바꿔 문장을 완성하시오.

fasten (동) 고정시키다, 매다

1 He said to me, "Fasten your seat belt."

seat belt (명) 안전벨트

→ He told me _____.

tired (형) 피곤한

2 She said to me, "I'm too tired to stay here."

→ She told me _____.

3 He said to me, "Do you have plans for next weekend?"

→ He asked me _____.

C 간접화법을 직접화법으로 바꿔 문장을 완성하시오.

make a noise 떠들다

1 The teacher told us not to make any noise.

move to ~로 이사하다

→ The teacher said to us, "_____."

2 She asked me when I was moving to a new house.

→ She said to me, "_____?"

3 Henry told me he would visit his grandparents the next day.

→ Henry said to me, "_____."

D 우리말과 같은 뜻이 되도록 주어진 단어를 배열하시오.

1 그는 내게 작가가 될 거라고 말했다. (would, me, a writer, that, told, be, he)

→ He _____.

2 그녀는 내게 애완동물을 키우냐고 물었다. (if, asked, I, a pet, had, me)

→ She _____.

3 나의 어머니가 내게 너무 빨리 먹지 말라고 말했다. (too, told, not, me, to, eat, fast)

→ My mother _____.

: Review Test

[01-03] 빈칸에 들어갈 알맞은 말을 고르시오.

01

Today, in science class, he learned oil and water _____ .

① do not mix   ② did not mix
③ hasn't mixed   ④ haven't mixed
⑤ hadn't mixed

02

I thought that he _____ me paint the fence.

① helps   ② will help
③ would help   ④ has helped
⑤ have helped

03

She told me the French Revolution _____ in 1789.

① begins   ② began
③ begun   ④ has begun
⑤ had begun

[04-06] 빈칸에 들어갈 말이 바르게 짝지어진 것을 고르시오.

04

· Fish and Chips _____ my favorite dish for lunch.
· Two thirds of the members _____ my idea.

① is – likes   ② are – like   ③ is – like
④ are – likes   ⑤ be – likes

05

· The blind often _____ it hard to get around.
· One of the most popular parks _____ turning into a garbage dump.

① find – be   ② finds – is   ③ find – are
④ finds – are   ⑤ find – is

06

· Something _____ just passed over her head.
· Both Rebecca and I _____ going to leave early.

① have – am   ② have – are   ③ has – am
④ has – are   ⑤ has – is

07 다음 중 어법상 어색한 문장은?

① The number of people who have dogs are increasing.
② I know something is going wrong.
③ Many of the companies were closed.
④ The rest of the people were talking in the living room.
⑤ Skipping breakfast is not good for your health.

[08-09] 우리말과 같은 뜻이 되도록 빈칸에 들어갈 알맞은 말을 고르시오.

08

나는 네가 경주에서 이길 줄 알았어.
→ I _____ you _____ the race.

① know – will win   ② know – won
③ knew – will win   ④ knew – would win
⑤ knew – have won

09

그는 워싱턴 D.C.가 미국의 수도인지 몰랐다.
→ He _____ Washington D.C. _____ the capital city of the U.S.A.

① doesn't know – is   ② doesn't know – was
③ didn't know – was   ④ didn't know – is
⑤ didn't know – be

10 다음 중 어법상 옳은 문장은 <u>모두</u> 몇 개인가?

· My father told me don't play games.
· My mother told me wake up early.
· My brother told me not to use his phone.
· My sister told me to eat breakfast.
· I told my family not worry about me.

① 1개   ② 2개   ③ 3개
④ 4개   ⑤ 5개

11 우리말을 영어로 옮긴 것 중 바르지 <u>않은</u> 것은?

① 그녀는 그에게 차를 원하냐고 물었다.
  → She asked him if he wanted some tea.
② 그는 누군가 우는 것을 들었다고 말했다.
  → He said he had heard someone crying.
③ 그는 나에게 왜 파티에 오지 않았냐고 물었다.
  → He asked me why I hadn't come to the party.
④ 그는 나에게 그 다음날 떠날 거라고 말했다.
  → He told me he was leaving the next day.
⑤ 그는 나에게 자신과 함께 점심을 먹겠냐고 물었다.
  → He asked me I was going to eat lunch with him.

[12-13] 두 문장의 의미가 통하도록 빈칸에 들어갈 알맞은 말을 고르시오.

12

He said to me, "Do you know how to fix computers?"
→ He asked me _____.

① that I knew how to fix computers
② whether I knew how to fix computers
③ if do you know how to fix computers
④ if did you know how to fix computers
⑤ did I know how to fix computers

13

My father said to me, "I'm proud of you."
→ My father told me _____.

① I was proud of you   ② I was proud of him
③ he is proud of you   ④ he is proud of him
⑤ he was proud of me

[14-15] 글을 읽고, 물음에 답하시오.

Today we got a new classmate. Our teacher said she is Korean but she ⓐ (come) from Canada. Every student ⓑ (be) looking at her with so much curiosity. I wanted to know more about her. So (A) 나는 그녀에게 캐나다에서 얼마나 오래 살았는지 물었다. She answered, "I ⓒ (be) born there and ⓓ (grow up) there." She also told me she doesn't speak Korean well and doesn't know much about Korea, either. So, I told her I would help whenever she needed any help. I want to be good friends with her.

14 밑줄 친 ⓐ~ⓓ를 바르게 바꿔 쓴 것은?

	ⓐ	ⓑ	ⓒ	ⓓ
①	came	was	was	grew up
②	came	was	was	grow up
③	comes	was	was	grew up
④	comes	were	am	grew up
⑤	comes	were	am	grow up

15 밑줄 친 (A)를 바르게 영작한 것을 <u>두 개</u> 고르시오.

① I asked her how long did you live in Canada.
② I asked her how long she lived in Canada.
③ I asked her how long she lives in Canada.
④ I said to her, "How long did you live in Canada?"
⑤ I said to her, "How long did she live in Canada?"

: 서술형 평가

[01-03] [보기]에서 알맞은 단어를 골라 우리말과 같은 뜻이 되도록 문장을 완성하시오.

보기	study	want	cost

01 각 품목은 15달러입니다.

→ Each item _____ fifteen dollars.

02 많은 학생들이 도서관에서 공부하고 있다.

→ A number of students _____ in the library.

03 우리 반 학생들 중 다수가 선생님이 되고 싶어 한다.

→ Many of the students in my class _____ to be a teacher.

[04-05] 우리말과 같은 뜻이 되도록 주어진 단어를 배열하시오.

04 나는 나쁜 소식은 빨리 퍼진다고 생각했다.

(travels, thought, bad news, fast)

→ I _____ .

05 나는 Einstein이 1921년에 노벨상을 받았다는 것을 안다.

(won, know, the Nobel Prize, Einstein, in 1921)

→ I _____ .

06 직접화법을 간접화법으로 바꿔 문장을 완성하시오.

(1) He said to me, "Have you ever been to Italy?"

→ He asked me _____

_____ .

(2) She said to me, "Don't take pictures in the museum."

→ She told me _____

_____ .

07 대화를 읽고, 주어진 단어를 이용하여 밑줄 친 우리말을 영작하시오.

> A What are you doing here? Mike is looking for you in the cafeteria.
>
> B Really? 그가 나에게 여기서 기다리라고 했어.
>
> A He must have been confused.

조건 간접화법으로 쓸 것

→ _____

(tell, wait)

[08-10] 글을 읽고, 물음에 답하시오.

> Yesterday I got my test results. **(A)** Most of the results was not bad. But **(B)** mathematics were awful. I was very disappointed because I thought I did pretty well this time. While we were having dinner today, **(C)** my mother said to me, "Why do you look so sad?" I said, "I studied hard, but I didn't get perfect scores." **(D)** My mother told me not to be depressed. And she said to me, "You can do better next time."

08 밑줄 친 (A), (B)에서 어법상 어색한 부분을 찾아 바르게 고쳐 쓰시오.

(A) _____ → _____

(B) _____ → _____

09 밑줄 친 (C)를 간접화법 문장으로 바꿔 쓰시오.

→ my mother _____

_____ .

10 밑줄 친 (D)를 직접화법 문장으로 바꿔 쓰시오.

→ My mother _____

_____ ."

Chapter 12

특수구문

UNIT 01 강조, 부정

1. 강조

(1) do를 이용한 동사 강조: 「do/does/did+동사원형」 정말 ~하다[했다]

I **do understand** you. 나는 너를 정말로 이해해.

She **did call** him yesterday. 그녀는 어제 정말로 그에게 전화를 했다.

(2) It ~ that 강조 구문: 「It is[was]+강조 어구+that ~」 ~한 것은 바로 …이다[였다]

I lost my umbrella in the library yesterday. 나는 어제 도서관에서 우산을 잃어버렸다.

➡ **It** was I **that** lost my umbrella in the library yesterday. [주어 강조]
어제 도서관에서 우산을 잃어버린 것은 바로 나였다.

➡ **It** was my umbrella **that** I lost in the library yesterday. [목적어 강조]
어제 도서관에서 내가 잃어버린 것은 바로 우산이었다.

➡ **It** was in the library **that** I lost my umbrella yesterday. [부사구 강조]
어제 내가 우산을 잃어버린 곳은 바로 도서관이었다.

> **Plus α**
> 「It ~ that」 강조 구문에서는 강조되는 대상에 따라 that 대신 who(m)(사람), which(사물), when(시간), where(장소) 등을 쓸 수 있다.
> It was at midnight **that**[**when**] the phone rang. 전화가 울린 것은 바로 한밤중이었다.

2. 부정

(1) 부분 부정: 「not+all/every/both/always」 모두[둘 다/항상] ~한 것은 아니다

Not everyone likes his idea. 모두가 그의 아이디어를 좋아하는 것은 아니다.

She does **not always** agree with me. 그녀가 항상 나에게 동의하는 건 아니다.

(2) 전체 부정: none/no one/neither/never 아무도[결코] ~하지 않다

None of us remembered what he said. [all의 전체 부정]
우리 중 어느 누구도 그가 한 말을 기억하지 못했다.

Neither of them came to his party. [both의 전체 부정]
그들 둘 다 그의 파티에 오지 않았다.

> **Tips**
> 부정어에는 이미 부정의 의미가 포함되어 있으므로 not을 중복해서 쓰지 않도록 주의한다.

Check-up 우리말과 같은 뜻이 되도록 ☐ 안에서 알맞은 말을 고르시오.

1 그녀는 혼자되는 것을 정말 싫어한다.

→ She does │ dislike / dislikes │ being alone.

2 그들 둘 다 틀렸다.

→ │ Neither / Either │ of them was correct.

: EXERCISES

A [　] 안에서 알맞은 것을 고르시오.

1 Maya [do / does] know that the work should be done by today.

2 She did [believe / believed] that Chris was the one who helped her last night.

3 It was at night [where / when] the kids ran around and sang loudly.

4 Fortunately, no one [was / wasn't] injured in the traffic accident.

loudly (부) 크게
fortunately (부) 다행히
injured (형) 다친
accident (명) 사고

B 밑줄 친 부분을 강조하는 문장으로 바꿔 쓰시오.

1 He <u>tried</u> his best to win the race.

→ He _____.

2 She <u>looks</u> excited about the holidays.

→ She _____.

3 <u>Jack</u> was elected class president.

→ It was _____.

4 She lost her student ID card <u>in the playground</u>.

→ It was _____.

try one's best
최선을 다하다
excited (형) 신 나는, 들뜬
holiday (명) 휴가
elect (동) 선출하다
playground (명) 운동장

C 두 문장의 뜻이 통하도록 문장을 완성하시오.

1 Jenny didn't learn how to ski, and Henry didn't, either.

→ _____ of them learned how to ski.

2 Some rich people are happy, but some aren't.

→ _____ all rich people are happy.

3 All the students in my class don't like horror movies.

→ _____ of the students in my class likes horror movies.

D 우리말과 같은 뜻이 되도록 주어진 단어를 배열하시오.

1 우리 중 아무도 그를 보지 못했다. (us, him, saw, of, none)

→ _____

2 나는 항상 일찍 일어나는 것은 아니다. (always, early, I, get up, don't)

→ _____

3 그 옷을 입으니 그녀는 정말 멋져 보인다. (that dress, look, does, nice, in, she)

→ _____

02 병렬구조, 도치

1. 병렬구조: 두 개 이상의 어구가 접속사로 연결되어 나란히 쓰이는 구조를 '병렬구조'라고 하고, 이때 연결된 어구는 성분이 같다.

(1) 등위접속사: and, but, or 등

The cat entered my room <u>slowly</u> **and** <u>silently</u>. 고양이는 내 방으로 천천히 그리고 조용히 들어왔다.

(2) 상관접속사: both A and B, either A or B, neither A nor B, not only A but also B 등

She is **not only** <u>beautiful</u> **but also** <u>considerate</u>. 그녀는 아름다울 뿐만 아니라 사려 깊다.

2. 도치: 문장의 어순이 뒤바뀌는 것을 '도치'라고 하는데, 주로 강조하고자 하는 말을 문장의 앞에 놓으면, 주어·동사의 어순이 바뀐다.

(1) 부사(구) 도치: 「부사(구)+동사+주어」

Under the sofa <u>was</u> <u>the puppy</u>.
← The puppy was under the sofa. 강아지는 소파 밑에 있었다.

(2) 부정어 도치: 「Never/Not/Hardly/Little/Seldom+동사+주어 ~」

Hardly (ever) <u>has</u> <u>she</u> <u>been</u> late for school.
← She has hardly (ever) been late for school. 그녀는 학교에 지각을 한 적이 거의 없다.

Never <u>will</u> <u>I</u> <u>see</u> her again.
← I will never see her again. 나는 그녀를 다시 만나지 않을 것이다.

Little <u>did</u> <u>I</u> <u>hear</u> about the accident.
← I heard little about the accident. 나는 그 사건에 대해 거의 듣지 못했다.

(3) so, neither, nor의 도치: 「So/Neither/Nor+동사+주어」

A I forgot to bring my gym clothes. 나 깜빡하고 체육복을 안 가져왔어.
B **So did I.** 나도 그랬어.

A I don't know who that gentleman is. 나는 저 신사가 누군지 모르겠어.
B **Neither do I.** 나도 그래.

A Can you and your brother speak Japanese? 너와 너의 형은 일본어를 할 수 있니?
B No. I can't speak Japanese, **nor can he.** 아니. 나는 일본어를 할 수 없고, 형도 마찬가지야.

> **Plus α**
>
> 1 전체 부정의 도치: not ~ anywhere [nowhere] 어디에도 ~없다
>
> I couldn't find my wallet **anywhere**.
>
> ➡ **Nowhere** <u>could I</u> find my wallet.
> 나는 어디에서도 지갑을 찾을 수가 없었다.
>
> 2 자동사 문장의 도치
> • 주어가 대명사인 경우 도치되지 않는다.
>
> A I'd like a cup of green tea, please.
> 녹차 한 잔 주세요.
> B Here you are.
> 여기 있습니다.
>
> • 주어가 명사인 경우 자동사가 주어 앞에 온다.
>
> Here comes the bus!
> 버스가 온다!

Check-up 안에서 알맞은 말을 고르시오.

1 I like playing the piano and singing / to sing songs for my family.

2 Seldom does she reads / she read fashion magazines.

: EXERCISES

A [   ] 안에서 알맞은 것을 고르시오.

1 Will you play as a member or [to watch / watch] as a spectator?

2 The machine can make both [high / highly] and low sounds.

3 You can decide either to buy it or not [to buy / buying] it.

4 Never [did I / I didn't] imagine I could win a gold medal in swimming.

5 It's the delivery man! Here [he comes / comes he].

spectator 명 관중
decide 동 결정하다
imagine 동 상상하다
delivery man 명 배달원

B 밑줄 친 부분을 강조하는 문장으로 바꿔 쓰시오.

1 He has <u>never</u> seen such clear sea water.

→ Never _____ such clear sea water.

2 She <u>hardly</u> regrets what she's already done.

→ Hardly _____ what she's already done.

3 A gigantic statue of the king stood <u>in front of us</u>.

→ In front of us _____ .

clear 형 투명한, 맑은
regret 동 후회하다
gigantic 형 거대한
statue 명 동상

C B의 대답이 "나도 그래"라는 의미가 되도록 대화를 완성하시오.

1 A I want to visit Spain someday.
  B _____

2 A I have never told such a big lie.
  B _____

3 A I can't make it to the party tonight.
  B _____

4 A I haven't eaten all day. I'm so hungry.
  B _____

lie 명 거짓말
make it 시간 맞춰 가다

D 우리말과 같은 뜻이 되도록 주어진 단어를 배열하시오.

1 경찰차가 온다! (comes, the police car)

→ Here _____ !

2 나는 유럽에 가 본 적이 없다. (I, been, have, Europe, to)

→ Never _____ .

3 나의 언니는 긴 생머리이고, 나도 그렇다. (so, I, do)

→ My sister has long straight hair, and _____ .

[01-02] 빈칸에 들어갈 알맞은 말을 고르시오.

01

> Hardly _____ since he failed the test.

① has he go out　② has he gone out
③ he didn't go out　④ he hasn't gone out
⑤ has gone he out

02

> She _____ the accident yesterday.

① do witnesses　② does witnessed
③ does witness　④ did witness
⑤ did witnesses

03 빈칸에 들어갈 말이 바르게 짝지어진 것은?

> · This orange is not only _____ but also sour.
> · Mark was neither shocked nor _____ by the news.

① sweet – surprise　② sweet – surprising
③ sweet – surprised　④ sweetly – surprised
⑤ sweetly – surprising

04 대화의 빈칸에 들어갈 알맞은 말은?

> A I don't like horror movies.
> B _____ Why don't we pick another one?

① So do I.　② So don't I.
③ Neither do I.　④ Neither don't I.
⑤ Neither I do.

05 다음 중 어법상 어색한 문장은?

① She said she did do her best.
② We're not always busy like this.
③ No one didn't complain about that.
④ It was he that found the missing file.
⑤ None of us understood what you wanted.

[06-07] 밑줄 친 부분의 쓰임이 나머지와 다른 하나를 고르시오.

06 ① She does like him.
② He did follow the rules.
③ He did say hello to them.
④ I did the dishes this evening.
⑤ I do regret what I did last night.

07 ① It is in the garden that I lost my key.
② It is sad that you need to leave earlier.
③ It was she that cooked dinner today.
④ It was Jack that I was looking for.
⑤ It was on the table that I left my wallet.

08 주어진 문장을 강조한 문장 중 어색한 것은?

> I ran into Peter on the street this morning.

① It was I who ran into Peter on the street this morning.
② It was ran into that I Peter on the street this morning.
③ It was Peter whom I ran into on the street this morning.
④ It was on the street where I ran into Peter this morning.
⑤ It was this morning when I ran into Peter on the street.

09 다음 중 대화가 가장 자연스러운 것은?

① A David is not lazy.
　B So is his brother.
② A I have a lot of things to do.
　B So have I.
③ A She can cook very delicious pizza.
　B Neither can I.
④ A I've thought about you all the time.
　B Neither have I.
⑤ A I did help Mom do the dishes yesterday.
　B So did I.

10 강조를 위해 도치한 문장이 <u>어색한</u> 것은?

① Your present is on your bed.
→ On your bed is your present.
② She has never ridden on a boat.
→ Never she has ridden on a boat.
③ She seldom drinks coffee.
→ Seldom does she drink coffee.
④ The princess came down the stairs.
→ Down the stairs came the princess.
⑤ I never do things I don't like to do.
→ Never do I do things I don't like to do.

11 다음 물음에 대한 답으로 가장 알맞은 것은?

Who did you meet in the shopping mall after school?

① It was my sister that you met in the shopping mall after school.
② It was in the shopping mall that I met my sister after school.
③ It was after school that I met my sister in the shopping mall.
④ It was I that met my sister in the shopping mall after school.
⑤ It was my sister that I met in the shopping mall after school.

[12-13] 우리말과 같은 뜻이 되도록 빈칸에 들어갈 알맞은 말을 고르시오.

12
그들은 조국의 역사에 대해 거의 알지 못했다.
→ _____ about the history of their country.

① They little didn't know
② Little they knew
③ Little didn't they know
④ Little they didn't know
⑤ Little did they know

13
모든 사람이 등산 가는 것을 좋아하는 것은 아니다.
→ _____ to go hiking.

① All of us like
② Not everyone likes
③ Not everyone doesn't like
④ Neither of us likes
⑤ None of us like

[14-15] 글을 읽고, 물음에 답하시오.

Do you know that the number of stray dogs is increasing? Sadly, many dogs are abandoned by people who ⓐ them. People buy dogs, and when they don't want to keep them, they just ⓑ them away on the street. Animal welfare workers catch the dogs and take them to shelters. But (A) 보호소에서 그들 모두를 돌볼 수 있는 것은 아니다. Only 10% of them can survive. The rest of them cannot be saved. Can we just blame people who own animals? No! It is ⓒ that have responsibility for the problem.

14 빈칸 ⓐ, ⓑ, ⓒ에 들어갈 말이 바르게 짝지어진 것은?

	ⓐ		ⓑ		ⓒ
①	did own	–	throw	–	we
②	did own	–	threw	–	us
③	did own	–	throw	–	us
④	did owned	–	threw	–	us
⑤	did owned	–	throw	–	we

15 밑줄 친 (A)를 바르게 영작한 것은?

① none of them can be taken care of in the shelters
② neither of them can be taken care of in the shelters
③ not all of them can be taken care of in the shelters
④ they can't always be taken care of in the shelters
⑤ hardly can they be taken care of in the shelters

[01-02] 우리말과 같은 뜻이 되도록 문장을 완성하시오.

01 내가 그를 본 것은 바로 어제였다.

→ It was _____ I saw him.

02 우리 둘 다 휴대 전화를 가져오지 않았다.

→ _____ brought cell phones.

[03-04] 우리말과 같은 뜻이 되도록 주어진 단어를 이용하여 문장을 완성하시오.

03 Emily는 넘어져서 다리가 부러졌다. (break one's legs)

→ Emily fell over and _____.

04 Peter는 사진 찍는 것뿐 아니라 카메라를 모으는 것도 즐긴다. (collect, cameras)

→ Peter enjoys not only taking photos _____

_____.

[05-06] 밑줄 친 부분을 강조하는 문장으로 바꿔 쓰시오.

05 A bird was on a branch.

→ On a branch _____.

06 She has never broken her promises.

→ Never _____.

[07-08] 두 문장의 의미가 통하도록 문장을 완성하시오.

07 She really dreamed about a big pig last night.

→ She _____.

조건 동사를 강조할 것

08 Some information on the Internet is useless, and some of it is not.

→ _____ of the information on the Internet is useless.

조건 부분 부정의 문장이 되게 할 것

[09-10] 글을 읽고, 물음에 답하시오.

Tom really likes soccer. (A) He enjoys both watching and play soccer. One day, he decided to join a soccer club. But (B) not everybody could not join the club. Only those who passed a test could join the club. Unfortunately, he failed to become a member. He never thought he would fail the test, and (C) 그의 친구들도 그랬다.

09 밑줄 친 (A), (B)에서 어법상 어색한 부분을 찾아 고쳐 쓰시오.

(A) _____

(B) _____

10 밑줄 친 (C)를 so 또는 neither를 이용하여 영작하시오.

_____

이것이 THIS IS 시리즈다!

THIS IS GRAMMAR 시리즈

▷ 중·고등 내신에 꼭 등장하는 어법 포인트 분석 및 총정리

강남인강
강의교재

THIS IS READING 시리즈

▷ 다양한 소재의 지문으로 내신 및 수능 완벽 대비

강남인강
강의교재

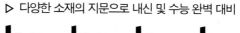

THIS IS VOCABULARY 시리즈

▷ 주제별로 분류한 교육부 권장 어휘

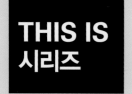

THIS IS
시리즈

무료 MP3 및 부가자료 다운로드
www.nexusbook.com
www.nexusEDU.kr

THIS IS GRAMMAR 시리즈
Starter 1~3   영어교육연구소 지음 | 205×265 | 144쪽 | 각 권 12,000원
초·중·고급 1·2   넥서스영어교육연구소 지음 | 205×265 | 250쪽 내외 | 각 권 12,000원

THIS IS READING 시리즈
Starter 1~3   김태연 지음 | 205×265 | 156쪽 | 각 권 12,000원
1·2·3·4   넥서스영어교육연구소 지음 | 205×265 | 192쪽 내외 | 각 권 10,000원

THIS IS VOCABULARY 시리즈
입문   넥서스영어교육연구소 지음 | 152×225 | 224쪽 | 10,000원
초·중·고급·어원편   권기하 지음 | 152×225 | 180×257 | 344쪽~444쪽 | 10,000원~12,000원
수능 완성   넥서스영어교육연구소 지음 | 152×225 | 280쪽 | 12,000원
뉴텝스   넥서스 TEPS연구소 지음 | 152×225 | 452쪽 | 13,800원

LEVEL CHART

초1	초2	초3	초4	초5	초6	중1	중2	중3	고1	고2	고3

VOCA

	초등필수 영단어 1-2 · 3-4 · 5-6학년용
	The VOCA + (플러스) 1~7
	THIS IS VOCABULARY 입문 · 초급 · 중급
	고급 · 어원 · 수능 완성 · 뉴텝스
	WORD FOCUS 중등 종합 5000 · 고등 필수 5000 · 고등 종합 9500

Grammar

	초등필수 영문법 + 쓰기 1~2
	OK Grammar 1~4
	This Is Grammar Starter 1~3
	This Is Grammar 초급~고급 (각 2권: 총 6권)
	Grammar 공감 1~3
	Grammar 101 1~3
	Grammar Bridge 1~3
	중학영문법 뽀개기 1~3
	The Grammar Starter, 1~3
	구사일생 (구문독해 Basic) 1~2
	구문독해 204 1~2
	그래머 캡처 1~2
	[특급 단기 특강] 어법어휘 모의고사

GRAMMAR

넥서스영어교육연구소 지음

Workbook

Level 3

NEXUS Edu

새 교과서 반영
중등 내신
완벽 대비서

GRAMMAR

새 교과서 반영
중등 내신
완벽 대비서

Workbook

Level 3

NEXUS Edu

UNIT 01 명사적 쓰임

A 주어진 단어를 이용하여 문장을 완성하시오.

1 We decided _____ this evening. (eat out)

2 I found it impossible _____ the computer. (fix)

3 He didn't know when and where _____. (start)

4 Can you tell me how _____ to the airport? (get)

5 My wish is _____ first prize in the contest. (win)

6 My goal is _____ alone around the world. (travel)

7 I like _____ butter and bread for breakfast. (have)

8 She wanted _____ the homework as soon as possible. (finish)

9 My plan is _____ earlier in the morning. (get up)

10 It was not easy _____ what he was talking about. (understand)

B 두 문장이 같은 의미가 되도록 주어진 문장 구조를 이용하여 문장을 다시 쓰시오.

[1~4] 「It(가주어) ~ that(진주어)」

1 To admit one's mistake is hard.

→ _____

2 To drink too much coke is not good for your health.

→ _____

3 To swim in the sea without a life jacket is dangerous.

→ _____

4 To sing and dance in front of lots of people is difficult.

→ _____

[5~7] 「의문사+to부정사」

5 Can you tell me which bus I should take?

→ Can you tell me _____?

6 She taught me how I should cook spaghetti.

→ She taught me _____.

7 I don't know what I should give him for his graduation.

→ I don't know _____.

C 보기 에서 알맞은 단어를 골라 「의문사+to부정사」로 바꿔 문장을 완성하시오.

> 보기   meet   buy   do   solve   get off   read and write   speak to

1 나는 다음에 무엇을 할지 모르겠다.
→ I don't know _____ next.

2 언제 내려야 하는지 알려 주시겠어요?
→ Could you tell me _____?

3 우리는 어디서 만날지 결정하지 못했다.
→ We haven't decided _____.

4 그들은 스페인 어를 읽고 쓰는 방법을 배웠다.
→ They learned _____ Spanish.

5 그녀는 누구에게 이야기를 해야 할지 모르겠다고 말했다.
→ She said she didn't know _____.

6 이 세 가지 중 어느 것을 살지 결정할 수가 없다.
→ I can't decide _____ among these three.

7 우리 오빠가 수학 문제 푸는 방법을 내게 가르쳐 주었다.
→ My brother taught me _____ the math problem.

D 우리말과 같은 뜻이 되도록 주어진 단어를 이용하여 문장을 완성하시오.

1 그는 자전거 타는 방법을 모른다. (ride, a bicycle)
→ He doesn't know _____ _____ _____ _____ _____.

2 우리는 여행하는 동안 어디서 머무를지 결정하지 못했다. (stay)
→ We haven't decided _____ _____ _____ during the trip.

3 인생에서 실패를 경험하는 것은 흔한 일이다. (experience, failure)
→ _____ is common _____ _____ in life.

4 이 지역에서 혼자 걸어 다니는 것은 위험하다. (walk around alone)
→ _____ is dangerous _____ _____ _____ in this area.

5 너무 늦기 전에 그녀에게 미안하다고 말하고 싶었어. (want, say, sorry)
→ I _____ _____ _____ _____ to her before it's too late.

6 그녀는 그와 친구가 되는 것이 어렵다는 것을 알게 되었다. (become, friends)
→ She found _____ difficult _____ _____ _____ with him.

7 인터넷은 전 세계에 있는 많은 사람들과 이야기하는 것을 가능하게 해 준다. (talk with)
→ The Internet makes _____ possible _____ _____ _____ many people around the world.

3

UNIT 02 형용사적, 부사적 쓰임

A 괄호 안에 주어진 단어를 알맞게 배열하여 문장을 완성하시오.

1 You have (to, worry, nothing) about.

→ You have ＿＿＿＿＿＿＿＿＿＿＿＿＿＿＿ about.

2 I am very (to, hear, glad) you're OK now.

→ I am very ＿＿＿＿＿＿＿＿＿＿＿＿＿＿＿ you're OK now.

3 She (be, to, grew up) a famous movie star.

→ She ＿＿＿＿＿＿＿＿＿＿＿＿＿＿＿ a famous movie star.

4 I have no (TV, time, watch, to) because of too much homework.

→ I have no ＿＿＿＿＿＿＿＿＿＿＿＿＿＿＿ because of too much homework.

B 밑줄 친 부분을 어법에 맞게 고쳐 쓰시오.

1 앉을 의자가 없다.

→ There's no <u>chair to sit</u>. ＿＿＿＿＿＿＿＿＿＿＿＿＿

2 그녀는 쓸 펜이 필요했다.

→ She needed <u>a pen to write</u>. ＿＿＿＿＿＿＿＿＿＿＿＿＿

3 물건들을 넣을 상자 좀 주실래요?

→ Will you give me <u>a box to put things</u>? ＿＿＿＿＿＿＿＿＿＿＿＿＿

4 나는 쓸 종이 한 장이 없다.

→ I don't have <u>a piece of paper to write</u>. ＿＿＿＿＿＿＿＿＿＿＿＿＿

C 문장의 의미가 통하도록 두 문장을 한 문장으로 바꿔 쓰시오.

1 I can help you. I am happy.

→ I am happy ＿＿＿＿＿ ＿＿＿＿＿ ＿＿＿＿＿.

2 She solved the problem. She was smart.

→ She was smart ＿＿＿＿＿ ＿＿＿＿＿ ＿＿＿＿＿ ＿＿＿＿＿.

3 He wanted to win the race. He tried his best.

→ He tried his best ＿＿＿＿＿ ＿＿＿＿＿ ＿＿＿＿＿ ＿＿＿＿＿.

4 We didn't want to be late for school. We had to run.

→ We had to run not ＿＿＿＿＿ ＿＿＿＿＿ ＿＿＿＿＿ ＿＿＿＿＿ ＿＿＿＿＿.

D 주어진 문장을 「be+to부정사」를 이용하여 바꿔 쓰시오.

1 He could not be trusted.

→ _____

2 Your dream cannot come true in a day.

→ _____

3 This medicine should be taken right after meals.

→ _____

4 All students should respect their teachers.

→ _____

5 If we intend to win the game, we have to practice a lot.

→ _____

6 The prince and the princess were destined to meet again.

→ _____

7 The Olympic Games are going to be held in three years.

→ _____

E 우리말과 같은 뜻이 되도록 주어진 단어를 배열하시오.

1 네 이름은 기억하기가 쉽다. (to, is, remember, easy)
→ Your name _____ .

2 나는 여행 가서 입을 옷이 없다. (nothing, have, on the trip, to, wear)
→ I _____ .

3 할머니를 돕는 걸 보니 그는 친절함이 틀림없다. (help, must, to, the old woman, be, kind)
→ He _____ .

4 그는 시험에 합격하기 위해 매우 열심히 공부했다. (pass, very hard, to, studied, the exam)
→ He _____ .

5 그녀는 자라서 유명한 무용수 중 한 명이 되었다. (grew up, the most popular, be, dancers, of, one, to)
→ She _____ .

6 나는 새 컴퓨터를 살 충분한 돈이 없다. (a new computer, buy, have, money, don't, to, enough)
→ I _____ .

7 그녀는 잠에서 깨어 집에 혼자 있는 자신을 발견했다. (at home, to, herself, woke up, alone, find)
→ She _____ .

UNIT 03 to부정사의 시제, 태, 의미상 주어

A 밑줄 친 부분을 어법에 맞게 고쳐 쓰시오.

1 It's very nice <u>for you</u> to say so. _____

2 I'm happy <u>to invite</u> to his party. _____

3 He seems <u>to not have heard</u> the news yet. _____

4 I want the report <u>to do</u> as early as possible. _____

5 It was very brave <u>for him</u> to admit his mistake. _____

6 He tries <u>to not pay</u> attention to what others say. _____

7 It's hard <u>of him</u> to get a perfect score on the exam. _____

8 The fire was thought <u>to have caused</u> by carelessness. _____

9 She didn't bring her book. She seems <u>to lose</u> her book. _____

B 두 문장의 의미가 통하도록 문장을 완성하시오.

1 It seems that you have a bad cold.

→ You seem _____ a bad cold.

2 It seemed that the class had already begun.

→ The class seemed _____ .

3 It seemed that he had lost his wallet on the way home.

→ He seemed _____ his wallet on the way home.

4 It seems that my parents were very worried about me.

→ My parents seem _____ very worried about me.

5 It seemed that everybody in the classroom liked the idea.

→ Everybody in the classroom seemed _____ the idea.

6 It seems that my mother has cooked something delicious.

→ My mother seems _____ something delicious.

7 It seems that Emma is very sensitive about her appearance.

→ Emma seems _____ about her appearance.

C 우리말과 같은 뜻이 되도록 주어진 단어를 이용하여 문장을 완성하시오.

1 친구에게 책을 빌려주다니 그는 착하구나. (nice, he, lend)
→ It is _____ _____ _____ _____ his book to his friend.

2 안전벨트를 매는 것은 필수적이다. (necessary, you, fasten)
→ It is _____ _____ _____ _____ your seat belt.

3 그녀가 약속을 연기하는 것은 불가능하다. (possible, she, delay)
→ It is not _____ _____ _____ _____ the appointment.

4 제 가방을 들어주시다니 당신 참 친절하시네요. (so, kind, you, help)
→ It is _____ _____ _____ _____ me with my luggage.

5 나에게 있어서 한 시간 안에 모든 문제를 다 푸는 것은 어려운 일이다. (hard, I, solve)
→ It's _____ _____ _____ _____ all the questions in an hour.

6 할머니에게 자리를 양보하다니 그는 참 예의가 바르구나.(polite, he, offer)
→ It is _____ _____ _____ _____ his seat to the old woman.

7 사람들이 도움을 요청할 때 안 된다고 말하는 것은 쉽지 않다. (easy, I, say no)
→ It is not _____ _____ _____ _____ _____ when people ask me for help.

D 우리말과 같은 뜻이 되도록 주어진 단어를 배열하시오.

1 내일까지 해야 할 일이 많다. (done, by tomorrow, lots of, to, work, be)
→ There is _____.

2 그녀는 내게 다시는 학교에 늦지 말라고 말했다. (to, be late for, told, school, me, again, not)
→ She _____.

3 그는 내게 할 말이 있는 것 같다. (seems, me, have, to, something, to, tell)
→ He _____.

4 혼자 여행을 다니는 것은 위험할 수 있다. (dangerous, travel alone, be, to, can)
→ It _____.

5 그녀는 우리의 약속을 잊어버린 것 같다. (have, seems, our appointment, forgotten about, to)
→ She _____.

6 그가 갑자기 약속을 취소한 것은 무례하다. (rude, him, the meeting, to, have, canceled, of)
→ It's _____ all of a sudden.

7 너는 심하게 다치지 않았으니 운이 좋았다. (lucky, to, hurt seriously, been, not, have, were)
→ You _____.

7

목적격보어로 쓰이는 부정사

A 주어진 단어를 이용하여 문장을 완성하시오.

1 I didn't want him _____ into trouble. (get)

2 She let their kids _____ whatever they want. (do)

3 I got my cell phone _____ on the subway. (steal)

4 The doctor told me _____ a balanced diet. (eat)

5 I don't know what you expect me _____. (bring)

6 I smell something _____ in the kitchen. (burn)

7 Please let me _____ if there's anything I can do. (know)

B 밑줄 친 부분을 어법에 맞게 고쳐 쓰시오.

1 He forced me <u>make</u> a decision. _____

2 She advised me <u>book</u> a ticket. _____

3 He felt someone <u>to follow</u> him. _____

4 Where did you have your hair <u>to cut</u>? _____

5 They didn't let me <u>to go</u> out at night. _____

6 She had Jake <u>to fix</u> the broken radio. _____

7 I saw him <u>to read</u> a book in the library. _____

8 I asked him <u>take care of</u> my dog during the holiday. _____

C 보기 에서 알맞은 단어를 골라 어법에 맞게 바꿔 문장을 완성하시오.

보기   play   eat   take   look   call   apply

1 The shoes make her _____ taller.

2 Can you tell him _____ me back?

3 I listened to him _____ the violin.

4 They encouraged me _____ for the college.

5 My mom doesn't let me _____ sweets before meals.

6 We stood near the statue to get our picture _____.

D 우리말과 같은 뜻이 되도록 주어진 단어를 배열하시오.

1 그는 세차를 했다. (his car, had, washed)
→ He _____.

2 우리 아버지는 내가 의사가 되기를 바란다. (me, to, wants, become)
→ My father _____ a doctor.

3 나는 누군가 문을 두드리는 소리를 들었다. (someone, knocking, heard)
→ I _____ on the door.

4 우리 부모님은 내가 애완동물 키우는 것을 허락하지 않으신다. (to, pets, me, allow, keep)
→ My parents don't _____.

5 그녀는 내게 다시는 이런 실수를 하지 말라고 말했다. (make, the same mistake, not, to)
→ She told me _____ again.

6 인터넷은 사람들이 서로 간에 의사소통할 수 있게 해 준다. (enables, to, with each other, people, communicate)
→ The Internet _____.

E 우리말과 같은 뜻이 되도록 주어진 단어를 이용하여 문장을 완성하시오.

1 그는 내가 이 문제를 푸는 것을 도와주었다. (help, solve)
→ He _____ _____ _____ _____ this problem.

2 그녀는 내게 책을 같이 보자고 부탁했다. (ask, share)
→ She _____ _____ _____ _____ my book with her.

3 너는 정오까지 청소를 끝내야 한다. (get, the cleaning, finish)
→ You have to _____ _____ _____ _____ by noon.

4 그들은 발밑에서 땅이 흔들리는 것을 느꼈다. (feel, the earth, shake)
→ They _____ _____ _____ _____ beneath their feet.

5 선생님은 내게 숙제를 다시 하라고 시켰다. (make, do one's homework)
→ The teacher _____ _____ _____ _____ _____ again.

6 나는 영화를 보는 도중 누군가 기침하는 소리를 들었다. (hear, someone, cough)
→ I _____ _____ _____ during the movie.

7 그는 내게 매일 가벼운 운동을 하라고 조언했다. (advise, get some light exercise)
→ He _____ _____ _____ _____ _____ every day.

05 too ~ to, enough to, 기타 표현

A 밑줄 친 부분을 어법에 맞게 고쳐 쓰시오.

1 There was <u>time enough</u> to finish the project.　　＿＿＿＿＿＿＿

2 The kid is <u>very short</u> to ride the roller coaster.　　＿＿＿＿＿＿＿

3 <u>Be frank with you</u>, the lecture was too boring.　　＿＿＿＿＿＿＿

4 The rope is <u>enough long</u> to get to the other end.　　＿＿＿＿＿＿＿

5 They arrived <u>too late</u> that they couldn't see the movie.　　＿＿＿＿＿＿＿

6 <u>So speak</u>, she is like a member of my family.　　＿＿＿＿＿＿＿

7 It is important to get <u>sleep enough</u> to stay healthy.　　＿＿＿＿＿＿＿

8 <u>Strangely to say</u>, I am afraid of birds and butterflies.　　＿＿＿＿＿＿＿

B 주어진 단어와 「too ~ to」 또는 「enough to」의 구문을 이용하여 문장을 완성하시오.

1 밖에 나가기에는 너무 늦었다. (late, go out)
→ It's ＿＿＿＿ ＿＿＿＿ ＿＿＿＿ ＿＿＿＿ ＿＿＿＿.

2 그녀는 투표할 만큼 충분히 컸다. (old, vote)
→ She is ＿＿＿＿ ＿＿＿＿ ＿＿＿＿ ＿＿＿＿.

3 나는 너무 놀라서 한 마디도 할 수 없었다. (surprised, say)
→ I was ＿＿＿＿ ＿＿＿＿ ＿＿＿＿ ＿＿＿＿ a word.

4 수프가 너무 뜨거워서 바로 먹을 수 없었다. (hot, eat)
→ The soup was ＿＿＿＿ ＿＿＿＿ ＿＿＿＿ ＿＿＿＿ right away.

5 나는 너무 피곤해서 더는 걸을 수 없다. (tired, walk)
→ I am ＿＿＿＿ ＿＿＿＿ ＿＿＿＿ ＿＿＿＿ any further.

6 James는 그 공을 피할 만큼 충분히 빨랐다. (fast, avoid)
→ James was ＿＿＿＿ ＿＿＿＿ ＿＿＿＿ ＿＿＿＿ ＿＿＿＿.

7 그는 선반에 손이 닿을 만큼 충분히 키가 크다. (tall, reach)
→ He is ＿＿＿＿ ＿＿＿＿ ＿＿＿＿ ＿＿＿＿ the shelf.

8 그는 산책을 갈 만큼 이제 충분히 좋아졌다. (well, go for a walk)
→ He is now ＿＿＿＿ ＿＿＿＿ ＿＿＿＿ ＿＿＿＿ ＿＿＿＿.

C 두 문장이 같은 뜻이 되도록 문장을 완성하시오.

1 You are so young that you can't travel alone.

→ You are _____ .

2 He acted so strangely that he couldn't be trusted.

→ He acted _____ .

3 It is so warm that we can eat out this evening.

→ It is _____ .

4 The museum is so large that it can't be toured in a day.

→ The museum is _____ .

5 The dog ran so fast that it could catch up with the car.

→ The dog ran _____ .

6 The problem is so easy that it can be solved in a minute.

→ The problem is _____ .

7 He was so busy that he couldn't spend time with his children.

→ He was _____ .

D 우리말과 같은 뜻이 되도록 주어진 단어를 이용하여 문장을 완성하시오.

1 우선, 도와주셔서 감사합니다. (begin)

→ _____ _____ _____ , I'd like to thank you for your help.

2 설상가상으로, 그녀는 휴대 전화를 잃어버렸다. (matters)

→ _____ _____ _____ _____ , she lost her cell phone.

3 스테이크가 너무 질겨서 씹을 수 없다. (tough, chew)

→ The steak is _____ _____ _____ _____ .

4 사실을 말하자면, 나는 그가 마음에 들지 않는다. (the truth)

→ _____ _____ _____ _____ , I don't like him.

5 말할 필요도 없이, 학생은 공부를 열심히 해야 한다. (needless)

→ _____ _____ _____ , students have to study hard.

6 그녀는 나를 파티에 초대할 만큼 충분히 친절하다. (kind, invite)

→ She is _____ _____ _____ _____ me to the party.

7 요약해서 말하면, 그들은 이후로 행복하게 살았다. (a long story)

→ _____ _____ _____ _____ _____ , they lived happily ever after.

UNIT 01 동명사의 쓰임

A 밑줄 친 부분을 바르게 고쳐 쓰시오.

1 He doesn't like <u>sleep</u> late.   _____

2 I hate <u>treated</u> like a child.   _____

3 Thank you <u>not for interrupting</u> me.   _____

4 I know I can't avoid <u>meet</u> him forever.   _____

5 I'm sorry for <u>coming not</u> to your party.   _____

6 She's afraid of <u>be criticized</u> by the public.   _____

7 <u>Exercise</u> regularly is good for your health.   _____

8 I remembered <u>she</u> talking about the rumor.   _____

9 His plan is <u>go</u> abroad to study after graduation.   _____

10 Having midnight snacks <u>are</u> not good for your health.   _____

B 두 문장이 같은 의미가 되도록 문장을 완성하시오.

1 I apologize that I called you at this hour.

   → I apologize for _____ at this hour.

2 He was sad that he disappointed his parents.

   → He was sad about _____.

3 She was happy that she won the competition.

   → She was happy about _____.

4 I am sorry that I canceled our appointment.

   → I am sorry for _____ our appointment.

5 She was surprised that he was absent from school.

   → She was surprised at _____ from school.

6 She was excited that she bought a new pair of jeans.

   → She was excited about _____.

7 Would you mind if I borrow your book for a day?

   → Would you mind _____ for a day?

8 My parents are proud that I graduated first in my class.

   → My parents are proud of _____ first in my class.

C 우리말과 같은 뜻이 되도록 주어진 단어를 이용하여 문장을 완성하시오.

1 좀 천천히 말씀해 주시겠어요? (mind, talk)

→ Would you _____ _____ slowly?

2 나는 파티에 초대되어 기뻐요. (be happy about, invite)

→ I _____ _____ _____ _____ to the party.

3 나는 실수를 한 것이 부끄러웠다. (be ashamed of, make)

→ I _____ _____ _____ _____ _____ a mistake.

4 영화 시간에 맞춰 오지 못해서 미안해. (be sorry for, be late for)

→ I _____ _____ _____ _____ _____ _____ the movie.

5 그는 시험에 합격하지 못할까 봐 두려웠다. (be afraid of, not, pass)

→ He _____ _____ _____ _____ the test.

6 나는 이렇게 추운 날씨에 코트를 입지 않은 것을 후회했다. (regret, not, wear a coat)

→ I _____ _____ _____ _____ _____ in this cold weather.

7 그녀는 혼자 힘으로 숙제를 한 것이 아님을 인정했다. (admit, not, do one's homework)

→ She _____ _____ _____ _____ _____ on her own.

D 우리말과 같은 뜻이 되도록 주어진 단어를 배열하시오.

1 제가 당신 사진을 찍어도 되겠습니까? (of you, my, mind, a picture, taking)

→ Would you _____?

2 나는 저녁 후에 산책 가는 것을 즐긴다. (after dinner, going, enjoy, for a walk)

→ I _____.

3 나는 내가 무엇을 해야 한다고 말을 듣는 것이 싫다. (I, what, being, hate, do, told, have to)

→ I _____.

4 우리 아버지는 담배를 끊겠다고 약속했다. (smoking, to, promised, quit)

→ My father _____.

5 어두운 곳에서 책을 읽는 것은 눈에 좋지 않다. (good, a book, is, in the dark, reading, not)

→ _____ for your eyes.

6 나는 부모님께 거짓말을 했던 것이 부끄럽다. (to, told a lie, am ashamed of, my parents, having)

→ I _____.

7 그녀는 그 문제를 풀기 위해 노력한 것이 자랑스러웠다. (solve, trying to, was proud of, the problem)

→ She _____.

UNIT 02 동명사 vs. to부정사

A 주어진 단어를 이용하여 문장을 완성하시오.

1 She denied _____ the rumors. (spread)

2 She hates _____ her mistakes. (admit)

3 She just gave up _____ the computer. (fix)

4 He refused _____ the rules at school. (follow)

5 I decided _____ regularly for my health. (work out)

6 I regret not _____ the sale items that day. (buy)

7 My mother dislikes _____ baseball games on TV. (watch)

8 If you don't understand it, why don't you try _____ it again? (read)

B 보기 에서 알맞은 단어를 골라 어법에 맞게 바꿔 문장을 완성하시오.

[1~5]

보기	eat	build	do	say	arrive

1 I expect _____ at the airport an hour late.

2 I regret _____ that I can't help you this time.

3 They agreed _____ more children's libraries.

4 You need to avoid _____ greasy food for some time.

5 I promised I wouldn't put off _____ homework again.

[6~10]

보기	buy	smoke	study	bake	play

6 He decided _____ abroad after graduation.

7 She is practicing _____ the piano for the concert.

8 Don't forget _____ some medicine before your trip.

9 I asked my father to quit _____, and he's trying hard.

10 My sister enjoys _____ cakes and cookies for her children.

C 두 문장의 의미가 통하도록 문장을 완성하시오.

1 My mother told me to pick up the laundry, but I forgot.

→ I _____ the laundry.

2 I didn't make a reservation in advance. Now I regret it.

→ I _____ in advance.

3 I used to play basketball with my friends, and I remember that.

→ I _____ with my friends.

4 He wanted to become the class president, so he tried so hard.

→ He _____ so hard.

5 I am sorry to inform you that you are rejected by this university.

→ I _____ you are rejected by this university.

D 우리말과 같은 뜻이 되도록 주어진 단어를 이용하여 문장을 완성하시오.

1 나는 문자 메시지를 확인하려고 멈췄다. (stop, check)

→ I _____ _____ _____ the text message.

2 나는 오늘 아침에 컴퓨터를 끈 것을 기억한다. (remember, turn off)

→ I _____ _____ _____ the computer this morning.

3 우리 어머니는 꽃과 채소 기르는 것을 즐긴다. (enjoy, grow)

→ My mother _____ _____ flowers and vegetables.

4 나는 어렸을 때 피아노 치는 법을 배우지 않은 것이 후회된다. (regret, learn)

→ I _____ _____ _____ how to play the piano when I was young.

5 그녀는 과거에 그 영화를 본 것을 깜박하고 그 영화를 또 봤다. (forget, see)

→ She _____ _____ the movie in the past and saw it again.

6 저녁 먹기 전에 손 씻는 것을 잊지 마라. (forget, wash)

→ _____ _____ _____ _____ your hands before you have dinner.

7 나는 학생 때 공부를 더 열심히 하지 않은 것이 후회된다. (regret, study)

→ I _____ _____ _____ harder when I was a student.

UNIT 03 여러 가지 동명사 표현

A 보기 에서 알맞은 단어를 골라 어법에 맞게 바꿔 문장을 완성하시오.

[1~5]

보기   cry   make   buy   hike   find

1 He had difficulty _____ the office.

2 I went _____ with my family on Saturday.

3 She spends a lot of money _____ new clothes.

4 It is no use _____ excuses. She knows everything.

5 She couldn't help _____ while watching the sad movie.

[6~10]

보기   fix   see   run   come   help

6 He devoted his life to _____ the poor.

7 My father is busy _____ his own business.

8 My mother keeps me from _____ home late.

9 There is no _____ the mistake you made at this point.

10 I'm looking forward to _____ the singer's new album.

B 밑줄 친 부분에 유의하여 해석을 완성하시오.

1 It's no use complaining about that.
→ 그것에 대해 _____.

2 She is busy taking care of her baby.
→ 그녀는 아기를 _____.

3 She is used to studying late at night.
→ 그녀는 밤늦게까지 _____.

4 She couldn't help but cancel the appointment.
→ 그녀는 약속을 _____.

5 We are looking forward to working with you.
→ 우리는 당신과 함께 _____.

6 I will go skiing with my friends this Friday.
→ 나는 이번 금요일에 친구들과 _____.

C 우리말과 같은 뜻이 되도록 주어진 단어를 이용하여 문장을 완성하시오.

1 나는 영화 보러 가고 싶지 않아. (not, feel like, go)

→ I _____ _____ _____ _____ to the movies.

2 오늘 저녁에 외식하는 게 어때? (how, eat out)

→ _____ _____ _____ _____ this evening?

3 나는 집에 도착하자마자 냉장고 문을 열었다. (arrive, home)

→ _____ _____ _____, I opened the fridge.

4 그 학생들은 소풍 가는 것을 기대하고 있다. (look forward to)

→ The students _____ _____ _____ _____ _____ on a picnic.

5 세계화 시대에 나는 영어를 배우지 않을 수 없다. (cannot, help, study)

→ I _____ _____ _____ English in the global era.

6 그는 새 휴대 전화를 사용하는 데 익숙해졌다. (get used to, use)

→ He _____ _____ _____ _____ the new cell phone.

7 그녀는 영화를 보는 동안 아이들을 조용히 시키는 데 어려움을 겪었다. (have, difficulty, keep)

→ She _____ _____ _____ the kids quiet during the movie.

D 우리말과 같은 뜻이 되도록 주어진 단어를 배열하시오.

1 그녀는 곧 젓가락 사용에 익숙해졌다. (used, using, got, to)

→ She soon _____ chopsticks.

2 우리 어머니는 지금 저녁을 하느라 바쁘다. (dinner, busy, is, making)

→ My mother _____ now.

3 네가 해결할 수 없는 문제에 대해 걱정해도 소용없다. (worrying about, no, it, use, is)

→ _____ the problem you can't solve.

4 그는 자선 단체를 설립하는 데 기여했다. (the charity, to, contributed, establishing)

→ He _____ .

5 그녀는 영어로 대화를 하는 데 어려움이 있다. (a conversation, having, difficulty, has)

→ She _____ in English.

6 나는 그의 무례한 행동을 보고 화를 내지 않을 수 없었다. (not, getting upset, help, could)

→ I _____ when I saw his rude behavior.

7 우리 어머니는 자신을 위해 옷을 사는 데 많은 돈을 쓰지 않는다. (clothes, much, money, buying, spends)

→ My mother hardly _____ for herself.

분사의 종류

A 주어진 단어를 이용하여 문장을 완성하시오.

1 The man is fixing the _____ chair. (break)

2 She helped me find the _____ child. (miss)

3 I'm _____ in cooking Italian food. (interest)

4 She found that she had no money _____ . (leave)

5 He opened the box with _____ hands. (shake)

6 The girl _____ a black jacket is my sister. (wear)

7 We were walking quickly past the _____ dog. (bark)

8 She has _____ her homework sooner than she expected. (finish)

B 우리말과 같은 뜻이 되도록 보기 에서 알맞은 단어를 골라 문장을 완성하시오.

> 보기   sleep   satisfy   steal   sell   depress

1 나는 시험 결과에 만족한다.
   → I'm _____ with the test result.

2 오늘 왜 그렇게 기운이 없어 보여요?
   → Why do you look so _____ today?

3 나는 자고 있는 아기에게 담요를 덮어주었다.
   → I put a blanket over the _____ baby.

4 콘서트 티켓은 이미 매진되었다.
   → The concert tickets have already _____ out.

5 도난당한 차는 범죄자들에 의해 또 다른 범죄에 사용된다.
   → _____ cars are used by criminals for other crimes.

C 밑줄 친 부분을 어법에 맞게 고쳐 쓰시오.

1 She had her hair <u>to cut</u>.   _____

2 I found this movie <u>bore</u>.   _____

3 Children like walking on <u>falls</u> leaves.   _____

4 The result of the game was <u>disappoint</u>.   _____

5 We were <u>excite</u> about the upcoming field trip.   _____

6 He decided to buy a <u>use</u> car because it's much cheaper.   _____

D 두 문장을 한 문장으로 만들 때 빈칸에 알맞은 말을 쓰시오.

1 She has a dog. It is called Goopie.

→ She has a dog _____.

2 I smell something. It is burning in the kitchen.

→ I smell something _____.

3 I'm reading a novel. It is written in English.

→ I'm reading _____.

4 He has a sister. She is working at the post office.

→ He has a sister _____.

5 The woman is my aunt. She is wearing a black skirt.

→ The woman _____ is my aunt.

6 My father bought me a violin. It was made in Austria.

→ My father bought me _____.

7 She kept her letters. They are hidden in a box under the bed.

→ She kept her _____ under the bed.

E 우리말과 같은 뜻이 되도록 주어진 단어를 이용하여 문장을 완성하시오.

1 우리는 그의 패배 소식을 듣고 충격을 받았다. (shock)

→ _____ _____ _____ to hear about his defeat.

2 버스를 기다리고 있는 그 소녀가 내 사촌이다. (the girl, wait for)

→ _____ _____ _____ _____ _____ _____ is my cousin.

3 그는 지하철에서 지갑을 도난당했다. (get, his wallet, steal)

→ He _____ _____ _____ _____ on the subway.

4 나는 책상 밑에서 잃어버린 목걸이를 찾았다. (lose, necklace)

→ I found my _____ _____ under the desk.

5 그는 놀라운 속도로 회복하고 있다. (get better, surprise, rate)

→ He _____ _____ _____ at a _____ _____.

6 나는 지금까지 그렇게 놀라운 건물은 본 적이 없다. (see, amaze, building)

→ I've never _____ such _____ _____ _____ until now.

7 그 파티에 초대된 일부 사람들은 아직 도착하지 않았다. (some people, invite, the party)

→ _____ _____ _____ _____ _____ _____ haven't come yet.

19

UNIT **02** 분사구문

A 두 문장이 같은 의미가 되도록 분사구문을 이용하여 문장을 완성하시오.

1 He shook my hand and smiled at me.

→ He shook my hand _____.

2 When she's alone, she likes to listen to the radio.

→ _____, she likes to listen to the radio.

3 Even though we are not rich, we are really happy together.

→ _____, we are really happy together.

4 Because she has poor eyesight, she has to wear glasses.

→ _____, she has to wear glasses.

5 If you are not able to come, you need to let them know.

→ _____, you need to let them know.

B 보기 에서 알맞은 접속사를 골라 두 문장이 같은 의미가 되도록 부사절을 완성하시오.

[1~3]

보기　　even though　　because　　while

1 Having dinner, she read a book.

→ _____, she read a book.

2 Being poor, he never loses his smile.

→ _____, he never loses his smile.

3 Feeling hot, she drank a glass of cold water.

→ _____, she drank a glass of cold water.

[4~6]

보기　　if　　although　　when

4 Being alone, he felt lonely and hopeless.

→ _____, he felt lonely and hopeless.

5 Coming to the party, you'll be able to see many celebrities.

→ _____, you'll be able to see many celebrities.

6 Not finishing his homework, he still wanted to play the computer game.

→ _____, he still wanted to play the computer game.

C 우리말과 같은 뜻이 되도록 주어진 단어를 이용하여 문장을 완성하시오.

1 그것은 비싸진 않지만, 품질은 좋다. (not, be, expensive)
→ _____ _____ _____, it is really good in quality.

2 그는 영화를 보다가 잠이 들었다. (watch, the movie)
→ _____ _____ _____, he fell asleep.

3 그는 긴장했으나, 절대 그것을 내보이지 않았다. (be, nervous)
→ _____ _____, he never let it show.

4 최선을 다한다면, 당신은 목표를 이룰 것입니다. (try one's best)
→ _____ _____ _____, you'll achieve your goal.

5 나는 내 친구를 기다리면서 휴대 전화로 게임을 했다. (wait for)
→ _____ _____ _____ _____, I played games on my cell phone.

6 그 경기에서 이겼기 때문에, 그는 상으로 뮤지컬 표를 받았다. (win)
→ _____ _____ _____, he got tickets to a musical for the prize.

7 우리는 저녁으로 스파게티를 먹고 후식으로 아이스크림을 먹었다. (have, for dessert)
→ We had spaghetti for dinner, _____ _____ _____ _____ _____.

D 우리말과 같은 뜻이 되도록 단어를 배열하시오. (분사구문이 문장의 앞에 오도록 쓸 것)

1 새 것은 아니지만, 이 기계는 작동이 잘 된다. (this machine, new, not, fine, being, works)
→ _____

2 프러포즈를 받고, 그녀는 매우 행복했다. (the proposal, she, happy, receiving, very, felt)
→ _____

3 크고 무섭게 생겼지만, 그 개는 사납지 않다. (wild, big and scary, is, looking, the dog, not)
→ _____

4 그의 전화번호를 알면, 제게 알려주세요. (know, knowing, me, his phone number, let, please)
→ _____

5 쇼핑할 시간이 없어서 나는 그것을 온라인으로 주문했다. (I, it, for shopping, online, having, no time, ordered)
→ _____

6 텔레비전을 볼 때 우리는 서로 대화를 하지 않게 된다. (talk to, tend, we, TV, watching, not, each other, to)
→ _____

7 회원 카드를 집에 놓고 와서, 그녀는 책을 대출할 수 없었다.
(the books, she, her membership card, check out, at home, leaving, couldn't)
→ _____

UNIT **03** 여러 가지 분사구문

A 두 문장이 같은 의미가 되도록 분사구문을 이용하여 문장을 완성하시오.

1 Because we had no money, we had to walk home.

→ _____, we had to walk home.

2 As I didn't sleep enough yesterday, I feel tired now.

→ _____, I feel tired now.

3 Because he lost his wallet, he has no money now.

→ _____, he has no money now.

4 Although she has been invited, she still will not go there.

→ _____, she still will not go there.

5 After he was told he failed the test, he was disappointed.

→ _____, he was disappointed.

6 As she skipped the breakfast this morning, she feels hungry now.

→ _____, she feels hungry now.

7 Even though he studied abroad, he still can't speak English very well.

→ _____, he still can't speak English very well.

8 As it was designed by a famous designer, it is very expensive.

→ _____, it is very expensive.

9 Because the summer vacation is just around the corner, the students are excited.

→ _____, the students are excited.

B 밑줄 친 분사구문을 어법에 맞게 고쳐 쓰시오.

1 He stood a book with under his arm.

2 Ignore by him, she was very angry.

3 Been sick, she went to the hospital.

4 She went out with the door unlocking.

5 Seeing from above, the cars look very small.

6 Saving a lot of money, I can buy a cell phone now.

7 Having too much coffee this morning, I'm not sleepy at all now.

C 두 문장이 같은 의미가 되도록 문장을 완성하시오.

1 Being advised, she practiced a lot.

→ As _____, she practiced a lot.

2 It being very cold outside, you'd better wear your coat.

→ Because _____, you'd better wear your coat.

3 Having argued a lot in the past, they are still best friends.

→ Although _____, they are still best friends.

4 Having attended the same middle school as me, he doesn't remember me.

→ Even though _____, he doesn't remember me.

D 두 문장이 같은 의미가 되도록 「with+명사+분사/전치사」 형태를 이용하여 문장을 완성하시오.

1 He fell asleep, and the lights were on.

→ He fell asleep _____.

2 He stood, and his back was to the wall.

→ He stood _____.

3 She was listening to music, and her legs were crossed.

→ She was listening to music _____.

4 She was looking out the window, and her scarf was flying in the wind.

→ She was looking out the window _____.

E 우리말과 같은 뜻이 되도록 주어진 단어를 이용하여 문장을 완성하시오.

1 칼과 가위를 사용할 때는 조심해라. (when, use)

→ Be careful _____ _____ knives and scissors.

2 엄격하게 말해서, 그것은 정확한 답은 아니다. (speak)

→ _____ _____, it is not the exact answer.

3 날씨가 좋아서 우리는 소풍을 갔다. (the weather, nice)

→ _____ _____ _____ _____, we went on a picnic.

4 그의 억양으로 판단하건대, 그는 호주에서 왔다. (judge, accent)

→ _____ _____ _____ _____, he is from Australia.

5 양을 고려하면, 그것은 비싼 것이 아니다. (consider, the quantity)

→ _____ _____ _____, it's not that expensive.

23

01 현재완료와 현재완료진행

A 밑줄 친 부분을 가장 적절한 시제로 고쳐 쓰시오.

1 He <u>never tries</u> Mexican food until now. _____

2 Have you ever <u>be</u> to London before? _____

3 I <u>have seen</u> her at the movie theater yesterday. _____

4 I <u>have graduated</u> from high school 10 years ago. _____

5 She <u>has lost</u> her bag on her way to work yesterday. _____

6 We <u>don't talk</u> to each other since we had a big fight. _____

7 He <u>is reading</u> that book since this morning. It must be very interesting. _____

B 두 문장의 의미가 통하도록 문장을 완성하시오.

1 She lost her passport, and she's still looking for it.

→ She _____ _____ her passport.

2 He went to his home country a week ago, so he is not here anymore.

→ He _____ _____ to his home country.

3 I started to wait for him an hour ago, and I'm still waiting for him.

→ I _____ _____ _____ for him for an hour.

4 I started to work for this company last year, and I'm still working here.

→ I _____ _____ _____ here since last year.

5 I left my cell phone on the desk, so I don't have it now.

→ I _____ _____ my cell phone on the desk.

6 She checked in to the hotel a week ago, and she's still staying at the same hotel.

→ She _____ _____ _____ at the same hotel for a week.

7 She picked up the phone half an hour ago, and she is still talking on the phone.

→ She _____ _____ _____ on the phone for half an hour.

C 우리말과 같은 뜻이 되도록 주어진 단어를 이용하여 문장을 완성하시오.

1 네 친구가 10분 전에 전화했었어. (call, ten minutes)

→ Your friend _____ _____ _____ _____ .

2 그녀는 한 시간 전에 여기 도착했다. (arrive, an hour)

→ She _____ _____ _____ _____ .

3 내가 이 사업을 시작한지 5년이 지났다. (pass, start)

→ Five years _____ _____ _____ _____ this business.

4 우리는 10년 동안 친구로 지내왔다. (be, friends, ten years)

→ We _____ _____ _____ _____ _____ _____ .

5 우리는 3년 동안 결혼 생활을 해왔다. (be married, three years)

→ We _____ _____ _____ _____ .

6 나는 내 카메라를 망가뜨려서 그것을 사용할 수가 없다. (break)

→ I _____ _____ _____ _____ , so I can't use it.

7 나는 2008년 이후로 가난한 사람들을 도와주고 있다. (help, the poor)

→ I _____ _____ _____ _____ _____ _____ _____ .

D 우리말과 같은 뜻이 되도록 주어진 단어를 배열하시오.

1 우리 개가 어제부터 아프다. (sick, yesterday, has, since, been)

→ My dog _____ .

2 내가 그녀와 헤어진 지 2주가 지났다. (her, broke up with, since, has, I, passed)

→ Two weeks _____ .

3 그들은 2년째 이 집에 살고 있다. (lived in, two years, this house, for, have)

→ They _____ .

4 나는 지금까지 내 차를 가져본 적이 없다. (until, have, never, had, now, my own car)

→ I _____ .

5 나는 네가 방금 내게 한 말을 믿을 수가 없어. (have, can't, said, you, just, believe, what)

→ I _____ .

6 나는 이 프로그램을 20분째 보고 있다. (for, have, this program, been, twenty minutes, watching)

→ I _____ .

7 나는 우리나라를 벗어나본 적이 없다. (out of, never, my country, have, been)

→ I _____ .

과거완료와 과거완료진행

A 밑줄 친 부분을 가장 적절한 완료 시제로 고쳐 쓰시오.

1 She <u>has already left</u> when I got there. _____

2 He said he <u>has seen</u> a man leaving the shop. _____

3 When I got there, the movie <u>has already finished</u>. _____

4 She <u>has been cleaning</u> the house when I came home. _____

5 They <u>have saved</u> enough money by the time they have a baby. _____

6 We <u>have been</u> very close before he moved to another city. _____

7 He <u>will have watched</u> a baseball game when his friend called him. _____

B 두 문장의 의미가 통하도록 문장을 완성하시오.

1 She lost her watch before but found it later.

→ She found her watch she _____ _____ before.

2 He paid for the food, but he forgot to get his change.

→ He realized he _____ _____ to get his change.

3 My mother called me after I started reading a book.

→ I _____ _____ _____ a book when my mother called me.

4 My dad just cleaned the house and a moment later, I got home.

→ When I got home, my dad _____ just _____ the house.

5 It's May now. They plan to buy a house a year from now.

→ By next May, they _____ _____ _____ a house.

6 He saw the program, and he began dreaming of becoming a doctor.

→ He _____ never _____ of becoming a doctor before he saw the program.

7 He was taking a shower, and a moment later, he heard a strange noise.

→ He _____ _____ _____ a shower when he heard a strange noise.

C 우리말과 같은 뜻이 되도록 완료 시제와 주어진 단어를 이용하여 문장을 완성하시오.

1 그가 집에 왔을 때 나는 잠들어 있었다. (fall, get)

→ I _____ _____ asleep by the time he _____ home.

2 내년 이맘때쯤엔 나무가 많이 자라있을 것이다. (grow)

→ The tree _____ _____ _____ tall by this time next year.

3 나는 그녀가 내게 보낸 편지들을 찾아냈다. (find, send)

→ I _____ the letters she _____ _____ me.

4 내가 전화했을 때 그는 짐을 풀고 있었다. (unpack, call)

→ He _____ _____ _____ when I _____ him.

5 우리는 부산으로 이사 오기 전에 서울에 살았었다. (live, move)

→ We _____ _____ in Seoul before we _____ to Busan.

6 그녀는 그녀에게 일어난 일을 친구들에게 말했다. (tell, happen)

→ She _____ her friends what _____ _____ to her.

7 그녀는 결혼하기 전에 요리를 해 본 적이 없었다. (never, cook, get married)

→ She _____ _____ _____ before she _____ _____ .

D 우리말과 같은 뜻이 되도록 주어진 단어를 배열하시오.

1 편지가 도착했을 때, 그는 이미 떠나고 없었다. (the letter, already, had, he, arrived, left)

→ When _____ .

2 그는 책을 집에 두고 왔음을 알게 되었다. (left, at home, he, found out, that, had, his book)

→ He _____ .

3 여기로 오기 전까지 우리는 방을 같이 썼었다. (shared, we, here, had, before, a room, moved)

→ We _____ .

4 나는 누군가 내 휴대 전화를 훔쳐갔음을 깨달았다. (my cell phone, stolen, someone, had, realized)

→ I _____ .

5 그들은 다음 달 이맘때쯤이면 결혼한지 10년이 될 것이다.

(by this time, next month, will, for ten years, been married, have)

→ They _____ .

6 나는 축제 전에는 그녀와 이야기를 나눠본 적이 없었다. (the festival, talked to, had, before, never, her)

→ I _____ .

7 그가 내게 전화했을 때, 나는 그를 한 시간 동안 기다린 상태였다.

(for an hour, him, me, when, had, he, waited for, called)

→ I _____ .

can, must, may, should

A 보기 에서 알맞은 말을 골라 문장을 완성하시오. (한 번씩만 쓸 것)

[1~4]

| 보기 | may | should | must not | can |

1 She insisted that I _____ go with her.

2 I will take this watch. _____ you gift-wrap it, please?

3 I'm not sure, but she _____ regret it if she misses this chance.

4 You are not disabled. You _____ park your car in a spot for the handicapped.

[5~8]

| 보기 | will be able to | don't have to | may | should |

5 You _____ go home if you've finished it.

6 You _____ exercise regularly even if you're busy.

7 You _____ understand him when you grow up.

8 You can do whatever you want. You _____ do what he said.

B 두 문장이 같은 의미가 되도록 문장을 완성하시오.

1 Can I speak to Mr. Kim, please?

→ _____ Mr. Kim, please?

2 She should get some rest for some time.

→ She _____ some rest for some time.

3 He couldn't agree with what she said.

→ He _____ what she said.

4 You must submit the report by this Friday.

→ You _____ the report by this Friday.

5 Some animals can hear high-pitched sounds.

→ Some animals _____ high-pitched sounds.

6 You shouldn't put off until tomorrow what you can do today.

→ You _____ until tomorrow what you can do today.

C 우리말과 같은 뜻이 되도록 주어진 단어를 이용하여 문장을 완성하시오.

1 급하면 일찍 집에 가도 좋습니다. (go, home)

→ You _____ _____ _____ _____ if you're in a hurry.

2 너는 그것에 대해 걱정할 필요 없다. (worry about)

→ You _____ _____ _____ _____ it.

3 낯선 사람을 집에 함부로 들이면 안 된다. (let)

→ You _____ _____ _____ a stranger into your house.

4 그녀가 Lisa일 리 없어. 그녀는 지금 프랑스에 있어. (be)

→ She _____ _____ Lisa. She's in France now.

5 그녀는 너를 다시 보면 틀림없이 기뻐할 거야. (be, happy)

→ She _____ _____ _____ to see you again.

6 그녀는 딸이 늦게까지 안 들어오는 것을 허락할 수 없었다. (allow)

→ She _____ _____ her daughter to stay out late.

7 그의 행동에는 틀림없이 무슨 이유가 있을 것이다. (be, some reason)

→ There _____ _____ _____ _____ for his behavior.

D 우리말과 같은 뜻이 되도록 주어진 단어를 배열하시오.

1 우리가 마지막 버스를 탈 수 있을까? (catch, be, will, to, able, we)

→ _____ the last bus?

2 원한다면 네가 이 방을 사용해도 좋아. (use, you, this room, may)

→ _____ if you want.

3 그는 시간이 별로 없어서 일찍 떠나야 했다. (had, early, he, leave, to)

→ _____ because he didn't have much time.

4 너는 돈을 낼 필요 없어. 내가 이미 지불했어. (pay, have, you, to, don't)

→ _____ the bill. I've already paid.

5 이곳에서는 허락 없이 사진을 찍으면 안 됩니다. (pictures, may, take, you, here, not)

→ _____ without permission.

6 나는 그녀에게 외국어를 배워보라고 제안했다. (learn, suggested, I, should, that, she)

→ _____ foreign languages.

7 마침내 우리는 살만한 좋은 집을 찾을 수 있었다. (a good place, find, could, to live in, we)

→ At last, _____ .

had better, used to, would rather, may as well

A 보기 에서 알맞은 말을 골라 문장을 완성하시오. (한 번씩만 쓸 것)

[1~4]

보기	had better not	would rather	may well	got used to

1 My mother finally _____ using a smartphone.

2 He often breaks his promises. You _____ doubt him.

3 I'm tired. I _____ stay home and get some rest.

4 The traffic is heavy. You _____ take a taxi to the airport.

[5~8]

보기	used to wear	had better not be	may as well take	would rather not buy

5 It's too expensive. I _____ it.

6 There's nothing to do at home. We _____ a walk.

7 She _____ a school uniform when she was young.

8 This is not the first time. You _____ late for school again.

B 우리말과 같은 뜻이 되도록 어법상 <u>어색한</u> 곳을 찾아 바르게 고쳐 쓰시오.

1 저울은 물건의 무게를 다는 데 사용된다.
→ A scale used to weigh things.
_____

2 그가 실망하는 것도 당연하다.
→ He may as well get disappointed.
_____

3 모퉁이에 높은 건물이 있었다.
→ There would be a tall building on the corner.
_____

4 요리를 하느니 차라리 저녁을 굶는 게 낫겠다.
→ I would rather skip dinner than cooking something.
_____

5 네가 할 수 있는 것은 이제 아무것도 없다. 너는 그냥 집에 가는 게 낫겠다.
→ There's nothing you can do anymore. You may well go home.
_____

C 우리말과 같은 뜻이 되도록 주어진 단어를 이용하여 문장을 완성하시오.

1 넌 곧 미국에 사는 데 익숙해질 거야. (live)
→ You'll _____ _____ _____ _____ in America soon.

2 너는 즉시 의사에게 가보는 것이 좋겠다. (go)
→ You _____ _____ _____ to see a doctor immediately.

3 여드름을 건드리지 않는 것이 좋겠다. (touch)
→ You _____ _____ _____ _____ the pimple.

4 우리는 겨울에 주말마다 스키를 타러 가곤 했어. (go skiing)
→ We _____ _____ _____ every weekend in winter.

5 그는 일요일마다 아버지와 농구를 하곤 했었다. (play basketball)
→ He _____ _____ _____ _____ with his father every Sunday.

6 어쨌든 가야 한다면, 가능한 한 일찍 가는 편이 낫겠다. (go)
→ If you have to go anyway, you _____ _____ _____ _____ as early as possible.

7 나는 축구를 하느니 낮잠을 자는 게 낫겠다. (take a nap, play soccer)
→ I _____ _____ _____ _____ _____ _____ _____.

D 우리말과 같은 뜻이 되도록 주어진 단어를 배열하시오.

1 나는 단것을 많이 먹었었다. (a lot, eat, to, sweets, used)
→ I _____.

2 나는 어렸을 때 만화책을 읽곤 했다. (was, would, read, young, I, when, comic books)
→ I _____.

3 자외선 차단제는 우리의 피부를 보호하는 데 사용된다. (protect, used, is, our skin, to)
→ Sunscreen _____.

4 거기 제시간에 갈 수 없다면, 가지 않는 편이 낫겠다. (as, there, may, not, you, go, well)
→ If you can't go there on time, _____.

5 너는 차라리 그녀에게 진실을 이야기하지 않는 것이 좋겠다. (the truth, rather, tell, would, her, not)
→ You _____.

6 우리는 지금 떠나는 게 좋겠어. 안 그러면 늦을지도 몰라. (be, had, might, late, leave, better, now, we, or)
→ We _____.

7 오후에 출발하느니 아침 일찍 출발하는 게 차라리 낫겠다.
(in the afternoon, than, rather, leave, early in the morning, would)
→ You _____.

31

UNIT 03 조동사+have+p.p.

A 보기 에서 알맞은 말을 골라 문장을 완성하시오.

[1~4]

> 보기   must have gone   may have forgotten   shouldn't have put   could have let

1 She _____ that much salt in it. It's too salty.

2 He didn't call me. He _____ my phone number.

3 I was disappointed in him. He _____ me know about it.

4 The light was off in her room. She _____ to bed early that night.

[5~8]

> 보기   must have rained   may have been   should have called   cannot have been

5 He _____ surprised when I told him the news.

6 She _____ there. She was shopping with me.

7 The ground was all wet. It _____ a lot last night.

8 I'm sorry to keep you waiting. I _____ you.

B 두 문장의 의미가 통하도록 문장을 완성하시오.

1 I am sure he saw the movie.

  → He _____ _____ _____ the movie.

2 I didn't study hard enough, and I regret it now.

  → I _____ _____ _____ hard.

3 He didn't leave early enough, and now he regrets it.

  → He _____ _____ _____ earlier.

4 I am sure that she didn't sleep much last night.

  → She _____ _____ _____ much last night.

5 You were able to ask me for help, but you didn't.

  → You _____ _____ _____ me for help.

6 It is possible that she left home already, but I'm not sure.

  → She _____ _____ _____ home already.

7 It is possible that she called me while I was in the bathroom, but I'm not sure.

  → She _____ _____ _____ me while I was in the bathroom.

C 우리말과 같은 뜻이 되도록 주어진 단어를 이용하여 문장을 완성하시오.

1 그녀가 내 고장 난 컴퓨터를 고쳤을지도 몰라. (fix)
→ She _____ _____ _____ my broken computer.

2 그가 우리의 약속을 깜빡한 것이 틀림없다. (forget)
→ He _____ _____ _____ our appointment.

3 나는 그녀의 말을 믿지 말았어야 했어. (not, believe)
→ I _____ _____ _____ what she said.

4 그녀가 거짓말을 했을 리가 없어. 그녀는 정직한 사람이야. (tell a lie)
→ She _____ _____ _____ _____. She is an honest person.

5 그가 반에서 일등을 했어. 열심히 공부를 했음이 틀림없어. (study, hard)
→ He was first in his class. He _____ _____ _____ _____.

6 나쁘진 않지만, 너는 더 잘 할 수 있었을 텐데. (do)
→ It's not bad, but you _____ _____ _____ it better.

7 그가 아팠을 리가 없어. 나는 그가 친구들과 농구를 하는 것을 보았어. (be, sick)
→ He _____ _____ _____ _____. I saw him playing basketball with his friends.

D 우리말과 같은 뜻이 되도록 주어진 단어를 배열하시오.

1 네가 다칠 수도 있었어. 좀 더 조심하도록 해. (hurt, have, could, been)
→ You _____. You need to be more careful.

2 그의 강의는 매우 지루했음이 틀림이 없다. (have, very, must, boring, been)
→ His lecture _____.

3 우리는 더 일찍 예약을 했어야 했다. (made, earlier, have, a reservation, should)
→ We _____.

4 그는 지하철을 탔어야 했어. 도로에 차가 너무 많아. (taken, have, should, the subway)
→ He _____. There are too many cars on the road.

5 그가 시험에 떨어졌을 리가 없어. 그는 매우 열심히 공부했어. (failed, have, the test, cannot)
→ He _____. He studied very hard.

6 누군가 네가 운동장에 있는 동안 네 시계를 훔쳐갔을지도 몰라. (watch, have, stolen, may, your)
→ Someone _____ while you were in the playground.

7 그녀는 수업 시간에 딴 생각을 하고 있었음이 틀림이 없다. (something else, been, must, thinking about, have)
→ She _____ during class.

UNIT 01 수동태의 의미와 형태

A 우리말과 같은 뜻이 되도록 주어진 단어를 이용하여 수동태 문장을 완성하시오.

1 스테이크는 너무 익었다. (overcook)
→ The steak _____ by her.

2 그 공은 골키퍼에 의해서 저지당했다. (block)
→ The ball _____ by the goalkeeper.

3 그 사고에서 차가 손상을 입었다. (damage)
→ The car _____ in the accident.

4 자세한 정보는 파일에 포함되어 있습니다. (include)
→ Detailed information _____ in the file.

B 우리말과 같은 뜻이 되도록 보기 에서 알맞은 단어를 골라 문장을 완성하시오.

보기	punish	cut off	separate	own

1 그 호텔은 그 외국인의 소유이다.
→ The hotel _____ by the foreigner.

2 수도 공급이 한 시간 동안 끊길 것입니다.
→ The water supply will _____ for an hour.

3 규칙을 어기는 사람은 처벌을 받게 될 것이다.
→ Those who break the rules will _____ .

4 종이는 다른 쓰레기와 분리되어야 한다.
→ Paper must _____ from other trash.

C 능동태 문장을 수동태 문장으로 바꿔 쓰시오. (by+행위자 생략)

1 She is charging her cell phone.
→ Her cell phone _____ .

2 Teachers should encourage students.
→ Students _____ .

3 He was repairing the car at that time.
→ The car _____ at that time.

4 The police have not found the missing child yet.
→ The missing child _____ yet.

D 우리말과 같은 뜻이 되도록 주어진 단어를 이용하여 문장을 완성하시오.

1 규정은 지켜져야 한다. (must, follow)
→ Rules _____ _____ _____.

2 화재가 신속히 진압되었다. (put out, quickly)
→ The fire _____ _____ _____ _____.

3 그 사고에서 많은 사람이 다쳤다. (injure, in the accident)
→ Many people _____ _____ _____ _____.

4 그 실수들은 즉시 수정될 것이다. (will, correct, immediately)
→ The mistakes _____ _____ _____ _____.

5 버터는 올리브오일로 대체될 수 있다. (can, replace, olive oil)
→ Butter _____ _____ _____ _____ _____.

6 그녀의 연설에서 그의 이름이 언급되었다. (mention)
→ His name _____ _____ in her speech.

7 많은 건물이 지진에 의해 부서졌다. (destroy, the earthquake)
→ Many buildings _____ _____ _____ _____ _____.

E 우리말과 같은 뜻이 되도록 주어진 단어를 배열하시오.

1 그녀는 교수로 채용되었다. (a professor, hired, has, as, been)
→ She _____.

2 벽에서 아주 작은 구멍이 발견되었다. (the wall, found, in, was)
→ A tiny hole _____.

3 이 시간들은 영원히 기억될 것입니다. (be, forever, remembered, will)
→ These times _____.

4 그 자전거는 우리 형이 수리 중이다. (being, my brother, is, by, repaired)
→ The bicycle _____.

5 이 기념비는 군인들을 기리기 위해 지어졌다. (to honor, built, the soldiers, was)
→ The monument _____.

6 그녀는 우주가 신에 의해 창조되었다고 믿는다. (by, the universe, created, God, was)
→ She believes that _____.

7 침대와 소파가 7일 안으로 배달될 것입니다. (seven days, delivered, within, be, will)
→ The bed and the sofa _____.

UNIT 02 4문형, 5문형 수동태

A 보기 에서 알맞은 단어를 골라 문장을 완성하시오.

보기   for   to   of

1 The dish was cooked _____ us by my mother.

2 Birthday presents were brought _____ me by my friends.

3 Several questions were asked _____ him by the reporter.

B 다음 문장을 수동태 문장으로 바꿔 쓰시오. (by+행위자 생략)

1 He threw his brother a pillow.

→ A pillow _____ .

→ His brother _____ .

2 I lent her my laptop computer.

→ My laptop computer _____ .

→ She _____ .

3 Somebody sent me crucial information.

→ Crucial information _____ .

→ I _____ .

4 My mother cooked me delicious pizza.

→ Delicious pizza _____ .

→ I _____ .

C 다음 문장을 수동태 문장으로 바꿔 쓰시오. (by+행위자 생략)

1 They made me lead the group.

→ I _____ .

2 He named his daughter Lisa.

→ His daughter _____ .

3 He advised me to tell him the truth.

→ I _____ .

4 I felt the earth shaking beneath me.

→ The earth _____ .

D 우리말과 같은 뜻이 되도록 주어진 단어를 이용하여 문장을 완성하시오.

1 나에게 좋은 가격이 제안되었다. (offer, me)

→ A good price ＿＿＿＿＿ ＿＿＿＿＿ ＿＿＿＿＿ ＿＿＿＿＿ .

2 내 컴퓨터는 James에게 팔렸다. (sell, James)

→ My computer ＿＿＿＿＿ ＿＿＿＿＿ ＿＿＿＿＿ ＿＿＿＿＿ .

3 나는 설거지를 하게 되었다. (make, wash the dishes)

→ I ＿＿＿＿＿ ＿＿＿＿＿ ＿＿＿＿＿ ＿＿＿＿＿ ＿＿＿＿＿ ＿＿＿＿＿ .

4 그는 대회에 참가하도록 격려를 받았다. (encourage)

→ He ＿＿＿＿＿ ＿＿＿＿＿ to participate in the competition.

5 나는 일주일을 더 기다리라는 이야기를 들었다. (tell)

→ I ＿＿＿＿＿ ＿＿＿＿＿ to wait another week.

6 Nick이 상사와 말다툼하는 소리가 들렸다. (hear, argue)

→ Nick ＿＿＿＿＿ ＿＿＿＿＿ ＿＿＿＿＿ with his boss.

7 그녀는 다음 주까지 과제를 제출하라고 요구를 받았다. (require)

→ She ＿＿＿＿＿ ＿＿＿＿＿ to submit her assignment by next week.

E 우리말과 같은 뜻이 되도록 주어진 단어를 배열하시오.

1 그 아이는 천재로 여겨진다. (a genius, considered, is)

→ The kid ＿＿＿＿＿＿＿＿＿＿＿＿＿＿＿＿ .

2 나는 그 집을 떠나도록 강요받았다. (forced, to, was, the house, leave)

→ I ＿＿＿＿＿＿＿＿＿＿＿＿＿＿＿＿ .

3 나는 축구 클럽에 가입하라고 요청을 받았다. (join, the soccer club, asked, to, was)

→ I ＿＿＿＿＿＿＿＿＿＿＿＿＿＿＿＿ .

4 그 놀이방은 나의 아들을 위해 만든 것이었다. (made, my son, for, was)

→ The playroom ＿＿＿＿＿＿＿＿＿＿＿＿＿＿＿＿ .

5 여러분은 안에서 사진을 찍어도 됩니다. (pictures, inside, allowed, take, are, to)

→ You ＿＿＿＿＿＿＿＿＿＿＿＿＿＿＿＿ .

6 발견하는 사람에게 보상이 제공될 것입니다. (be, the finder, offered, to, will)

→ A reward ＿＿＿＿＿＿＿＿＿＿＿＿＿＿＿＿ .

7 그녀가 개를 뒤쫓아 달려가고 있는 것이 목격되었다. (running after, was, her dog, seen)

→ She ＿＿＿＿＿＿＿＿＿＿＿＿＿＿＿＿ .

UNIT 03 주의해야 할 수동태

A 보기 에서 알맞은 단어를 골라 문장을 완성하시오.

보기   of   with   to   about   that

1 The vase is made _____ glass.

2 The ground was covered _____ snow.

3 Viruses are known _____ be the cause of colds.

4 My mother is worried _____ my condition.

5 It is expected _____ the rainy season will last for more than a month.

B 다음 문장을 수동태 문장으로 바꿔 쓰시오. (by+행위자 생략)

1 We think that she is the best teacher.

→ She _____.

→ It _____.

2 People know that Bach is the father of classical music.

→ It _____.

→ Bach _____.

3 They say that she graduated from Harvard University.

→ It _____.

→ She _____.

C 다음 문장을 수동태 문장으로 바꿔 쓰시오.

1 The oven gave off too much heat.

→ Too much heat _____.

2 The settlers drove away lots of Native Americans.

→ Lots of Native Americans _____.

3 The train ran over the cat.

→ The cat _____.

4 The moving company took out all the belongings.

→ All the belongings _____.

D 우리말과 같은 뜻이 되도록 주어진 단어를 이용하여 문장을 완성하시오.

1 상점은 손님들로 붐볐다. (crowd)

→ The store _____ _____ _____ customers.

2 경기가 비 때문에 취소되었다. (call off)

→ The game _____ _____ _____ because of rain.

3 그녀는 아름다운 목소리로 유명하다. (know)

→ She _____ _____ _____ a beautiful voice.

4 그 배우가 이번 가을에 결혼할 예정이라고들 한다. (say)

→ It _____ _____ _____ the actor is getting married this fall.

5 그가 대부분의 돈을 기부할 거라고 여겨진다. (think, donate)

→ He _____ _____ _____ _____ most of his money.

6 그녀는 조부모님에 의해 키워졌다. (bring up, her grandparents)

→ She _____ _____ _____ _____ _____ .

7 그 강아지는 내 동생이 돌보고 있다. (take care of, my sister)

→ The puppy _____ _____ _____ _____ _____ _____

_____ _____ .

E 우리말과 같은 뜻이 되도록 주어진 단어를 배열하시오.

1 산이 벚꽃으로 뒤덮여 있다. (covered, cherry blossoms, with, is)

→ The mountain _____ .

2 그들은 그의 발전에 놀랐다. (astonished, progress, were, his, at)

→ They _____ .

3 그 방은 검은 연기로 가득 차 있다. (with, smoke, filled, black, is)

→ The room _____ .

4 그는 진실을 숨기고 있다고 믿어진다. (believed, to, the truth, is, hide)

→ He _____ .

5 그는 아들의 행동에 실망했다. (disappointed, his son's behavior, with, was)

→ He _____ .

6 그녀는 새 아파트에 만족했다. (satisfied, apartment, was, new, her, with)

→ She _____ .

7 나는 같은 노래를 듣는 것에 싫증이 났다. (tired, the same song, of, listening to, was)

→ I _____ .

UNIT 01 가정법 과거, 과거완료, 혼합가정

A 주어진 단어를 이용하여 문장을 완성하시오.

1 If I _____ you, I wouldn't buy that bag. (be)

2 If we _____ a noise, the teacher will be angry. (make)

3 If I knew how to play the drums, I could _____ the band. (join)

4 If I was invited to her birthday party, I _____ there. (will, go)

5 If he _____ one more goal, we would have won the game. (score)

B 두 문장이 같은 뜻이 되도록 가정법 문장을 완성하시오.

1 As I don't have a brother, I am lonely.

→ If I _____ a brother, I _____ lonely.

2 As today is not Sunday, we go to school.

→ If today _____ Sunday, we _____ to school.

3 As you are not old enough, you can't watch this movie.

→ If you _____ old enough, you _____ this movie.

4 As he overslept, he was late for school.

→ If he _____, he _____ late for school.

5 As I moved to London, I don't go to the same school as you now.

→ If I _____ to London, I _____ to the same school as you now.

C 우리말과 같은 뜻이 되도록 주어진 단어를 이용하여 문장을 완성하시오.

1 오늘이 내 생일이라면, 선물을 많이 받을 텐데. (be, will, get)
→ If today _____ my birthday, I _____ many presents.

2 내가 정답을 맞혔다면, 저 상은 내 것이 되었을 텐데. (get, will, be)
→ If I _____ the correct answer, that prize _____ mine.

3 내가 미국에서 태어났더라면, 영어를 잘했을 텐데. (be, will, speak)
→ If I _____ born in America, I _____ English well.

4 숙제를 가져 왔다면, 선생님한테 혼나지 않았을 텐데. (bring, will not, scold)
→ If I _____ my homework, I _____ by my teacher.

5 걱정하지 마. 서두르면, 우리는 제시간에 도착할 거야. (hurry up, will, arrive)
→ Don't worry. If we _____, we _____ on time.

D 우리말과 같은 뜻이 되도록 주어진 단어를 배열하시오.

1 복권에 당첨된다면, 나는 큰 집을 살 텐데. (a, house, would, I, buy, big)
→ If I won the lottery, _____.

2 그녀가 내 옆에 앉는다면, 그녀와 말을 할 수 있을 텐데. (next to, sat, me, she)
→ If _____, I could have a talk with her.

3 그가 숙제를 다 했다면, 그는 벌을 받지 않았을 텐데. (his, had, he, done, homework)
→ If _____, he wouldn't have been punished.

4 뒷마당이 있는 집에서 산다면, 우리는 개를 기를 수 있을 텐데. (lived, with, in, a backyard, a house, we)
→ If _____, we could have a dog.

5 좀 더 조심했다면, 너는 창문을 깨지 않았을 텐데. (broken, you, have, the window, wouldn't)
→ If you had been more careful, _____.

6 어렸을 때 수영을 배웠다면, 지금 물을 무서워하지 않을 텐데. (as, I, how to swim, learned, a young kid, had)
→ If _____, I wouldn't be scared of water now.

E 우리말과 같은 뜻이 되도록 주어진 단어를 이용하여 문장을 완성하시오.

1 내가 학생이라면, 공부를 열심히 할 텐데. (study, hard)
→ If I _____ _____ _____, I _____ _____ _____.

2 그가 집에 있다면, 나는 그와 농구를 할 텐데. (at home, play, basketball, with him)
→ If he _____ _____ _____, I _____ _____ _____ _____
_____.

3 경기에서 이겼다면, 그들은 지금 사람들에게 환영을 받을 텐데. (win, the game, be welcomed)
→ If they _____ _____ _____ _____, they _____ _____ _____
_____ _____ now.

4 내가 수의사라면, 나의 아픈 고양이에게 약을 처방해 줄 수 있을 텐데. (a vet, prescribe, medicine)
→ If I _____ _____ _____, I _____ _____ _____ for my sick cat.

5 내가 문을 잠갔더라면, 컴퓨터를 잃어버리지 않았을 텐데. (lock the door, lose, my computer)
→ If I _____ _____ _____ _____, I _____ _____ _____
_____ _____.

6 그가 잠자기 전에 창문을 닫았더라면, 그는 감기에 걸리지 않았을 텐데. (close, the window, catch a cold)
→ If he _____ _____ _____ _____ before going to bed, _____
_____ _____ _____ _____ _____.

I wish, as if, but for, without 가정법

A 주어진 단어를 이용하여 가정법 문장을 완성하시오.

1 I wish I _____ a lot of money now. (have)

2 He acts as if he _____ superman. (be)

3 I wish I _____ this book earlier. I'm sorry I didn't read it. (read)

4 If it were not for the air conditioner, we _____ the heat of this summer. (bear)

5 Without the alarm clock, I _____ late for the meeting. But I wasn't late. (be)

B 두 문장의 의미가 통하도록 문장을 완성하시오.

1 I'm sorry that I can't help you now.

→ I wish _____.

2 I'm sorry that I gave up writing my novel.

→ I wish _____.

3 In fact, he is not a patient.

→ He talks as if _____.

4 In fact, she didn't eat dinner.

→ She talks as if _____.

5 If it were not for water, we couldn't live longer than a week.

→ _____, we couldn't live longer than a week.

6 If it had not been for the navigation, I could have got lost.

→ _____, I could have got lost.

C 보기 에서 알맞은 말을 골라 문장을 완성하시오.

| 보기 | were his mother | left for the airport | couldn't travel | had said |

1 It's time you _____.

2 I wish I _____ nothing to him then.

3 The baby is looking at me as if I _____.

4 But for airplanes, we _____ around the world.

D 우리말과 같은 뜻이 되도록 주어진 단어를 이용하여 가정법 문장을 완성하시오.

[1~4] I wish 가정법

1 그녀가 나의 여자 친구라면 좋을 텐데. (be)

→ I _____ _____ _____ _____ _____.

2 그 모자를 안 샀더라면 좋을 텐데. (buy, the cap)

→ I _____ _____ _____ _____ _____.

3 내가 어제 일찍 잤더라면 좋을 텐데. (go to bed)

→ I _____ _____ _____ _____ _____ early yesterday.

4 나의 할머니께서 살아 계신다면 좋을 텐데. (be, alive)

→ I _____ _____ _____ _____.

[5~8] as if 가정법

5 그는 운전을 매우 잘하는 것처럼 말한다. (drive, well)

→ He talks _____ _____ _____ _____ _____.

6 그는 마치 나보다 나이가 많은 것처럼 말한다. (be, older)

→ He talks _____ _____ _____ _____ _____ _____.

7 그녀는 마치 그 배우를 직접 만난 것처럼 말한다. (meet, herself)

→ She talks _____ _____ _____ _____ _____ _____ _____.

8 그는 전에 그 사진을 본 적이 있었던 것처럼 느꼈다. (see, before)

→ He felt _____ _____ _____ _____ _____ _____

_____.

E 우리말과 같은 뜻이 되도록 주어진 단어를 배열하시오.

1 해가 없다면, 나무들은 잘 자라지 못할 것이다. (trees, the sun, grow, without, wouldn't)

→ _____ well.

2 그 알약이 없다면, 나는 매우 고통스러울 것이다. (feel, the pills, would, I, without)

→ _____ a lot of pain.

3 네 도움이 없었다면, 나는 그 사고에서 살아남지 못했을 것이다. (survived, I, but, have, your help, couldn't, for)

→ _____ the accident.

UNIT 01 관계대명사

A 보기 에서 알맞은 관계대명사를 골라 문장을 완성하시오.

> 보기   what   who   which   whose

1 This is my cousin _____ lives next door.
2 I bought a dog _____ hair is all black.
3 _____ I want for lunch is Chinese food.
4 The bird _____ I want to have is a parrot.

B 밑줄 친 부분을 어법에 맞게 고쳐 쓰시오.

1 It's not easy to get <u>that</u> you want.   _____
2 Carrot is the vegetable <u>who</u> I hate.   _____
3 This is not the thing <u>what</u> I asked for.   _____
4 I met a girl <u>who</u> dream is to become a doctor.   _____
5 The girl <u>which</u> Vanessa became friends with was Melanie. _____

C 두 문장을 관계대명사를 이용하여 한 문장으로 만드시오.

1 This is the wallet. I got it on my birthday.

   → This is the wallet _____.

2 I have a friend. Her mother is a professor.

   → I have a friend _____.

3 It is a seat belt. You use it for protection.

   → It is a seat belt _____.

4 This is the girl. I talked about her yesterday.

   → This is the girl _____.

5 Did you see the calculator? It was on the table.

   → Did you see the calculator _____?

6 He wanted to build a house. The windows of the house would be big.

   → He wanted to build a house _____.

7 The bicycle is in the garden. It is the gift from my father.

   → The bicycle _____ is the gift from my father.

D 우리말과 같은 뜻이 되도록 주어진 단어를 이용하여 문장을 완성하시오.

1 그는 내게 어제 산 것을 보여주었다. (buy)

→ He showed me ＿＿＿＿＿ ＿＿＿＿＿ ＿＿＿＿＿ yesterday.

2 나는 Sarah가 입고 있는 치마가 마음에 든다. (wear)

→ I like the skirt ＿＿＿＿＿ ＿＿＿＿＿ ＿＿＿＿＿ ＿＿＿＿＿.

3 내가 지금 듣고 있는 강의는 매우 지루하다. (take)

→ The lecture ＿＿＿＿＿ ＿＿＿＿＿ ＿＿＿＿＿ ＿＿＿＿＿ now is very boring.

4 우리는 흥행한 영화를 보았다. (be, a box-office hit)

→ We watched a movie ＿＿＿＿＿ ＿＿＿＿＿ ＿＿＿＿＿ ＿＿＿＿＿ ＿＿＿＿＿.

5 밖에 줄을 서서 기다리고 있는 사람들이 많이 있다. (wait in line)

→ There are lots of people ＿＿＿＿＿ ＿＿＿＿＿ ＿＿＿＿＿ ＿＿＿＿＿ outside.

6 엄마가 내 방 창문에 걸려 있는 커튼을 만드셨다. (hang)

→ Mom made the curtains ＿＿＿＿＿ ＿＿＿＿＿ ＿＿＿＿＿ in the windows of my room.

7 우리 어머니가 특별한 것은 내 낮은 점수에 대해 전혀 걱정하지 않는다는 것이다. (be, special about)

→ ＿＿＿＿＿ ＿＿＿＿＿ ＿＿＿＿＿ ＿＿＿＿＿ my mother is that she is never worried about my low grades.

E 우리말과 같은 뜻이 되도록 주어진 단어를 배열하시오.

1 오늘 아침에 네가 한 말이 맞았다. (this morning, said, was, you, what)

→ ＿＿＿＿＿＿＿＿＿＿＿＿＿＿＿＿＿ right.

2 저 사람은 아들이 유명한 배우이다. (whose, famous, is, actor, the man, son, a)

→ That's ＿＿＿＿＿＿＿＿＿＿＿＿＿＿＿.

3 Lisa 옆에 서 있는 남자 아이는 나와 동갑이다. (next to, the boy, is standing, that, Lisa)

→ ＿＿＿＿＿＿＿＿＿＿＿＿＿ is the same age as me.

4 이것이 우리 아버지가 지난달에 산 차이다. (which, bought, last month, my father, the car)

→ This is ＿＿＿＿＿＿＿＿＿＿＿＿＿.

5 나는 그 유명 소설가가 쓴 책을 많이 읽었다. (the famous novelist, many, books, by, were, that, written)

→ I read ＿＿＿＿＿＿＿＿＿＿＿＿＿.

6 그는 내가 우리 학교에서 가장 좋아하는 선생님이다. (in my school, the teacher, like most, whom, I)

→ He is ＿＿＿＿＿＿＿＿＿＿＿＿＿.

7 내가 들은 것은 그의 집이 화재로 다 타버렸다는 것이다. (that, what, his house, heard, burnt down, is, I)

→ ＿＿＿＿＿＿＿＿＿＿＿＿＿ in the fire.

UNIT 02 관계부사

A 우리말과 같은 뜻이 되도록 관계부사를 이용하여 문장을 완성하시오.

1 여기는 내가 태어난 병원이다.

→ This is the hospital _____ I was born.

2 그가 오늘 왜 수업에 빠졌는지 알고 있니?

→ Do you know _____ he missed the class today?

3 내가 자란 마을은 경관이 아름답다.

→ The town _____ I grew up has beautiful scenery.

4 그는 그녀가 갑자기 사라진 이유를 알고 싶었다.

→ He wanted to know _____ she suddenly disappeared.

5 나는 마이크처럼 키가 클 수 있는 방법을 알고 싶다.

→ I want to know _____ I can grow tall like Mike.

6 나는 그가 나에게 자신을 소개하던 날을 기억한다.

→ I remember the day _____ he introduced himself to me.

7 나는 우리 부모님에게 어떻게 처음 만났는지를 물었다.

→ I asked my parents _____ they first met.

B 두 문장을 관계부사를 이용하여 한 문장으로 만드시오.

1 The hotel was expensive. We stayed in that hotel.

→ The hotel _____ was expensive.

2 I know the reason. She is so upset for that reason.

→ I know the reason _____ .

3 Could you tell me the way? You get to the post office in that way.

→ Could you tell me _____ ?

4 Yesterday was the date. You had to hand in your homework on that date.

→ Yesterday was the date _____ .

5 She missed the city. She studied in that city when she was young.

→ She missed the city _____ when she was young.

6 Do you remember the year? The Korean War broke out in that year.

→ Do you remember the year _____ .

7 I want to know the reason. Many people are waiting in line here for that reason.

→ I want to know the reason _____ .

C 우리말과 같은 뜻이 되도록 관계부사와 주어진 단어를 이용하여 문장을 완성하시오.

1 네가 내게 전화한 이유를 말해 줄 수 있니? (call)

→ Could you tell me the reason _____ _____ _____ _____?

2 나에게 그 이야기가 어떻게 끝나는지 말해 줘. (the story, end)

→ Please tell me _____ _____ _____ _____.

3 그녀는 그 기계가 어떻게 작동하는지 모른다. (the machine, work)

→ She doesn't know _____ _____ _____ _____.

4 2002년은 월드컵이 한국에서 열린 해이다. (the World Cup, be held)

→ 2002 is the year _____ _____ _____ _____ _____ in Korea.

5 나는 처음으로 비행기를 탄 날을 잊지 못할 것이다. (get on)

→ I won't forget the day _____ _____ _____ _____ the plane for the first time.

6 나는 그들이 왜 서로 말을 안 하는지 이유를 알고 있다. (talk)

→ I know the reason _____ _____ _____ _____ _____ each other.

7 그는 갓 구운 빵이 나오는 시간을 안다. (fresh bread, come out)

→ He knows the time _____ _____ _____ _____ _____.

D 우리말과 같은 뜻이 되도록 주어진 단어를 배열하시오.

1 이것이 내가 컴퓨터를 고친 방법이야. (fixed, is, I, the computer, how)

→ This _____.

2 내가 여기에 온 이유를 말해 줄게. (the reason, for, I, here, which, came)

→ I'll tell you _____.

3 8월은 한국에서 가장 더운 달이다. (the hottest, when, is, in Korea, the month, it)

→ August is _____.

4 우리는 대통령이 태어난 곳을 방문했다. (the president, where, born, the place, was)

→ We visited _____.

5 너는 그녀가 미국에서 돌아올 날을 아니? (be, the day, from America, she, back, when, will)

→ Do you know _____?

6 나는 그녀가 연설을 하는 방식이 마음에 든다. (gives, she, a speech, the way)

→ I like _____.

7 이 근처에 물을 한 병 살 수 있는 편의점이 있나요?

(I, a bottle of, near here, any convenient store, buy, where, water, can)

→ Is there _____?

UNIT 03 주의해야 할 관계사의 쓰임

A 밑줄 친 부분을 어법에 맞게 고쳐 쓰시오.

1 He asked me the place in <u>that</u> I was born. _____

2 Do you know <u>to who</u> your brother is talking? _____

3 This is the post office <u>which</u> my friend works. _____

4 I have a close friend <u>with who</u> I can discuss everything. _____

5 That's the novel <u>by which</u> the movie was inspired by. _____

6 I like the romantic comedy movie *Love Actually*, <u>that</u> makes me feel good. _____

B 생략 가능한 부분을 생략하여 문장을 다시 쓰시오.

1 The boy that you are looking at is my cousin.

   → _____

2 She is the girl whom I talked about yesterday.

   → _____

3 The man who is wearing a blue tie is my brother.

   → _____

4 Do you know the man who is standing next to Nick?

   → _____

5 The woman who is standing over there is my teacher.

   → _____

6 This is the sonata which Beethoven composed in 1801.

   → _____

7 The man who is looking for his lost wallet is my friend.

   → _____

8 This is the movie that I saw with my friends yesterday.

   → _____

9 Thailand is the only country which I have ever been to.

   → _____

10 France is the country that I lived in when I was young.

   → _____

C 두 문장의 의미가 통하도록 관계대명사를 이용하여 문장을 완성하시오.

1 I knew William's daughter, and she is very smart and pretty.

→ I knew William's daughter, _____.

2 This is the flight. The goods will be shipped on the flight.

→ This is the flight _____ on.

3 It was Christmas Eve. I became friends with Jenny on that day.

→ Christmas Eve was the day on _____.

4 The Eiffel Tower is the tallest building in Paris, and she saw it.

→ She saw the Eiffel Tower, _____.

5 I bought the fashion magazine "Vogue" yesterday, and I read it.

→ I read the fashion magazine "Vogue," _____.

6 This is the art gallery. His paintings were displayed in this art gallery.

→ This is the art gallery _____ in.

7 This is the restaurant. I had dinner with my sister yesterday in the restaurant.

→ This is the restaurant in _____.

D 우리말과 같은 뜻이 되도록 주어진 단어를 배열하시오.

1 모자를 쓰고 있는 그 남자는 내 남동생이다. (a cap, wearing, the man)

→ _____ is my younger brother.

2 Einstein은 과학자이고, 천재라고 불린다. (a scientist, who, was)

→ Einstein, _____, is said to be a genius.

3 영어는 전 세계적으로 사용되는 언어이다. (all over the world, spoken, the language)

→ English is _____.

4 그는 학생들이 가장 존경하는 선생님이다. (respect most, all the students, the teacher)

→ He is _____.

5 그녀는 지난 일요일에 산 새 치마를 입고 있었다. (last Sunday, bought, she, a new skirt)

→ She was wearing _____.

6 네가 떠나기로 예정되어 있는 날을 알려줘. (are scheduled to, which, leave on, you, the day)

→ Let me know _____.

7 그는 내게 자기가 뉴욕에 살았다고 말했는데, 그것은 사실이 아니었다. (not, was, which, true)

→ He told me that he lived in New York, _____.

UNIT **04** 복합관계사

A 밑줄 친 부분을 한 단어로 바꿔 쓰시오.

1 We welcome <u>anyone whom</u> you come with. _____

2 Just tell me <u>anything that</u> is on your mind. _____

3 <u>No matter who</u> criticizes me, I won't give up. _____

4 <u>No matter how</u> old I get, I want to keep working. _____

5 <u>No matter when</u> he visits his grandmother, he brings roses for her. _____

B 보기 에서 알맞은 복합관계사를 골라 문장을 완성하시오.

보기	whichever	whenever	however	whoever	wherever

1 _____ you go, I'll be with you.

2 _____ asked, he didn't try to help.

3 _____ you come, you'll be welcomed.

4 I'll buy _____ costs less between them.

5 _____ angry you get, you should control yourself.

C 두 문장이 같은 의미가 되도록 복합관계사를 이용하여 문장을 완성하시오.

1 She looks beautiful no matter what she wears.

→ She looks beautiful _____ .

2 Anyone who comes first will take the window seat.

→ _____ will take the window seat.

3 No matter how hard you try, he won't listen to you.

→ _____ , he won't listen to you.

4 No matter which you buy, you can get a 10% discount.

→ _____ , you can get a 10% discount.

5 She always has her dog with her no matter where she goes.

→ She always has her dog with her _____ .

D 우리말과 같은 뜻이 되도록 복합관계사와 주어진 단어를 이용하여 문장을 완성하시오.

1 어디든 좋으신 곳에 앉으세요. (like)

→ You can sit _____ _____ _____.

2 그녀는 아무리 많이 먹어도 살이 찌지 않는다. (eat, much)

→ She never gains weight _____ _____ _____ _____.

3 네가 원하는 때 언제든지 우리 집에 와도 된다. (want)

→ You can come to my house _____ _____ _____.

4 그는 내가 먹고 싶은 것은 무엇이든지 주문하게 했다. (want, eat)

→ He let me order _____ _____ _____ _____ _____.

5 네가 어떤 것을 선택하든지 그들은 네 결정을 존중할 것이다. (choose)

→ _____ _____ _____, they will respect your decision.

6 그녀의 부모님은 그녀가 원하는 것은 무엇이든 사주고 싶어 했다. (want)

→ Her parents wanted to buy her _____ _____ _____.

7 누구에게 도움을 청해도, 아무도 너를 도와주지 않을 것이다. (ask for help)

→ _____ _____ _____ _____ _____, nobody will help you.

E 우리말과 같은 뜻이 되도록 주어진 단어를 배열하시오.

1 이 집이 얼마이든 간에 나는 이 집을 사고 싶다. (costs, much, it, however)

→ I want to buy this house _____.

2 네가 아무리 바쁘더라도 교통 신호를 지켜야 한다. (however, you, busy, are)

→ _____, you must observe the traffic signals.

3 네가 어디 있든지 너는 혼자가 아니라는 것을 기억해야 한다. (are, you, wherever)

→ _____, you should remember you are not alone.

4 네가 그를 위해 무엇을 요리해도 그는 먹지 않을 것이다. (him, cook, whatever, for, you)

→ _____, he won't eat.

5 그녀는 내가 그녀를 찾아갈 때면 언제나 나를 따뜻하게 환영해 준다. (her, I, whenever, visit)

→ She warmly welcomes me _____.

6 클럽에 참가하고 싶은 사람은 누구든지 올 수 있다. (participate in, wants, the club, whoever, to)

→ _____ can come.

7 이것들 가운데 네가 좋아하는 것은 무엇이든 가질 수 있다. (these, like, whichever, among, you)

→ You can have _____.

간접의문문, 상관접속사

A 밑줄 친 부분을 어법에 맞게 고쳐 쓰시오.

1 He said he needed neither money <u>or</u> fame.　　　　　　_____

2 I wonder <u>that</u> they can arrive on time or not.　　　　_____

3 She not only sings but also <u>play</u> the piano every day.　　_____

4 Both my father and my mother <u>enjoys</u> swimming a lot.　　_____

5 <u>Do you think who</u> will be elected the class president?　　_____

6 I felt both upset <u>or</u> disappointed when I heard the news.　_____

7 Either she or I <u>has to</u> go there even though we don't want to.　_____

B 두 문장의 의미가 통하도록 주어진 상관접속사를 이용하여 문장을 완성하시오.

1 The food was tasty, and it was cheap, too. (both ~ and)

　→ The food was _____.

2 You can choose A type, or you can choose B type. (either ~ or)

　→ You can choose _____.

3 The animal can live on land, and it can live in water, too. (both ~ and)

　→ The animal can live _____.

4 She didn't show up at the party and he didn't, either. (neither ~ nor)

　→ _____ showed up at the party.

5 The TV program is interesting, and it is educational, too. (not only ~ but also)

　→ The TV program is _____.

6 Brian doesn't like to ride a bicycle, and I don't like to, either. (neither ~ nor)

　→ _____ like to ride a bicycle.

7 He is interested in classical music, and I am interested in it, too. (not only ~ but also)

　→ _____ am interested in classical music.

8 You can choose a cup as a free gift or you can choose a tray as a free gift. (either ~ or)

　→ You can choose _____ as a free gift.

C   두 문장을 한 문장의 간접의문문으로 바꿔 쓰시오.

1   She wonders. Is the rumor true?

→ She wonders _____ .

2   I wonder. When will the movie be released?

→ I wonder _____ .

3   Do you think? Who called her at this hour?

→ _____ her at this hour?

4   I asked. Why did she miss the class yesterday?

→ I asked _____ yesterday.

5   I don't know. How can I get to the museum?

→ I don't know _____ .

6   He wonders. Has she received his postcard?

→ He wonders _____ his postcard.

7   Everybody wants to know. Will this plan succeed?

→ Everybody wants to know _____ .

D   우리말과 같은 뜻이 되도록 주어진 단어를 이용하여 문장을 완성하시오.

1   나도, 그녀도 이번 주말에 계획이 없다. (have, plans)

→ _____ _____ _____ _____ _____ for this weekend.

2   너는 "네", 또는 "아니요"로 대답해야 한다. (Yes, No)

→ You have to answer _____ _____ _____ _____

3   그는 재미있을 뿐 아니라 총명하다. (funny, intelligent)

→ He is _____ _____ _____ _____ _____ _____ .

4   나는 그것을 사야 할지 말아야 할지 결정할 수 없었다. (should, buy)

→ I couldn't decide _____ _____ _____ _____ or not.

5   그는 어디 앉아야 할지 몰라 두리번거렸다. (has to, sit)

→ He looked around because he didn't know _____ _____ _____ _____ _____ .

6   그는 지난밤에 무슨 일이 일어났는지 호기심이 생겼다. (happen, last night)

→ He became curious about _____ _____ _____ _____ .

7   그녀는 티켓이 매진되었는지 알고 싶었다. (the tickets, be sold out)

→ She wanted to know _____ _____ _____ _____ _____ _____ .

UNIT 02 종속접속사

A 보기 에서 알맞은 접속사를 골라 문장을 완성하시오. (한 번씩만 쓸 것)

[1~5]

| 보기 | as soon as | since | until | if | unless |

1 You can ask me _____ you want to borrow my book.

2 _____ she saw her mother, she started to cry.

3 _____ you arrive early, you won't be able to take a seat.

4 I have dreamed about becoming a singer _____ I was a kid.

5 He had been playing basketball with his friends _____ his mother called him.

[6~10]

| 보기 | unless | because | when | while | although |

6 _____ he ignored me, I was very angry.

7 _____ you like my idea, you don't have to accept it.

8 She got good grades _____ she studied very hard.

9 _____ he helped me, I couldn't solve the problem.

10 I enjoyed watching the people who passed by _____ I was waiting for him.

[11~15]

| 보기 | as soon as | until | even if | as | because |

11 _____ I tell him the truth, he won't believe me.

12 _____ my mother grew older, she felt tired very often.

13 You can't go out of the classroom _____ I allow you to do so.

14 I couldn't sleep last night _____ I drank too much coffee.

15 _____ he finished his homework, he went out to play with his friends.

B 우리말과 같은 뜻이 되도록 주어진 단어를 이용하여 문장을 완성하시오.

1 나의 어머니가 요리를 하는 동안 아버지가 상을 차렸다. (cook)

→ _____ _____ _____ _____ _____, my father set the table.

2 시간이 지남에 따라 그는 점점 나아졌다. (go by)

→ _____ _____ _____ _____, he got better and better.

3 그는 너무 어리기 때문에 거기 혼자 갈 수 없다. (too young)

→ He can't go there alone _____ _____ _____ _____ _____.

4 그녀는 아이였을 때, 할머니와 함께 살았다. (a kid)

→ _____ _____ _____ _____ _____, she lived with her grandmother.

5 그가 연설을 마치자마자 모두가 환호하며 박수를 쳤다. (finish one's speech)

→ _____ _____ _____ _____ _____ _____,

everybody cheered and clapped.

6 비가 많이 왔음에도 우리는 계획대로 소풍을 갔다. (rain, a lot)

→ _____ _____ _____ _____ _____, we went on a picnic as we planned.

7 비록 그가 그녀를 도와 줬음에도, 그녀는 여전히 해야 할 일이 많다. (help)

→ _____ _____ _____ _____ _____, she still has a lot of things to do.

C 우리말과 같은 뜻이 되도록 주어진 단어를 배열하시오.

1 나는 아파서 오늘 점심을 먹지 않았다. (sick, felt, as, I)

→ _____, I didn't have lunch today.

2 그는 비록 나이가 많지만 매일 아침 조깅을 간다. (is, he, old, although)

→ _____, he goes jogging every morning.

3 택시를 탄다 해도, 너는 제시간에 도착할 수 없을 것이다. (even if, a taxi, take, you)

→ _____, you won't be able to arrive on time.

4 그녀는 돈이 없어서 새 노트북 컴퓨터를 살 수 없었다. (money, she, no, had, because)

→ _____, she couldn't buy a new laptop computer.

5 선생님이 교실을 나가자마자 학생들은 소란을 떨기 시작했다. (the classroom, the teacher, as soon as, left)

→ _____, the students started to make a lot of noise.

6 우리 어머니가 내가 거기 가는 것을 허락하지 않으시면, 나는 갈 수 없다. (lets, there, unless, go, me, my mother),

→ _____, I can't go.

7 그녀는 비록 영어를 못하지만 외국인들과 대화하는 것을 두려워하지 않는다.

(can't, English, even though, speak, she)

→ She is not afraid of speaking to foreigners _____.

UNIT 01 원급, 비교급, 최상급

A 주어진 단어를 이용하여 문장을 완성하시오.

1 It is not as _____ as you think. (hard)

2 My bag is _____ than yours. (heavy)

3 I think tea is _____ than coffee. (good)

4 Today's temperature is _____ than usual. (much, high)

B 주어진 문장과 의미가 통하도록 문장을 완성하시오.

1 Your luggage is not as heavy as mine.

→ Your luggage _____ _____ _____ _____ mine.

→ Your luggage _____ _____ _____ _____ mine.

→ My luggage _____ _____ _____ yours.

2 The bus is not as crowded as the train.

→ The bus _____ _____ _____ _____ _____ the train.

→ The bus _____ _____ _____ _____ the train.

→ The train _____ _____ _____ _____ the bus.

3 Hallasan is not as dangerous as the Himalayas.

→ Hallasan _____ _____ _____ _____ _____ the Himalayas.

→ Hallasan _____ _____ _____ _____ the Himalayas.

→ The Himalayas _____ _____ _____ _____ Hallasan.

C 두 문장이 의미가 통하도록 주어진 단어를 이용하여 문장을 완성하시오.

1 I can jump 50 cm high. My brother can jump 1 m high.

→ My brother can jump _____ _____ I can. (high)

2 The pizza is $30. The spaghetti is $20.

→ The spaghetti is _____ _____ _____ _____ the pizza. (expensive)

3 Betty is 160 cm tall. Peter is 185 cm tall. Eden is 175 cm tall.

→ Peter is _____ _____ of the three. (tall)

4 I received $50, and my sister received $100 for pocket money.

→ My sister received _____ _____ _____ _____ I received. (pocket money)

D 우리말과 같은 뜻이 되도록 주어진 단어를 이용하여 문장을 완성하시오.

1 너는 그만큼 게으르지 않다. (lazy)
→ You are _____ _____ _____ _____ him.

2 나는 그만큼 많은 사람들을 만났다. (many)
→ I met _____ _____ _____ _____ him.

3 나는 너보다 춤을 잘 출 수 있다. (well)
→ I can dance _____ _____ you can.

4 가장 가까운 우체국이 어디 있나요? (near, post office)
→ Where is _____ _____ _____ _____?

5 Teresa는 내 친구 중에서 가장 사려 깊은 사람이다. (thoughtful)
→ Teresa is _____ _____ _____ _____ of all my friends.

6 나는 피아노를 치는 것보다 노래하는 것이 훨씬 더 좋다. (much)
→ I like singing _____ _____ _____ playing the piano.

7 그 문제는 네가 생각하는 것보다 훨씬 더 심각하다. (a lot, serious)
→ The problem is _____ _____ _____ _____ _____ you think.

E 우리말과 같은 뜻이 되도록 주어진 단어를 배열하시오.

1 조금 더 빨리 걷자. (faster, walk, lets, a little)
→ _____

2 레몬이 오렌지보다 훨씬 더 시다. (than, a lot, are, oranges, sour, lemons, more)
→ _____

3 누가 세계에서 가장 부자인가요? (in the world, is, the, who, man, richest)
→ _____

4 올해는 평소보다 눈이 훨씬 많이 왔다. (has rained, usual, more, it, than, a lot)
→ This year, _____

5 음식은 내가 예상한 것보다 더 별로였다. (worse, I, the food, expected, was, than)
→ _____

6 우리 아버지는 사무실에서 가장 바쁜 사람이다. (is, in, man, his office, the, busiest, my father)
→ _____

7 영화는 원작 소설만큼 흥미롭지 않았다. (interesting, the original novel, was, not, as, the movie, as)
→ _____

02 여러 가지 비교급, 최상급 표현

A 우리말과 같은 뜻이 되도록 보기 에서 알맞은 말을 골라 문장을 완성하시오.

보기 as thick as worse and worse the sweeter the wiser

1 상황이 점점 더 악화되고 있다.
→ Things are getting _____.

2 둘 중에 이 복숭아가 더 달다.
→ This peach is _____ of the two.

3 너는 더 많이 배우면 배울수록 현명해 질 것이다.
→ The more you learn, _____ you become.

4 이 사전이 그 소설보다 세 배 두껍다.
→ This dictionary is three times _____ that novel.

B 주어진 문장과 의미가 통하도록 문장을 완성하시오.

1 Alicia is the cutest girl in my class.

→ _____ other _____ in my class is _____ _____ _____ Alicia.

→ _____ other _____ in my class is _____ _____ Alicia.

→ Alicia is _____ _____ _____ _____ in my class.

→ Alicia is _____ _____ all the other _____ in my class.

2 Seoul is the busiest city in Korea.

→ _____ other _____ in Korea is _____ _____ _____ Seoul.

→ _____ other _____ in Korea is _____ _____ Seoul.

→ Seoul is _____ _____ _____ _____ in Korea.

→ Seoul is _____ _____ all the other _____ in Korea.

3 Masa is the most expensive restaurant in this city.

→ _____ other _____ in this city is _____ _____ _____ Masa.

→ _____ other _____ in this city is _____ _____ _____ Masa.

→ Masa is _____ _____ _____ _____ _____ in this city.

→ Masa is _____ _____ _____ all the other _____ in this city.

C 우리말과 같은 뜻이 되도록 주어진 단어를 이용하여 문장을 완성하시오.

1 가능한 한 일찍 와주세요. (early)
→ Please come _____ _____ _____ _____ .

2 나는 점점 더 살이 찌고 있다. (fat)
→ I'm getting _____ _____ _____ .

3 의사는 가장 인기 있는 직업 중 하나다. (popular, job)
→ A doctor is _____ _____ _____ _____ _____ _____ .

4 돈을 더 많이 벌수록, 더 바빠진다. (much, money, busy)
→ _____ _____ _____ you earn, _____ _____ you become.

5 그는 나이가 들수록 점점 더 아버지를 닮아간다. (old, much)
→ _____ _____ he gets, _____ _____ he looks like his father.

6 라 토마티나는 가장 유명한 축제 중 하나이다. (famous, festival)
→ La Tomatina is _____ _____ _____ _____ _____ _____ .

7 그것은 내가 지금까지 본 것 중에 가장 아름다운 사원이다. (beautiful, temple)
→ It is _____ _____ _____ _____ I have ever seen.

D 우리말과 같은 뜻이 되도록 주어진 단어를 배열하시오.

1 둘 중 이 간단한 디자인이 더 낫다. (two, the, the, of, better, is)
→ This simple design _____ .

2 그녀에 대해 알면 알수록 그녀가 더 좋다. (I, more, her, the, like)
→ The more I know about her, _____ .

3 내 컨디션이 점점 더 나아지고 있다. (better, is, better, and, getting)
→ My condition _____ .

4 가능한 한 많은 책을 읽도록 노력해라. (possible, many, as, as, books)
→ Try to read _____ .

5 이 건물은 우리 집보다 두 배만큼 오래됐다. (as, twice, my house, old, is, as)
→ This building _____ .

6 Bill Gates는 성공한 사업가 중 한 명이다. (most, of, businesspeople, is, successful, the, one)
→ Bill Gates _____ .

7 "True Men"은 내가 본 것 중 가장 재미있는 쇼였다. (I, was, ever, show, funniest, seen, the, have)
→ *True Men* _____ .

UNIT 01 수 일치

A 빈칸에 **is**와 **are** 중 알맞은 것을 써 넣어 문장을 완성하시오.

1 One of the tires _____ flat.

2 Physics _____ not easy for me to study.

3 Most of his friends _____ from France.

4 It seems that something _____ missing in my room.

5 Thirty minutes _____ enough time for me to go there.

6 A number of people _____ watching the soccer game.

7 Two thirds of the oranges _____ not in good condition.

B 밑줄 친 부분을 어법에 맞게 고쳐 쓰시오.

1 The old <u>has</u> wisdom of life. _____

2 The rest of the books <u>is</u> in my school. _____

3 George and Brian <u>is</u> in the same class. _____

4 <u>Are</u> somebody going to pick it up tomorrow? _____

5 One of the popular sports <u>are</u> soccer around the world. _____

6 Politics <u>are</u> not a popular major among college students. _____

7 Every computer in all classrooms <u>are</u> linked to the Internet. _____

C 우리말과 같은 뜻이 되도록 보기 에서 알맞은 동사를 골라 문장을 완성하시오.

| 보기 | live | increase | need | play |

1 각각 10달러씩 내야 한다.
  → Each person _____ to pay ten dollars.

2 학생들의 3분의 2가 아파트에 산다.
  → Two thirds of the students _____ in an apartment.

3 학생들 중 몇 명은 밤늦게까지 게임을 한다.
  → Some of the students _____ games until late at night.

4 해외여행을 하는 사람들의 수가 증가하고 있다.
  → The number of people traveling abroad _____ _____.

D 우리말과 같은 뜻이 되도록 주어진 단어를 이용하여 문장을 완성하시오.

1 40분은 기다리기에 긴 시간이다. (forty minutes, be)

→ _____ _____ _____ a long time to wait.

2 각각의 테이블에는 4개의 의자가 있다. (have)

→ _____ _____ _____ four chairs.

3 누구 그 답을 아는 사람이 있니? (anyone, know)

→ _____ _____ _____ the answer?

4 수학은 우리 삶에 꼭 필요하다. (mathematics, be)

→ _____ _____ necessary for our lives.

5 그 학생들의 절반이 방과 후에 영어 수업을 듣는다. (half, take)

→ _____ _____ _____ _____ _____ English classes after school.

6 젊은이들은 노인들을 존중해야 한다. (the young, have to, respect)

→ _____ _____ _____ _____ the old.

7 많은 사람들이 줄을 서서 기다리고 있다. (number, wait)

→ _____ _____ _____ _____ _____ in line.

E 우리말과 같은 뜻이 되도록 주어진 단어를 배열하시오.

1 무엇인가 이상한 일이 일어났다. (happened, strange, something, has)

→ _____

2 부자라고 항상 행복한 것은 아니다. (rich, happy, not, the, always, are)

→ _____

3 지구 표면의 4분의 3은 바다이다. (is, the earth's surface, three fourths, oceans, of)

→ _____

4 많은 사람들이 그의 의견에 찬성했다. (were for, number, his, a, people, opinion, of)

→ _____

5 도시에서 나무의 수가 줄어들고 있다. (of, is, trees, number, in the city, decreasing, the)

→ _____

6 그 돈의 대부분은 가난한 사람들을 돕는 데 사용된다. (the money, the poor, help, of, help, most, is used to)

→ _____

7 카레라이스가 카페테리아에서 가장 맛있는 요리이다.

(in the cafeteria, dish, curry and rice, most, is, delicious, the)

→ _____

UNIT 02 시제 일치

A 주어진 단어를 이용하여 문장을 완성하시오.

1 He said that blood _____ thicker than water. (be)

2 She thought he _____ come home early. (will)

3 I thought you _____ _____ to watch the movies with me. (not, want)

4 My mother said everyone _____ mistakes sometimes. (make)

5 My teacher said Sejong the Great _____ Hangul in 1443. (invent)

B 우리말과 같은 뜻이 되도록 보기 에서 알맞은 단어를 골라 문장을 완성하시오.

보기　　tell　　like　　see　　bake

1 나는 무엇인가를 보았다고 생각했다.
　　→ I thought that I _____ something.

2 그는 엄마가 과자를 구워 주기를 바란다.
　　→ He hopes that his mom _____ cookies.

3 나는 그가 거짓말을 하고 있다는 것을 알았다.
　　→ I knew that he _____ _____ a lie.

4 그는 그녀가 자신을 좋아한다고 믿었지만, 아니었다.
　　→ He believed that she _____ him, but she didn't.

C 주절의 시제를 과거 시제로 바꿔 문장을 완성하시오.

1 She doesn't believe I am sick.
　　→ She didn't believe _____.

2 I think that you will trust me.
　　→ I thought that _____.

3 I think that she is already gone.
　　→ I thought that _____.

4 He wonders how you solved the problem.
　　→ He wondered _____.

5 He says to me that Parents Day is on the eighth of May in Korea.
　　→ He said to me that _____.

D 우리말과 같은 뜻이 되도록 주어진 단어를 이용하여 문장을 완성하시오.

1 나는 그들이 나를 초대해 줘서 기뻤다. (be, invite)

→ I _____ pleased that they _____ _____.

2 너는 에디슨이 전구를 발명했다는 것을 아니? (know, invent)

→ _____ _____ _____ that Edison _____ light bulbs?

3 그녀는 자신의 아들이 매우 똑똑하다고 믿는다. (believe, be, smart)

→ She _____ that her son _____ _____ _____.

4 그는 그녀가 자신을 기억할까 궁금했다. (wonder, will, remember)

→ He _____ if she _____ _____ _____.

5 그는 그녀가 자신을 도와줄 거라고 믿었다. (believe, will, help)

→ He _____ that she _____ _____ him.

6 나는 다른 회원들이 Adam을 좋아하지 않는다고 생각했다. (think, not, like)

→ I _____ that other members _____ _____ Adam.

7 나는 여기서 그를 만날 것이라고는 전혀 생각하지 못했다. (thought, will, meet)

→ I never _____ that I _____ _____ _____ here.

E 우리말과 같은 뜻이 되도록 주어진 단어를 배열하시오.

1 그는 사고가 일어나서 슬펐다. (the accident, was, that, happened, he, sad)

→ _____

2 나는 Bill이 결혼을 안 할 거라고 생각했다. (Bill, get married, thought, not, would, I)

→ _____

3 그녀는 주말마다 자전거를 탄다고 말했다. (said, weekend, she, a bike, every, she, rides, that)

→ _____

4 그는 주말마다 영화를 보러 간다고 말했다. (said, goes to, he, every weekend, the movies, he)

→ _____

5 나는 그가 왜 그날 결석을 했는지 몰랐다. (know, he, that day, why, had, I, absent, didn't, been)

→ _____

6 나의 형은 고래가 포유류라고 말했다. (said to, are, that, mammals, whales, my brother, me)

→ _____

7 우리는 한국이 1945년에 일본으로부터 독립을 했다는 것을 잊지 않아야 한다.

(in 1945, that, not, we, from Japan, forget, won, should, independence, Korea)

→ _____

UNIT 03 화법 전환

A 직접화법을 간접화법으로 바꿔 문장을 완성하시오.

1 He said to me, "I like you."

→ He _____.

2 She said, "I have made up my mind."

→ She _____.

3 Clara said, "I forgot to bring your book."

→ Clara _____.

4 He said to me, "Why are you so busy?"

→ He _____.

5 Brian said to me, "Will you help me do my homework?"

→ Brian _____.

6 My mother said to me, "Get enough sleep."

→ My mother _____.

7 The teacher said to us, "Do not use cell phones in class."

→ The teacher _____.

B 간접화법을 직접화법으로 바꿔 문장을 완성하시오.

1 He said that he had lots of things to do that day.

→ He _____

2 She said that there was a fire in her neighborhood.

→ She _____

3 My mother asked me when I would clean my room.

→ My mother _____

4 The man asked me where the nearest post office was.

→ The man _____

5 I asked Sam if he had a pen.

→ I _____

6 He told me to close the curtains.

→ He _____

7 She told me not to turn the volume up.

→ She _____

C 우리말과 같은 뜻이 되도록 주어진 단어를 이용하여 문장을 완성하시오.

1 그녀는 새 옷을 사고 싶다고 말했다. (say, want)

→ She _____ _____ _____ to buy new clothes.

2 나는 그녀에게 내가 그녀의 컴퓨터를 고칠 수 있다고 말했다. (tell, can, fix)

→ I _____ _____ _____ _____ _____ her computer.

3 Lisa는 내게 그 가방을 어디서 샀냐고 물었다. (ask, buy)

→ Lisa _____ _____ _____ _____ _____ _____ that bag.

4 그는 내게 자기와 콘서트에 가겠냐고 물었다. (ask, go)

→ He _____ _____ _____ _____ _____ _____ to the concert with him.

5 그는 내게 액션 영화를 좋아하냐고 물었다. (ask, like)

→ He _____ _____ _____ _____ action movies.

6 나의 의사는 나에게 물을 많이 마시라고 충고했다. (advise, drink)

→ My doctor _____ _____ _____ _____ a lot of water.

7 그는 내게 새치기하지 말라고 말했다. (tell, cut in line)

→ He _____ _____ _____ _____ _____ _____ _____ .

D 우리말과 같은 뜻이 되도록 주어진 단어를 배열하시오.

1 그들은 내게 다음 날 그곳을 떠날 거라고 말했다. (the next day, there, leave, me, would, they, told)

→ They _____ .

2 그녀는 그에게 언제 집에 갈 거냐고 물었다. (was, home, he, asked, going, when, him)

→ She _____ .

3 그는 그녀에게 전에 무슨 말을 했냐고 물었다. (said, before, asked, she, what, had, her)

→ He _____ .

4 그녀는 내게 그의 전화번호를 아는지 물었다. (me, his, if, knew, asked, I, phone number)

→ She _____ .

5 그는 내게 돈을 빌려줄 수 있냐고 물었다. (me, some money, lend, whether, I, could, asked, him)

→ He _____ .

6 의사는 그에게 술을 마시지 말라고 했다. (not, ordered, drink, him, to)

→ The doctor _____ .

7 그녀는 내게 불을 모두 끄라고 말했다. (me, all the lights, turn off, to, told)

→ She _____ .

UNIT 01 강조, 부정

A 밑줄 친 부분을 강조하는 문장으로 바꿔 쓰시오.

1 He <u>has</u> a good memory.

→ He _____ a good memory.

2 She <u>looks</u> young for her age.

→ She _____ young for her age.

3 I <u>regret</u> that I didn't go there.

→ I _____ that I didn't go there.

4 I <u>hoped</u> that he would win the competition.

→ I _____ that he would win the competition.

5 We <u>climbed</u> the mountain in China for eight hours.

→ We _____ the mountain in China for eight hours.

6 They <u>welcomed</u> the students from other countries.

→ They _____ the students from other countries.

B 밑줄 친 부분을 강조하는 「It ~ that」 문장을 완성하시오.

1 I shared my book with <u>Sarah</u>.

→ It was _____ .

2 He left for the U.S. <u>a week ago</u>.

→ It was _____ .

3 They like playing <u>basketball</u> in the park.

→ It is _____ .

4 She is supposed to meet her friend <u>at six</u>.

→ It is _____ .

5 She found a kitten <u>in the garage</u> last night.

→ It was _____ .

6 He bought <u>a science book</u> at the bookstore.

→ It was _____ .

7 <u>Jackie</u> bought me a handkerchief for my birthday.

→ It was _____ .

C 주어진 단어를 이용하여 두 문장의 의미가 통하도록 문장을 완성하시오.

1 I don't like spicy food, and my sister doesn't, either.

→ _____ _____ _____ likes spicy food. (neither)

2 Some of the students got an A, and the others didn't.

→ _____ _____ of the students got an A. (all)

3 I haven't been to Europe and neither have all of my friends.

→ _____ _____ _____ has been to Europe. (none)

4 Jack didn't bring his book, and Kelly didn't bring her book, either.

→ _____ _____ _____ brought their books. (neither)

5 Most of the time the bus comes on time, but sometimes it doesn't.

→ The bus _____ _____ _____ on time. (always)

D 우리말과 같은 뜻이 되도록 주어진 단어를 이용하여 문장을 완성하시오.

1 아무도 그가 한 일에 대해 불평하지 않았다. (no, complain)

→ _____ _____ _____ about what he did.

2 나의 자전거를 고쳐준 사람은 바로 우리 아버지였다. (my father. fix)

→ It was _____ _____ _____ _____ my bike.

3 진실을 말하는 것이 항상 옳은 일은 아니다. (telling the truth)

→ _____ _____ _____ _____ _____ the right thing to do.

4 나는 정말로 너에게 며칠 전에 이메일을 보냈어. (do, send)

→ I _____ _____ an email to you a few days ago.

E 우리말과 같은 뜻이 되도록 주어진 단어를 배열하시오.

1 그는 정말로 새벽에 운동을 한다. (at dawn, exercise, does, he)

→ _____

2 그가 정직하다고 믿는 사람은 아무도 없다. (one, is, believes, he, no, honest)

→ _____

3 모두가 장학금을 받을 수 있는 것은 아니다. (a scholarship, can, not, get, everyone)

→ _____

4 그녀의 집 앞에 꽃을 갖다 놓은 사람은 바로 나였다. (was, in front of, I, it, her house, that, flowers, left)

→ _____

UNIT 02 병렬구조, 도치

A 밑줄 친 부분을 어법에 맞게 고쳐 쓰시오.

1 Either he or me will pick you up. _____

2 He wrote his report quickly and accurate. _____

3 He is not only funny but also intelligence. _____

4 She enjoys playing the guitar and do puzzles. _____

B 밑줄 친 부분을 강조하는 문장으로 바꿔 쓰시오.

1 An old man stood on the hill.

→ On the hill _____.

2 The cat hid under the bookcase.

→ Under the bookcase _____.

3 She seldom breaks her promise.

→ Seldom _____.

4 A black car was in front of my house.

→ In front of my house _____.

5 I little knew what was happening.

→ Little _____.

6 The kid has never been to the museum.

→ Never _____.

C So 또는 Neither를 이용하여 대화를 완성하시오.

1 A I was sick yesterday.

B _____. I took medicine.

2 A I love reading books.

B _____. I try to read two books a month.

3 A I didn't see the game show last night.

B _____. I had to finish writing a report.

4 A I can't solve this problem.

B _____. I think It's too difficult for us.

D 우리말과 같은 뜻이 되도록 주어진 단어를 이용하여 문장을 완성하시오.

1 내 이름은 명단 맨 아래에 있었다. (be)

→ At the bottom of the list _____ _____ _____.

2 그는 움직일 수도, 말을 할 수도 없었다. (speak)

→ He could neither move _____ _____.

3 그는 주말에 거의 외출을 하지 않는다. (go out)

→ Hardly _____ _____ _____ _____ during the weekends.

4 여기서 드시거나 집으로 가져갈 수 있습니다. (take, home)

→ You can either eat here _____ _____ it _____ with you.

5 그는 그 문장을 영어와 스페인 어로 쓸 수 있다. (Spanish)

→ He can write the sentence both in English _____ _____ _____.

6 그 아이들은 하이킹 가는 것뿐 아니라 수영 가는 것도 좋아한다. (go swimming)

→ The kids like not only going hiking _____ _____ going _____.

7 너는 피아노 연습하는 것과 영어 공부하는 것 중에서 선택해야 해. (study)

→ You have to choose between practicing the piano _____ _____ _____.

E 우리말과 같은 뜻이 되도록 주어진 단어를 배열하시오. (부사(구)를 강조하는 문장으로 쓸 것)

1 봬! 우편집배원이 온다. (comes, the, here, postman)

→ Look! _____

2 한 소녀가 해변에 앉아 있다. (sat, on the shore, a girl)

→ _____

3 그 돌 아래에 작은 물고기가 있다. (under the rock, small, were, fish)

→ _____

4 인기 있는 빵집이 모퉁이를 돌면 있다. (around the corner, bakery, the, is, popular)

→ _____

5 그녀는 한 번도 노인들을 무례하게 대한 적이 없다. (been, old people, she, never, to, has, rude)

→ _____

6 너는 산책을 하거나 낮잠을 잘 수 있다. (for a walk, or, a nap, take, go, either)

→ You can _____.

7 그녀는 음악을 듣는 것뿐만 아니라, 기타 치는 것도 좋아한다.

(listening to, playing, but also, the guitar, not only, music)

→ She loves _____.

새 교과서 반영
중등 내신 완벽 대비서
GRAMMAR 공감

- 최신 교과서의 학습 내용을 반영한 체계적인 문법 설명

- 2,500여 개의 전국 중학교 기출 문제 완전 분석 후 문법 포인트, 문제 반영

- 공부감각을 업그레이드 시켜주는 다양한 서술형 평가 코너 수록 및 워크북 제공

- 놓치기 쉬운 문법 포인트를 잡아 주는 Plus α, Tips 코너 수록

- 말하기, 쓰기, 읽기의 실용적 쓰임을 생각한 통합형 문법 학습

- 2,000여 개 이상의 충분한 문제풀이를 통한 문법 감각 향상

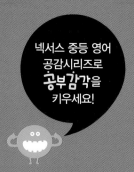

넥서스 중등 영어
공감시리즈로
공부감각을
키우세요!

NEXUS makes your next day
www.nexusEDU.kr | 책에 대해 궁금한 사항은 넥서스에듀 홈페이지 1:1 고객상담 게시판을 이용하세요.

	초1	초2	초3	초4	초5	초6	중1	중2	중3	고1	고2	고3

Writing

공감 영문법+쓰기 1~2

도전만점 중등내신 서술형 1~4

영어일기 영작패턴 1-A, B · 2-A, B

Smart Writing 1~2

Reading

Reading 101 1~3

Reading 공감 1~3

This Is Reading Starter 1~3

This Is Reading 전면 개정판 1~4

This Is Reading 1-1 ~ 3-2 (각 2권; 총 6권)

원서 술술 읽는 Smart Reading Basic 1~2

원서 술술 읽는 Smart Reading 1~2

[특급 단기 특강] 구문독해 · 독해유형

Listening

Listening 공감 1~3

The Listening 1~4

After School Listening 1~3

도전! 만점 중학 영어듣기 모의고사 1~3

만점 적중 수능 듣기 모의고사 20회 · 35회

TEPS

NEW TEPS 입문편 실전 250⁺ 청해 · 문법 · 독해

NEW TEPS 기본편 실전 300⁺ 청해 · 문법 · 독해

NEW TEPS 실력편 실전 400⁺ 청해 · 문법 · 독해

NEW TEPS 마스터편 실전 500⁺ 청해 · 문법 · 독해

www.nexusEDU.kr
t.02-330-5500 f.02-330-5555
NEXUS Edu

새 교과서 반영 공감 시리즈

Grammar 공감 시리즈
▶ 2,000여 개 이상의 충분한 문제 풀이를 통한 문법 감각 향상
▶ 서술형 평가 코너 수록 및 서술형 대비 워크북 제공

Reading 공감 시리즈
▶ 어휘, 문장 쓰기 실력을 향상시킬 수 있는 서술형 대비 워크북 제공
▶ 창의, 나눔, 사회, 문화, 건강, 과학, 심리, 음식, 직업 등의 다양한 주제

Listening 공감 시리즈
▶ 최근 5년간 시 · 도 교육청 듣기능력평가 출제 경향 완벽 분석 반영
▶ 실전모의고사 20회 + 기출모의고사 2회로 구성된 총 22회 영어듣기 모의고사

• Listening, Reading – 무료 MP3 파일 다운로드 제공